Emotional Awareness

EMOTIONAL
AWARENESS

Overcoming the Obstacles
to Psychological Balance
and Compassion

A Conversation Between
The Dalai Lama and Paul Ekman, Ph.D.

Edited by Paul Ekman

A Holt Paperback
Times Books / Henry Holt and Company / New York

Holt Paperbacks
Henry Holt and Company, LLC
Publishers since 1866
175 Fifth Avenue
New York, New York 10010
www.henryholt.com

A Holt Paperback® and ⑩® are registered trademarks of Henry Holt and Company, LLC.

Library of Congress Cataloging-in-Publication Data

Emotional awareness : overcoming the obstacles to psychological balance
and compassion : a conversation between the Dalai Lama and Paul Ekman /
edited by Paul Ekman.—1st ed.

    p. cm.
Includes bibliographical references and index.
ISBN-13: 978-0-8050-9021-5
ISBN-10: 0-8050-9021-5

 1. Emotions.   2. Compassion.   3. Ekman, Paul—Interviews.
4. Bstan-'dzin-rgya-mtsho, Dalai Lama XIV, 1935– —Interviews.   I. Ekman, Paul.
BF531.E498   2008
152.4—dc22   2008008848

Henry Holt books are available for special promotions and premiums.
For details contact: Director, Special Markets.

Originally published in hardcover in 2008 by Times Books
First Holt Paperbacks Edition 2009
Designed by Victoria Hartman

B. Alan Wallace's commentary on pages 56–57 is adapted from "What Did the Buddha Really
Mean by 'Mindfulness'?," *Tricycle,* 17(3), Spring 2008. Reproduced by permission.
Photograph on page 244 by Eve Ekman. All other interior photographs of the Dalai Lama
and Paul Ekman by Tenzin Choejor, Office of His Holiness the Dalai Lama.

Printed in the United States of America
9 10 8

Contents

✳

Foreword

DANIEL GOLEMAN

"Emotional intelligence" refers to being intelligent about our emotional life: more self-aware, better able to handle disturbing emotions, more sensitive to the emotions of others—and able to put all that together to create effective, nourishing interactions. Some people are far better than others at these fundamental human skills, but the good news is that all these abilities are learned—and learnable.

In any domain of human skill, when it comes to cultivating expertise it helps to have guidelines from experts themselves. As an old Zen saying puts it, "If you want to get to the top of the mountain, ask someone who goes up and down the path to the summit."

And so the dialogue recorded here has special value to anyone wanting to become more intelligent about emotion. I can think of no two people on the planet who offer more expertise on the nature of emotion than the Dalai Lama and Paul Ekman.

His Holiness the 14th Dalai Lama may on first glance seem an unlikely source for insights into emotions. But I've had the pleasure to witness firsthand his expertise on this corner of our inner life, in the course of several weeklong dialogues between him and scientists. Each time, I've come away impressed by the clarity and nuance with which he engages any aspect of human consciousness, particularly emotions. His Holiness brings to the topic a unique perspective, first as a contemplative master who has probed his own psyche with analytic thoroughness and candor, and also as a representative of a thousand-year-old intellectual tradition that takes the positive transformation of human emotion as its focus. The Dalai Lama approaches emotions as a steadfast student and practitioner of an inner science.

On the other hand, Paul Ekman represents the higher reaches of a complementary intellectual tradition, modern psychology. For decades he has been a leading scholar of the experimental study of emotion and the unquestioned expert on his specialty, the universal facial expressions of emotion. Paul Ekman carries on a scientific lineage begun by Charles Darwin, who read the legacy of our evolutionary past in the signals of love and hate, fear and anger, which to this day pass across the faces of humans and animals alike. Paul, a personal friend for years, has become the world-class practitioner of emotional understanding as well as an expert in the detection of lies. He has developed effective tools for upgrading our ability to read a person's emotions with accuracy. Paul brings to this conversation the hard-nosed perspective of an open-minded empiricist.

I feel particular satisfaction in having been the person who first introduced Paul and His Holiness, in March 2000, in my role as the moderator of a dialogue of the Mind and Life Institute on the topic "Destructive Emotions." As will be told in these pages, that was the occasion for an encounter between these two remarkable men that was emotionally transformative for Paul and that has shaped his personal and professional life. Their dialogue represents one consequence of that initial meeting.

This is a rich feast for the mind; the conversation touches on a fascinating spectrum of compelling topics and meets hard questions head-on. What makes anger constructive? How can we better manage our destructive emotions, and how does increasing the time gap between an impulse and the act help? Why should we react differently to the person who upsets us than to the upsetting act—and what would help us do this? How can we widen the circle of people for whom we feel genuine compassion?

Paul has chosen to share the flavor of the meeting by carefully preserving for the reader exactly what went on. This format brings us as readers to the table side, able to share in the authentic flavor of what actually was said, rather than what someone says about what was said. This also preserves a historical record of this singular meeting of two intellectual traditions—and two remarkable minds and hearts grappling with some of humanity's most critical challenges.

Introduction

PAUL EKMAN

Emotions unite and divide the worlds in which we live, both personal and global, motivating the best and the worst of our actions. They save our lives, enabling quick action in emergencies. Yet how we behave when we are emotional can make our lives, and the lives of those we care about, miserable. Without emotions there would be no heroism, empathy, or compassion, but neither would there be cruelty, selfishness, nor spite. Bringing different perspectives to bear—Eastern and Western, spirituality and science, Buddhism and psychology—the Dalai Lama and I sought to clarify these contradictions and illuminate some paths that might enable a balanced emotional life and a feeling of compassion that can reach across the globe.

As the leader of a millennia-old spiritual tradition as well as a nation in exile, the Dalai Lama holds something resembling divine status among his fellow Tibetans. He is the world's principal living advocate of nonviolence and the winner, in 1989, of the Nobel Peace Prize and, in 2007, of the Congressional Gold Medal, the highest award given to a civilian by the U.S. government. He is denounced and at times publicly despised by the leaders of the People's

Republic of China, which has occupied Tibet since 1950. Yet he is also more than a religious and political leader: In the Western world his celebrity approaches that of a rock star. He has authored several bestselling books and is nearly always traveling, speaking, and inspiring audiences that number in the thousands. He is also strongly interested in integrating the findings of modern science into the Buddhist worldview. In our conversations, it became clear to me that he considers himself first and foremost a Buddhist monk and an interpreter of Buddhist thinking to the rest of the world. He believes that Buddhist wisdom provides an ethical framework through which the world might be able to better deal with the problems that divide us.

I am a professor emeritus at the University of California-San Francisco School of Medicine, having spent more than forty years establishing the universality of humans' emotional behavior, mapping the expressions of the face, discovering how lies are betrayed in our demeanor, and proposing theories to explain both the nature of emotion and why and when people lie. This research has helped to reawaken scientific interest in both emotion and deception. I am the author or editor of fourteen books, five of them—*Unmasking the Face, Face of Man, Telling Lies, Why Kids Lie,* and *Emotions Revealed*—written for the general public, and over my career I have become an expert on Charles Darwin's writings on emotional expression. My work has been of interest to a wide range of organizations, from animation studios to police departments, and I now run a business that designs interactive training tools for improving emotional understanding and evaluating truthfulness. I also advise several governments' antiterrorism agencies. I am Jewish in background but not observant, and as skeptical about Buddhism as I am about any religion. I have spent my life as a behavioral *scientist*, developing and applying hard, objective methods to the investigation of what had been considered the soft phenomenon of emotion.

Despite our differences, we discovered important common ground in our perspectives. We share a commitment to reducing human suffering, intense inquisitiveness, and a conviction that we were likely to learn from each other. Our conversations reveal the unfolding of what developed into an intense friendship over the course of the nearly forty hours we spent exploring these issues. Our common concerns for personal and social welfare, borne from decades of thought and work in the most contrasting of conditions, united our efforts and brought forth new ideas, new ways to understand ourselves, practical steps for creating better worlds, in our closest and most distant relationships.

I first met the Dalai Lama in 2000, when I attended a small conference on destructive emotions organized by the Mind and Life Institute, in Boulder, Colorado.[1] Since 1987, the institute has brought scientists to Dharamsala, India, where the Dalai Lama lives in exile, for conferences on diverse scientific topics. At the 2000 conference I was one of six scientist-participants who talked with the Dalai Lama over five days. My responsibility was to present the Darwinian view of emotion and to explain my scientific research on the universality of emotional expression and physiology. Whether through a shared sense of playful and probing curiosity, our commitment to reducing human suffering, or a conviction that we were likely to learn from each other, the Dalai Lama and I immediately found an unexpectedly strong rapport across the wide gulf of the intellectual heritages we each represent.

In the following few years, I participated as one of a group of scientists in three other conferences with the Dalai Lama. In addition, I was in the audience at a panel session, "Opening the Heart," that was held in Vancouver, British Columbia, in 2004, in which the Dalai Lama was one of a number of religious leaders in attendance. One by one, the spiritual leaders addressed the group: Bishop Desmond Tutu talked about how his religion had helped him open his heart; Dr. Jo-Ann Archibald, a Northwest American Indian, talked about how her religion had opened her heart; the

Iranian justice Shirin Ebadi and then Rabbi Zalman Schachter-Shalomi each spoke about how their religions had opened their hearts. His Holiness was the last to speak.* He looked around at each of the individuals who had preceded him and, with a broad smile on his face, said something like, "But religions often divide the world. What unifies us are our emotions. We all want to have happiness and reduce suffering." I thought to myself, exactly right—but our emotions also divide us.

When I left the Vancouver meeting, my mind was filled with the issues about the nature of emotion that had been raised by the Dalai Lama's remarks, issues that I thought merited exploration. He was right in saying emotions are what we had in common, but he had left out all the ways in which our emotions can separate us, and cause us to have conflicts with one another. I was concerned that perhaps I had oversimplified matters in my presentation about emotions four years earlier. I began a list of the unexplored questions, some of them focusing on how humanity might be able to reduce the divisions among us through the unifying nature of our emotions, others on how to decrease the destructive influence emotions can bring into our lives. My initial outline came to twenty pages.

Motivated by the sense that, coming from our distinct traditions of Western psychology and Buddhist philosophy, a back-and-forth discussion could spark between us new ideas, I sought the opinions of two colleagues I had met at the Mind and Life Institute conference in 2000. One was Matthieu Ricard. Matthieu received his doctorate in biology in 1972 and then chose to leave the academic world, becoming a Tibetan Buddhist monk and a renowned author and photographer.[2] He has resided at the Shechen

---

* I was told the honorific "His Holiness" was adopted for addressing the Dalai Lama when he leaves the home of the government in exile in Dharamsala to represent the Tibetan cause around the world since the Tibetan term for addressing him is very long and cumbersome; "His Holiness" was adopted because it is how the pope, the head of another world religion, is addressed. I rarely used the honorific in our conversations as, being nonreligious myself, I view him as an extraordinary person but not a holy one.

Monastery in Nepal for more than thirty years and has served as a French translator for the Dalai Lama. Matthieu has been a guest in my home many times and agreed to be the subject of scientific study of his expressions and physiology in a series of experiments.[3] I also sent the outline to B. Alan Wallace, who was ordained as a monk in 1973 and studied with the Dalai Lama before leaving the monastery to return to the United States, completing his education, and marrying. Alan is the author of many books on meditation and founded the nonprofit Santa Barbara Institute for Consciousness Studies. He too has become a good friend and had in the past served as the meditation trainer for one of my research projects. Both Matthieu and Alan added ideas to the outline and then urged me to contact the Dalai Lama through his office.

Knowing that the Dalai Lama's schedule was already overfilled, I was reluctant to request the ten to twelve hours I thought would be required for a conversation on these questions. But I sent it on to Thupten Jinpa, the renowned Tibetan scholar and former monk who serves as an English translator for the Dalai Lama when he travels outside of India. Jinpa is a sweet and gentle man with whom it was easy to establish a warm relationship. In my letter to him I asked if he thought the issues I had outlined were important enough to merit a private conference with the Dalai Lama. Jinpa's response was enthusiastic. He suggested other issues that should be included and then advocated for three days of meetings. It took fourteen months for a time to open up in the Dalai Lama's calendar.

As a result of Jinpa's determination, during the weekend of April 22–23, 2006, the Dalai Lama and I sat down for eleven hours of intense discussion on my twenty-four pages of questions about emotion and compassion, as well as several other questions that came out of the natural flow and surprise of our conversation. It ended up being the first of three dialogues, a total of thirty-nine hours of intimate exchange that we shared over a period of fifteen months.

Our first meeting was held in Libertyville, Illinois, in the luxurious living room of a farm belonging to the Pritzker family, which heads the Hyatt Corporation. The walls were adorned with a portion of what is reputedly the best private Asian art collection in the United States. I sat to the immediate left of the Dalai Lama. "Perched" is a better word, for I was on the edge of my chair, bent toward the Dalai Lama, throughout our conversation. In front of me on a coffee table was the twenty-four-page outline I had prepared. Next to my outline were a few handouts that I distributed as the discussion progressed, which appear in the text alongside our conversation. We talked about every item on the outline and many other issues, some directly relevant and others too fascinating not to pursue.

We were both clearly excited by the challenge of reorganizing our thinking in light of the other, and our focus and concentration were palpable. But we also brought enthusiasm and enjoyment, expressed through our loud voices and equally loud (and frequent) peals of laughter. We came to the table with highly developed viewpoints, stemming from totally different sources, each of us at the top of our field. We also knew that there might never again be such an opportunity: The Dalai Lama was seventy-one at the time of our conversation, and I was seventy-two.

When we decided to devote the better part of three days to intense discussion—something I had never before done with anyone, and reportedly quite a rare event for the Dalai Lama—we were already aware of the strong connection we had felt in our previous meetings at more public conferences. A few days into the 2000 conference, a sense of deja vu emerged in me, as if I had already known the Dalai Lama for a long time. The Dalai Lama also sensed our strong connection. In his book *The Universe in a Single Atom*, he wrote, "I felt an immediate affinity with him and sensed that a genuine ethical motivation underlies his work, in that if we understand the nature of our emotions and their universality better we may be able to develop a greater sense of kinship in humanity." And in the very next sentence, he slipped in a joke, which, like all his jokes, riffs on something true: "Also, Paul speaks at exactly the right pace for me to follow his presentation in English without difficulty."

As one would expect for the leader of a world religion, particularly one who is a head of state and has received death threats, we were not alone. At one entrance sat a U.S. State Department protective service officer, who was regularly relieved, every thirty minutes, by a fellow officer. Other members of the protective service surrounded the house; a car was kept idling twenty-four hours a day outside the front door in case there should be need for a quick exit. At the other end of the room, forty feet away, a member of the Tibetan government-in-exile entourage gazed down from a high balcony.

To the Dalai Lama's right sat my ally in this endeavor, Thupten Jinpa, who served as the translator for the meeting, and next to him sat another Tibetan, Geshe Dorji Damdul. (*Geshe* is the term used for those scholars who, in their study of Tibetan Buddhism, have reached a level equivalent to that of a Western doctorate.) Occasionally in our discussion, Dorji responded to a question posed by the Dalai Lama about how my comment fit with Tibetan scholarship. He is fluent in English and needed no translation to understand what I said, but spoke directly to the Dalai Lama in Tibetan and never spoke without being asked to do so.

The conversation was also witnessed by several individuals, including the Dalai Lama's American doctor, Barry Kerzin, who three years earlier had been ordained as a Buddhist monk, and his personal Tibetan physician, Dr. Tsetan Sadutshang. The doctors were there both because of their interest in the topic and out of concern for the Dalai Lama's health; he had just a day before been discharged from the Mayo Clinic, where he had gone for a regular examination. Twenty-five feet away, at the other end of the large room, sat my family: my son, Tom Ekman, who had recently graduated from law school and had not before met the Dalai Lama; my wife, Mary Ann Mason, who was then dean of the graduate division at the University of California-Berkeley and in 2003 had attended (as a silent observer) my twenty-minute audience with the Dalai Lama to discuss an issue I had raised for scientific investigation ("Why does meditation focusing on the breath benefit emotion?"); and my daughter, Eve Ekman, an artist, writer, and social worker who had observed the five-day conference on destructive emotions at which I first met the Dalai Lama in 2000.

The last member of the group was Dr. Clifford Saron, a psychologist, neuroscientist, "super tech," and personal friend. Cliff, whose knowledge of the brain and of Buddhism far exceeds mine, was invited to provide not only the essential, high-quality audio recording of the conversation but also to provide me with advice during the breaks on phrasing my questions about Buddhism.

The experience of talking day after day about issues that I had spent most of my life thinking and writing about, engaging in more than conversation but less than debate, is hard to describe. There were challenges back and forth, and as I had hoped, new ideas were sparked that had not emerged before in my thinking. I am always excited when a new idea crystallizes, but this time the excitement was multiplied by learning more about Buddhist thinking, getting to know this remarkable man better, and witnessing his ideas change during the course of our discussions. If I were to say I felt "high," it would capture only some of what I felt when it was over; "satisfied" also only captures part of it. I was far from exhausted, and though I sensed this would not be the last of our discussions, I did not anticipate that this would turn out to be less than a third of the time we were to spend together in the following year. In the next months I played the tapes to a group of colleagues and friends interested in the topic, who raised many questions about what either he or I had said, which made it clear that I would need to meet with the Dalai Lama again.[4]

A year later, we met in India, at a five-day conference in April 2007 sponsored by the Mind and Life Institute. During that conference, each scientist in the group was asked to explain his or her reactions to the Dalai Lama's *The Universe in a Single Atom,* his book in which he described what he had learned from his many meetings with scientists.

The Dalai Lama and I managed to meet twice during breaks in the conference, each time for an hour and a half. These private conversations were held in a room used for meetings with individuals or small groups; *thangkas** covered the walls, and air-conditioning was available. (The Dalai Lama likes it to be much colder than I do, even though his monk's robes provide less coverage than traditional Western clothing.) As always in these intimate meetings, he removed his shoes and crossed his legs beneath him. We sat very close to each other, neither of us leaning back in our chairs. I had been warned that if he ever sits back, you have lost his interest, but that never occurred.

Geshe Dorji Damdul joined us, translating and sometimes contributing to the conversation. Occasionally the two of them would fall into a long conversation in Tibetan, trying to decide if my scientific perspective had any correspondence in the Buddhist texts. At the end of the sessions, I explained my plan to splice much of what we had said into the original dialogue, so that our amplified points would come just as the reader needed them. I proposed to provide the integrated text to Jinpa, who could check for inaccuracies against the transcripts, but wanted to know if the Dalai Lama himself would like to review the manuscript before I sent it to the publisher. "Who are the authors?" he asked for clarification. "The Dalai Lama and Paul Ekman," I replied. He then said that he would like to invite me to come back to India and read the entire manuscript to him aloud so that he could review and elaborate on it.

I had not expected this. I was already committed to making a trip a few weeks later to Europe and could not cancel it. Later, one of the Dalai Lama's senior managers told me not to worry: I would have to wait at least a year, as there was no time free in the Dalai Lama's schedule for what would likely take a week of reading and commenting. When Jinpa, who was also attending the conference,

---

* A *thangka* is a painted or embroidered Buddhist banner that is hung in a monastery or at a family altar and carried by lamas in ceremonial processions. *Thangka* painting originally became popular among traveling monks because the scroll paintings were easily rolled and transported from monastery to monastery. *Thangkas* served as important teaching tools and depicted the life of the Buddha, influential lamas, deities, and Bodhisattvas. To Buddhists, these banners are believed to be a manifestation of the divine.

heard about this, he once again intervened as a champion for the book, arguing that it would be wrong to delay its publication. And so, at the end of June 2007 I traveled again to India, just before the start of the monsoon season. We met every day for five hours, five days in a row. It was exhilarating and it was exhausting.

This time yet another set of people observed and participated. Dr. Bernard Schiff, a retired psychologist and a close friend, read aloud my part in the previous discussions. I thought he might well provide me with useful suggestions from both of his backgrounds, but as it turned out I was too completely engaged to want any suggestions. Bernard thoroughly enjoyed this opportunity to meet the Dalai Lama, though he was sometimes frustrated that he too could not become a participant, only a reader. I read aloud what the Dalai Lama had said. We rarely got through a page before either he or I or both of us interrupted the reading to question or expand on what had been said. Joining us was the Dalai Lama's brother—who a few times commented on the exchange—as well as his son. A Tibetan scholar from the nearby Institute of Dialectics attended in order to resolve any uncertainty about how particular issues were explained in the Buddhist texts; he never spoke in English during the reading. This last set of meetings added another very valuable third to this book and convinced me to reorganize the original discussions by topic, weaving together what we had to say about each issue considered, whether it was said during the first, second, or third set of conversations.[5] They also helped me identify moments in our dialogue at which further explanation, beyond the interplay between the Dalai Lama and myself, would be enriching. These appear as occasional footnotes (introducing or expanding upon Buddhist or scientific terms or identifying the individuals mentioned) and commentaries from Buddhist thinkers, including Geshe Dorji Damdul and meditation teachers Margaret Cullen and B. Alan Wallace, and other scientists, including Frans de Waal, Richard J. Davidson, Margaret Kemeny, Robert Levenson, and Cliff Saron.

When I was speaking, I tried to make clear when my comments were based on scientific evidence—my own or that of others. But on many of the most interesting and important issues that we considered, there is no science yet. Thus I invited the viewpoints of other scientists to comment on some of these issues as well as questions about their work that came up in our discussion. While I believe my ideas are extrapolations from the existing evidence, they should be evaluated as more in the tradition of philosophy than of science, accepted or rejected as they are useful or interesting. I was to learn from the Dalai Lama that the Buddha cautioned his readers to accept only what they found useful.

We began by discussing how people view the world, a topic I found is fundamental to the Dalai Lama's conception of compassion, and by digging into the assumed antagonism between science and religion. Once this ground was settled, we turned our focus to the nature of our emotions, the topic that had inspired us to meet one-on-one. As we explored the differences between emotions and other mental states, I reported to the Dalai Lama some of the findings from an experiment I conducted, with my colleague Robert Levenson, on Matthieu Ricard's ability to calm a difficult person with whom he is engaged in conversation. Is it an engrained part of Matthieu's temperament or a product of his Buddhist training? Matthieu's case seemed instructive as we looked at the problems faced by people who become emotional very quickly. We discussed tactics for obtaining emotional balance available from the Buddhist and Western psychology traditions.

Later, we considered the emotions of anger, resentment, and hatred before turning to the question of how to cultivate compassion. While we agreed from the outset that anger can be constructive, the Dalai Lama persuaded me that, in the long term, hatred always corrodes our lives, and we contemplated how people can let go of resentments and grievances, which are responsible for many conflicts between peoples in the world. As we shifted to our discussion of compassion, I witnessed the Dalai Lama become, at this point, a Darwinian, quoting Darwin back to me! As we reviewed examples of compassion and moral virtues in other animals, we soon considered the prospects for extending compassion to all human beings.

In the closing chapter of our conversation, I share the story of my personal transformation six years earlier during a break in my first meeting with the Dalai Lama. As my daughter, Eve, asked, and the Dalai Lama answered, a question about anger and love, I experienced an unusual awareness that changed my own emotional life. Always the scientist, I provided to the Dalai Lama my evidence and my explanation for what had occurred then and asked the Dalai Lama to provide his own.

While these topics have been considered in some previous books, including books by the Dalai Lama and myself, our conversation offers a level of immediacy, passion, and depth that is conveyed in the back-and-forth of our exchange. The dialogue also offers a uniquely vivid view of the Dalai Lama's remarkable personality. At one point, I told him how relieved I was that in our conversations I did not need to tamp down my enthusiasm or my force of argument. Usually I feel obliged to do so, as people can misinterpret my excitement and passion for anger. The Dalai Lama replied, "Why talk unless you feel passionately!"

Because I spoke more clearly, loudly, and distinctly than my usual mumble, translation was not often required, allowing more fluidity in our conversation than there would have been if every word I spoke had to be translated. While often the flow was interrupted when the Dalai Lama replied in Tibetan, which then had to be translated, sometimes he became so eager to proceed that he spoke in English, providing a unique picture of how he thinks. About a third of the time he spoke in English, more so in our later meetings. I have avoided the temptation to correct his grammar. He speaks with many shadings of intonation and emphasis, which of course are missing on the printed page, but the sense of what it is like to talk with this man comes across most clearly in the untranslated sections.

I hope you find our conversations as invigorating and thought-provoking as we did.

Emotional Awareness

· 1 ·

EAST AND WEST

Knowing of the Dalai Lama's interest in gadgets, I decided to begin our first dialogue by presenting the Dalai Lama with a small tool, which contained a knife, a screwdriver, tweezers, scissors, and other devices. Many times in the first session, the Dalai Lama picked the tool up, apparently sorely tempted to play with it, but each time he restrained himself. Though it was not my intention, the gadget seemed later to represent a theme of our conversation: the Dalai Lama's openness to engaging with the scientist's tools and my interest in engaging with Buddhism's tools.

EKMAN: I have a small gift for you.

DALAI LAMA: Thank you. How kind.

EKMAN: When I showed this gadget to Jinpa before you came in, he asked me to tell you not to put this in your carry-on bag. Otherwise, they will take it away.

DALAI LAMA: One time, in Japan, I had a tweezer; it was attached to a knife. At the airport, they took it away. As soon as I arrived I made sure that this thing was being sent to me. (*Everyone laughs.*) Thank you much.

TWO TRADITIONS

EKMAN: I am very grateful for the time you are giving for this series of conversations. My hope is that by bringing to bear our two very different intellectual traditions—Buddhism and Western Psychology—we will spark in each other ideas we have not already had, hopefully ideas that might be of benefit in understanding emotion and compassion.

You have written that we must train our minds to observe. Would you agree that both how we train our minds and how we can motivate people to want to undertake such training can be addressed scientifically?

DALAI LAMA: (*Translated.*) No one denies the existence of emotion, feeling, or mind. In daily life, we have emotion; it is *there.* Science and technology are concerned, basically, with physical comfort. When it comes to difficulties or problems with emotions, then, technology cannot do much. I think injection, some drugs, to reduce your anxiety, these are temporary. So now the time has come to explore the trouble, which is faced by our emotional mind, the method or means to tackle this wicked mischievous nature of mind.

EKMAN: Television teaches everyone the message, "If I become rich, if I become famous, I'll be very happy." Very few people find out that that is untrue because most people do not get rich. (*Dalai Lama laughs.*)

How can we reach people who want happiness but have been misled by television to think the path to it involves fame and riches and power? How do we reach them with the message that this is a false path? Can you think of any way that scientists can help correct this misperception?

DALAI LAMA: For the last almost a hundred years, the whole concept of material development was that it would solve all our problems. The real problem is poverty. But we didn't realize that solving poverty doesn't provide inner peace. I can give one example—the Chinese case. I think Deng Xiaoping felt once people are rich, then all problems reduce. He even extend[ed] it that, no matter what method you adopt, the goal, so long you get rich, okay. In the seventies, he started, or developed, a movement. He said, It doesn't matter what color the cat is as long as it catches mice. So, the implication, even through the wrong method [capitalism], you can get rich. (*Laughs.*) So now today in China, they are getting richer—and more corruption. Poor people suffer more. And rich people, many are not happy.

EKMAN: Yes.

DALAI LAMA: For many people simply, they think if you are rich, you will have plenty of money and then they suppose all their problems are solved. Or if you have power, then no problem. That is not the case. Rich people, powerful people, very famous people have been mentally very unhappy. It is obvious. Hatred and other emotions create more problems.

EKMAN: Yes.

DALAI LAMA: In the eighteenth century, nineteenth century, the early part of the twentieth century, no government says what is the importance of peace of mind. Only say: economy, economy, economy. Why? Because poverty is urgent. So, therefore, people everywhere, putting every effort, including our education, into eliminating poverty. No?

EKMAN: Yes.

DALAI LAMA: Also, on the television, all you see, is about improvement of the poverty: to improve the economy, prosperity. But, you see, people, at least those people, who are no longer much worried about their physical needs, now they are experiencing problems, but mainly at the mental level. That mental unrest brings a lot of suffering on humanity. Therefore, now we have to think or explore another field, and that is mental health. We cannot change mental health overnight.

Scientists have focused on what is relevant to material welfare. Now [scientists] begin to realize, there is possibility, to develop proper, healthy mental attitudes, which [are of] benefit when we are facing problems. You, as a scientist, you do that—and you should do that.

SCIENCE, RELIGION, AND TRUTH

DALAI LAMA: In the past, the circumstances were such that science was applied toward material development, not toward mental things. In the West, traditionally, religion means Christianity, Judaism, and Islam. Those are traditions of, mainly, faith. There is not much emphasis on investigation. Science demands trying to find the reality through investigation, through experiments. According to that, we can say that science has nothing to do with religious faith.

EKMAN: No, it does not.

DALAI LAMA: Clearly. But, that does not mean, of every person who is in the world of science, that a scientist is *necessarily* a nonbeliever.

EKMAN: Yes. That is true.

DALAI LAMA: Science, in the past, was mainly involved with material development. So, you see, in that domain, science has nothing to do with religious faith.

EKMAN: Yes. Yes.

DALAI LAMA: In individual cases, some scientists are very religious-minded. But their profession, their professional field, has nothing to do with religion. Now, I think, society is now facing a new crisis, or a new problem; it is mainly an emotional problem. Therefore, science begins to deal with that. So modern science—their exploration or their sort of interest or their concern not only matters, but also emotions. I think that is the way. Is it not?

EKMAN: Yes. That is a very accurate way of putting it. With the works of Wilhelm Wundt, Sigmund Freud, and Charles Darwin at the end of the nineteenth century, psychology began. That was the beginning attempt to deal with the mind, but we had science before then. And even in the twentieth century, the preponderance of science dealt with the material. For a hundred years, a question was largely ignored in academic research: How can we achieve happiness? There has not been much progress.

Scientists are now beginning to look outside of Western thinking to see what they could learn and study scientifically that might be relevant. A growing number of scientists are interested in what we can learn from Buddhist thinking on this.

DALAI LAMA: Now, "soft" science and "hard" science—what is the demarcation?

EKMAN: It used to be a clearer demarcation. "Hard" sciences were the natural and biological sciences. "Soft" sciences were the social and behavioral sciences. Now cognitive neuroscience crosses the two, because it is using some very biological measures—brain measures, blood chemistry measures—to look at psychological phenomena.

I measure the movement of the facial muscles—you cannot get harder science—but I do it to study emotions. We cannot see an emotion; the facial movement is just a display, but we can learn a lot if we can measure that display precisely. Many scientists today, certainly in cognitive neuroscience, and even in fields like emotion and memory in psychology, are using very objective methods, some of them biological, some of them not.

There is the greatest disregard among some scientists for findings on the basis of what people tell you in a questionnaire. I think what people tell you is interesting; it may not be what they really think, or what they know may only be part of what they actually are and do, so it has limits, but it is not without merit. Studies that only use questionnaires are considered to be very "soft."

DALAI LAMA: And Darwin?

EKMAN: Psychology came out of philosophy. I myself consider Darwin to have been the first writer in psychology, in his book on the expression of emotions, in 1872. For large parts of psychology, I think it is very hard to determine, Is it biological or is it psychological? They are just two sides of the same coin. Everything is both; the questions are in what way, in which phenomena does each play their role.

DALAI LAMA: In the West, there is not much of a tradition of investigation in religion. Whereas, in the nontraditional religions, in India, particularly in Buddhism, it was different—they experimented or investigated in the traditions.

The reality is that science is not all antireligious. Simply, is it trying to know the reality, find out the reality through investigation, through experiment? Not by faith. That is not antireligion. Even the pope—the new pope is a very intelligent person, a very wonderful person—emphasizes that faith and reason must go together. Actually, he mentions he started this idea with some of his followers: If people have faith without reason, then people would not get the feeling of relevance of religion to their life, so reason must be there.

But only reason, no faith, like with some scientists—they are great scientists, but mentally unhappy. (Laughs.) So faith also is necessary.* That is the way; I think that way. So, even Christians are now compelled to realize the importance of reason. As far as Buddhism is concerned, there is no problem. We have the courage to say, True investigation is something. If our findings—through investigations, through experimentation—contradict Buddhist ideas, then we have the liberty to reject the old ideas. That is the Buddha's own words.

Chinese Communists say that Tibetan Buddhism, because there is a lack of science knowledge—"those foolish Tibetans, they were full of blind faith or superstition." So that is their attitude in the early sixties, seventies, eighties. I think that from the beginning they feel that not recognizing Buddhism encourages an investigative attitude and rejection of dogma.

---

* Neuroscientist Clifford Saron, of the University of California-Davis Center for Mind and Brain, commented, "Scientists have faith in their method and hypothesis—it's full of faith—just not necessarily faith in God."

On one occasion, I was in Moscow meeting with some scientists. I think that was my first visit or my second visit. So, at that time the Marxists or Communist ideology was still fresh. Some scientists believe or feel science is something that must be anti-religion, but that is not the case. Science is only the method to investigate what is the reality. Religious matters deal mainly with the subjective side.

EKMAN: The motivation of most scientists and physicians, at least when they start, and for many it remains, is to relieve suffering. Some would say they are motivated religiously.

DALAI LAMA: Religiously?

EKMAN: They want to do good.

DALAI LAMA: Oh, yes.

EKMAN: They want to relieve suffering.

DALAI LAMA: Oh—compassion.

EKMAN: Yes.

DALAI LAMA: Their sense of concern. About suffering. That's right. I think that is in every human activity, all human actions, activities. I think human beings, everyone, do not want suffering and do not want to see pain.

EKMAN: Virtually everyone does not want to suffer themselves.

Although science is an investigatory method, there are very few scientists whose motivation is not to do good in the world, which gives them some overlap with religious motivations. Whether they believe in a Creator does not really matter. In the Jewish religion, if you do service to your community, you are a religious Jew. You need not believe in a Creator. It depends on the religion. In my view, most good scientists are motivated by the spiritual value of wanting to be of service, to be of help, in the world.

DALAI LAMA: There are now some institutions, some schools, some people, people dealing with education, quite a number now, showing interest about how to cultivate the awareness of the importance of compassion. Hopefully, some media people eventually may take interest.

We cannot change all our lives or worldviews. Our message, our voice, is very small. Very small! The other is very shiny! But as time goes by, when I talk about this inner value in the West, people want this very strong, whereas in India, they want it not that much. In Africa, I think it is very difficult; the people's main concern is if there is food or shelter—these things. So why the interest in the West? Because as far as material comfort is concerned, this is already achieved, yet they are not happy. So now, through their own experience, they are looking for an alternative.

EKMAN: In *The Threepenny Opera*, the German playwright Bertolt Brecht wrote, "First feed the face. Then, tell right from wrong." The next line is, "Even honest men may act like sinners unless they've had their customary dinners."

DALAI LAMA: (*Chuckles.*) Very good.

THE FILTER OF MOODS

EKMAN: Before we go much further, I think it is important to consider how emotions differ from moods. Unless we do so, we may not always know whether we are talking about emotions or moods, as they are easily confused. I recall seven years ago, when I first met you and described this distinction, you told me it did not exist in the Tibetan view of mental states, and that you found it very useful. As I describe it in more detail, I hope you will continue to find it of interest.

I believe moods get us into a lot of trouble, even more so than some of our emotions. One difference between emotions and moods is a person's understanding of what triggers each of them. He or she may not know what triggers an emotion when it first begins, but afterward can almost always easily figure it out. The person may not think he or she should have become angry, but knows, at least afterward, what set it off. By contrast, when someone is in an irritable mood, he or she may never know what triggered it.

DALAI LAMA: Would you not say that they can reinforce each other? Because of a bad mood, you would be much more prone to an explosion of particular emotions? For example, yesterday, your mood was not good. At that time, if your friend comes, you may lose your temper. But then, the next day, your mood is calm. Then, you see, yesterday's appearance completely changes. So much depends on your own mental attitude, your outlook. According to our experience, that is clear.

EKMAN: Yes. That's one of the problems with moods.

DALAI LAMA: Similarly, when you have a strong emotional experience, that can affect your mood.

EKMAN: Yes, you are right on both. When we are in an apprehensive mood we are looking to be afraid. We are responding to the world with fear more than anything else, often misperceiving the world. It is as if we *need* to be afraid when we are in an apprehensive mood, just like we *need* to get angry when we are in an irritable mood.

Most scientists believe that moods typically occur for reasons that the person experiencing the mood does not understand—perhaps generated by neurohormonal changes not directly tied to an event in our environment. However, there are certain events that can trigger a mood; for example, if you are sleep-deprived, you are more likely to get either irritable or giddy and to laugh at things you would never laugh at.

DALAI LAMA: Can sleeplessness, or sleep deprivation, lead to giddiness?

EKMAN: Yes, particularly in children and adolescents. They may laugh and laugh. They stay up all night, and they are in a wonderful, excited mood.

DALAI LAMA: (*Translated.*) Can the causal relation go the opposite way? Because you are in a very excited state, the sleep does not come easily?

EKMAN: (*Laughs.*) Here I am speculating. And I do want to distinguish when I'm talking on the basis of facts that have some scientific basis, when I'm talking on the basis of theory that all those who study emotion would agree with, from when I'm talking on the basis of just my own ideas. I may be right, but I don't believe anyone else has yet considered the matter; the idea that when a person is sleep-deprived he or she may become giddy is my own speculation.

ON SCIENTIFIC CERTAINTY

by Paul Ekman

Richard J. Davidson, a professor of psychology at the University of Wisconsin, who had originally nominated me to attend the 2000 meeting in Dharamsala during which I first met the Dalai Lama, had cautioned me to be certain to make clear to the Dalai Lama when I was speculating and when I was speaking on the basis of accepted scientific fact. I have known Richie since he was a graduate student, and regard him more as a friend than as a congenial colleague, although we coauthored a few scientific papers twenty years ago. Our principal theoretical difference is his acceptance and my rejection of the value of distinguishing between positive and negative emotions, a question that arises in the course of this conversation.

Richie's interest in meditation dates back more than thirty years. His primary research focuses on the brain and emotion, and in recent years much of it has examined the impact of meditation on the brain.

✦ ✦ ✦

EKMAN: Unfortunately, some of the most interesting issues are matters that no one has yet written about, let alone studied scientifically, so we do not know if they are completely true.

DALAI LAMA: So, not very sure. (*Laughs heartily.*)

EKMAN: On the issue of sleep deprivation, it is my belief that when a person has been deprived of sleep, if the person is provoked or frustrated, an irritable mood will be instigated that may last for hours. If the person is delighted by something, a giddy mood may occur. Whatever emotion is aroused sets the mood when a person has been sleep-deprived. When people get off an airplane, they ought to hear beautiful music and people telling jokes to put them into a wonderful mood, rather than have them become frustrated that their luggage has not come. You do not want to frustrate people; you want to delight them when they haven't had much sleep.

DALAI LAMA: (*Laughs heartily.*) Oh!

EKMAN: You said that a strong emotion can create a mood. I wrote about this in my last book, *Emotions Revealed.*[1] No one has yet responded to my proposal specifying when an emotional experience can create a mood. I think the emotional experience must be (1) very intense and (2) very dense, that is, you experience the emotion again and again and again in a short period of time. When this happens, you cross a threshold—you are now in a mood. If you were to make me very, very happy again and again and again, I am going to be in a euphoric mood for hours. If in a short period of time you make me very frightened again and again and again, I'm going to be in a very worried, apprehensive mood. But this is just my idea; I do not know whether it is true.

DALAI LAMA: (*Translated.*) Sometimes an emotion can be very intense because the triggering event itself is very intense; then the emotional *reaction* is very intense. But sometimes the trigger may not be a dramatic event, but is the result of dwelling upon a situation or event, ruminating about it over and over again. Then, too, the emotion can be very intense.

EKMAN: Yes, I completely agree. I use the term "fester" to describe when that happens. When an emotion festers, it dominates your life, at least for a period of time.

We have known for a long time, but scientists have just recently acknowledged, that animals other than humans have emotions. Everyone who has a pet knows this, but scientists were afraid for many years of being accused of being anthropomorphic, of falsely attributing human characteristics to animals. Now the evidence is overwhelming that animals have emotions. We do not know whether they have moods. It would be very interesting to find out from people who have pets, Are there some days you can recognize that your dog is in a bad mood, or is very jittery or afraid? We do not know if animals have moods.*

DALAI LAMA: Of course, the visibility and obviousness of emotions and moods may be different for humans and animals, but the general pattern ought to be the same. If human beings have emotions and moods, one would expect that animals, too, have emotions and moods.

You know, I am wondering, if very small insects, like mosquitoes or some others, similar sorts of small animals, have emotions, I don't know if compassion is one of them. Or caring. I don't know. You see, if we show affection, then animals also eventually appreciate it. But mosquitoes?

EKMAN: I do not know about a mosquito, whether it ever appreciates it. (*Laughs.*)

DALAI LAMA: (*Translated.*) Probably the difference is due to the size of the brain. Some simple organisms like mosquitoes, as compared to mammals, do not have more complex emotional responses, apart from their immediate needs, in terms of reproduction or feeding.

EKMAN: It may also be the effect of selective breeding. My wife and I were recently in Tanzania, and we saw hyenas that were the size of many dogs, but they were very vicious and you would not want to approach them. Someone who had for a long time been feeding a hyena in a laboratory had her arm chewed off by it. With dogs, there has been a selection, over a long, long period of time, for the breeds that most like humans and that most want to work

---

* University of British Columbia forensic psychologist John Yuille, a devoted dog owner, reports that his poodle definitely has moods.

with us. Maybe if someone was to selectively breed mosquitoes, you could get mosquitoes or bees that were friendlier!

Let me introduce a controversial speculation, one that I believe but that many of my colleagues do not accept. I believe that moods are what Stephen Jay Gould called a "spandrel," something that is not itself adaptive or useful to our species, but that arises as a by-product of something else that is. My claim is that moods are not useful to us; they filter what we see in the world, and they make us respond on the basis of a narrow if not distorted view of reality. Although I do not think we could live without emotions, I suggest that we would lead better lives if we had no moods at all, and were therefore more responsive to what is actually happening in the world rather than what little we can see through the narrow filter of one or another mood.

DALAI LAMA: (*Translated.*) We cannot find a Tibetan word that captures the concept of "mood" accurately. There is a concept of "latent emotions" in Buddhist psychology, but then we also speak about a person's state of mind.

EKMAN: Emotions also filter the knowledge that is available to us. When we are in the grip of an emotion, I have proposed that we are in a "refractory period," during which we can only remember information that fits the emotion; we can only interpret others in a way that fits the emotion.[2] Often a refractory period is very short-lived, and when that is so, it can be helpful, by focusing our attention. For moods, a refractory period can last a whole day, and all of that time we are misperceiving the world. We do not have access to everything we know, only to what fits our mood.

That is why, as a Darwinian, I believe that moods must be a by-product of something else. They are a plague for us, distorting how we see the world and respond to others. People have heard me say I want to banish moods and have asked me, What about a good mood? But in a good mood, we are not sensitive to potential problems; we are in a deluded state. We enjoy it, but just because we enjoy it does not mean it is really useful.

There is a great deal of emphasis in the popular press and

within the field of psychology about feeling good, achieving happiness. Although the language used does not always make it clear, what usually is under consideration is an overall sense of well-being, of believing life is going well or as well as can be expected, not the emotion of happiness or the mood of euphoria.[3]

In terms of this distinction between emotions and moods, to me what is fundamental about a mood is that it lasts a long time—though usually not for weeks, just for hours—and we do not see the world the way we would if we were not in that mood. It distorts and narrows our responses. Therefore it is not good for us.

So, a question: There is a lot of interest in America today about learning meditative practices, believing it may benefit the practitioner's emotional life. I think we are beginning to acquire scientific evidence that meditation can help our emotions, but what type of meditative practice could help us shorten a mood? Sometimes you are aware of being in a mood. Someone says, Why are you always getting so short-tempered? and you realize you are in an irritable mood. But what can you do to shorten the mood? If you wake up in the morning and you are feeling irritable, what type of meditative practice would help you get out of that mood?

DALAI LAMA: (*Translated.*) We still have not resolved what exact Tibetan term correlates with the term "mood." . . . But despite that, my personal view is that practices such as mindfulness meditation, and meditation in which you focus on breathing, are very effective in bringing the mind to a more neutral state from a more turbulent emotional fluctuation. Because mindfulness is able to bring the mind to a more restful, neutral state, one would also expect that this effect would be felt on the mood as well. The idea here is that the mood is in some sense an imprint, an aftereffect of an emotional state of mind.

There could be some types of mood that may be purely biologically related, not the product of some external event; for example, when you wake up and somehow you feel very dull. Even the Shamatha meditation manuals recognize that there are certain types of mental states or temperaments that simply cannot be corrected through meditation alone. One of the two main obstacles for Shamatha practice, which trains attention, is referred to as mental laxity, sometimes translated as mental "sinkingness." It is the feeling of sinking and dullness. I think Alan Wallace* translates it as laxity, a much more lax state of mind, a dullness and non-clarity. The meditation manuals state that in many cases when the meditator is experiencing a much more intense form of dullness or laxity, these may be related to the health and physical constitution of the person—maybe she is not getting enough sleep or something is wrong with her diet. And in these cases, the advice is not to continue to meditate, but to go out into a more open space, to throw water on your face to wake up. There is a recognition that these are—I don't know whether they can be called "moods"—but these are states of mind.

EKMAN: They sound like moods.

JINPA: Yes.

EKMAN: Even if meditation does not correct or eliminate the mood, it may still have an effect on the tendency to respond with an emotion while you are in that mood, without being mindful of it. Do you agree?

DALAI LAMA: (*Translated.*) This is very true. For example, in meditation one constantly reflects upon the disadvantages and destructive nature of anger and hatred. Then, even though the person may sometimes find himself in an irritable mood, he may not respond with anger to a trigger. In the Buddhist psychology and meditation texts, there is a term that literally means "mental unhappiness," but it is probably better translated as "disquiet," which is a basic sense of dissatisfaction. "Frustration" is probably a better word. This is seen as the fuel for anger. So when there is

---

* A scholar and the author of many books on Buddhism, B. Alan Wallace, PhD, is the founding director of the nonprofit Santa Barbara Institute for Consciousness Studies. He was a Buddhist monk for many years and has served as a translator for the Dalai Lama and as a meditation teacher. Wallace and I have become close friends, and I serve on the board of the institute.

a frustration, it fuels anger. A small trigger can immediately bring it up. In the meditation texts, it is mentioned that a meditator who constantly reflects upon the destructive nature of anger, even when he may find himself with this frustrated state of mind, may not actually express it in anger.

EKMAN: In an irritable mood, a person is prone to getting angry. But, through meditation practice he might be able to learn to observe himself and *see* that he is in an irritable mood. He would be less likely to get angry. Even if he has not eliminated the mood, he would know he is in the mood, and he could apply intelligence and be less likely, even during the mood, to get angry.

DALAI LAMA: (*Translated.*) Is mood emotional?

EKMAN: Yes. Each mood is saturated with a particular emotion. So, when a person is in an irritable mood, his distortion of reality is to promote anger. He is looking for a chance to be angry. But you often do not even realize you are in an irritable mood.

DALAI LAMA: (*Translated.*) Hmm. So it is an inclination.

EKMAN: It is more than an inclination: You are biologically prepared to be angry. The mood causes you to distort reality to fit the mood. But if through meditation practice a person is more observant of himself, he will see that he is in an irritable state, and had better try not to just jump into anger. Meditative practices might, over time, change the appraisals. As the meditation that involves a knowledge of destructiveness of harming others becomes a part of a person, over time it will allow him to evaluate things differently. The same frustrating trigger will not be frustrating. Do you agree?

DALAI LAMA: That is right. Exactly; it works that way. What is said here is absolutely correct. So there are, of course, some problems we can avoid. "Avoid" means then "to overcome." But for some problems, there is no way to overcome, just to simply divert your thinking. "Let us just avoid," but the problems still remain there. Looking at the problem itself, but from a different angle, through that way, you may see some positive things about that problem. Still, you are facing the problem. You have meditated on the problem. But you see much less of a disturbance on your peace of mind. That is the way—what is referred to in the Buddha's text as transforming the adverse conditions into the path.

EKMAN: I think this is very important. Let me take an example, so we will be sure that we understand each other.

DALAI LAMA: Yes.

EKMAN: Suppose you are walking down the street. Someone is standing in the middle of the street, blocking your way. It is hard to get around him, because you are carrying suitcases. You say to this person, "Pardon me," and the person says, "What's your problem?!" in a nasty way. Now, you could respond with anger to his seeming anger. But if you do express your anger, what you do not want to do is say, "My problem is you! You are being a problem!" because the conflict could escalate. If you respond to *him* rather than to the *problem* itself, it will be harmful. If instead you could reevaluate the situation, imagining that he probably had trouble today that made him irritable and easily provoked, you would start to empathize with him. But you could still say, "I do not want to inconvenience you, but I've got these heavy suitcases, so I need some help." You might call forth from him a positive response. Why was he being impolite? Probably because he has some trouble. If you can be sympathetic to his trouble, he may be able to help you with yours. It is a totally different way of dealing with the situation. And this is what you are talking about. It is a tall order; I do not know if I would be capable of it.

From a Western point of view, what you are doing is *cognitively reframing* the situation. An enormous amount of the Buddhist emphasis is on a wiser understanding, a fuller understanding of others.

DALAI LAMA: Yes.

WHEN EMOTIONS ARE DESTRUCTIVE

EKMAN: I want to turn now to the distinction between what Buddhists call afflictive and nonafflictive emotions, or what in the

West has been called destructive and nondestructive emotions. In the psychology of emotion, it is very common to contrast positive and negative emotions. In your recent book, *The Universe in a Single Atom,* I was pleased that you dismissed that distinction. I also think it is much too simple.[4] A so-called negative emotion can save your life; for example, in a near-miss car accident, your fear causes you to make adjustments to your driving that save your life. And humor can be used to ridicule; humor can be very enjoyable, but it can be at someone else's expense.

DALAI LAMA: Like a sarcastic remark.

EKMAN: Yes. Absolutely.

DALAI LAMA: Would you say it is a humor if it is hurting the other person?

EKMAN: Yes, if it is funny and others like it. I know a person who writes book reviews for a major newspaper, and if her review is not cutting—and that is a very important word because you can write in a way where you "cut" the other person—they want her to rewrite it. There was a review recently of a movie in which the reviewer was cruel in his words—cruel in a clever way, and people like to read that. I think it is bad for people to read and enjoy such cruel writing; it feeds cruelty in the reader, and it is terrible for the person you have cut. Yet, this particular journalist gets things sent back, saying, "Not cutting enough!"

DALAI LAMA: Should we really call that humor? Because in actual fact, it is harsh words.

EKMAN: It is very harsh, but in a funny way.

DALAI LAMA: That is right. Definitely.

EKMAN: You agree.

DALAI LAMA: Yes, yes.

EKMAN: I believe you hold this view because of your belief that an awareness of the interdependence of all peoples will prevent cruel actions. Also, the Buddhist view of hatred is that it obscures recognizing that there is some good in everyone. I have got that correctly?

DALAI LAMA: Definitely. (*Laughs.*)

(*Translated.*) Since destructive, or afflictive, emotion is a kind of "Buddhalogical English"—Buddhist-jargon English—how would it sound to an average English listener, "afflicted"? Does it convey the idea?

EKMAN: I want to discuss what it means to identify a mental state as afflictive. My interpretation of what is meant in Buddhalogical English by the term "afflictive" is that it is both harmful to the person feeling the emotion and harmful to others. If that is the case, then it is termed afflictive when it does harm, perhaps even more harm to the person who feels it than to the recipient or target. It cultivates bad traits and destructive attitudes. Unfortunately, I think that human beings are capable of having that cultivated. There is pliability as to what characteristics you cultivate, and either cruelty or compassion can be cultivated.

DALAI LAMA: (*Translated.*) Between the afflictive emotions and mental states on the one side and the nonafflictive mental states and emotions on the other, I doubt there would be any difference in their immutability to cultivation, and the degree to which they can be cultivated. I was wondering whether an afflictive emotion or mental state, like cruelty, can be really cultivated to a high point, at which it becomes spontaneous and like advanced states of compassion. I wonder whether the afflictive states follow the same pattern as the nonafflictive, or whether they follow a different pattern.

EKMAN: It is a wonderful question. There is no scientific evidence available to answer that question. In my thinking, cruelty means that you enjoy inflicting suffering. We do know that some extremely cruel people are generous and warm to some people at the same time they are cruel to others. Hitler was reported to be kind to children and to dogs. A number of people who were world champions of cruelty were also, in some relationships with some people, kind; the cruelty was not there.

DALAI LAMA: (*Translated.*) To relate this discussion back to our earlier one about an emotion's or a mood's tendency to obscure our vision of reality, certainly in the case of cruelty, it really obscures our vision of reality. In the case, say, of empathy, or a sense of caring for others, would you say it shares this tendency to obscure?

EKMAN: I suspect not; but again I do not know of any scientific evidence that is directly relevant to your question. A prerequisite for compassion or cruelty—for either—is to be able to know how the other person feels. Knowing how you feel does not mean I am going to help you.

Do you agree that any emotion can be afflictive or nonafflictive—it depends on how it is enacted? For example, you wrote that if anger is directed at an act, but not to harm the actor, it is constructive. We certainly know that fear can be constructive; it can save your life. When you are feeling anguish at a loss, that can be constructive—if it does not fester—because other people will come and comfort you. From a Darwinian perspective, one would assume that we would not have emotions unless they were at least sometimes useful in our ancestral environment, and that is why they have been preserved in our species.

When I said this to you in Dharamsala six years ago, you said back to me, very quickly, "Well, just because it is part of us does not necessarily mean it is good! Death—we all die, and nobody wants to die."

I was so startled by your reply, not yet knowing how quickly you think and what a great debater you are, that I did not think to argue back that there can be a good death. If you die after a long and fulfilling life, if you die when your body is worn out, it is time to die. When people reach that point in life, they can welcome death. They may not welcome the fact that their body does not work anymore or that they are getting mentally confused, but, in a sense, death is very functional and adaptive for us, if it is not premature.

I discussed this issue with the evolutionary philosopher Helena Cronin, who said that we need to think about death on a gene level.[5] If you want to think about death on an individual level, Cronin said, a Darwinian explanation is that adaptations that are good for the individual early in life, particularly when the individual is still able to reproduce, can take a heavy toll later in life—including senescence and death. The individual dies but he or she has been more successful reproductively than he or she would have been had they not had those adaptations. The burden for males of carrying testosterone is thought to be such an adaptation, and one of the reasons for earlier male than female deaths. It is good for the individual only in the sense of his having left more offspring than he would have done otherwise. It is not good in the sense of having a "good death."*

I have a very hard time thinking about how the emotion "contempt" can be constructive. It is a terrible word in English because it sounds like "content," but that is not what it means. When someone feels contempt, she feels morally superior to the object of her contempt: I look down on you because you are not even worth my bothering with, you are so morally deficient. I cannot think of how that could ever be constructive.

ON CONTEMPT

by Paul Ekman

An evolutionary view of emotion does not overlap entirely with the distinction between destructive (or, as they are referred to by Buddhists, afflictive) emotional episodes and constructive ones. The traditional evolutionary view of emotions is that they have been adaptive to the individual who experiences them. If a person shows contempt, others may adjust their behavior to no longer act in a way that he or she disapproves of. If they change their behavior, that is useful to the contemptuous person; and if that results in

---

* The Dalai Lama asked if animals fear death. I queried the primatologist Frans de Waal, who replied, "They seem to recognize death in others; they react to it; sometimes they mourn others. Their own death? No one knows."

more reproductive success for him or her, then expressing contempt can be considered adaptive. Since no one wants to be the target of contempt, from the standpoint of our discussion contempt would be considered afflictive. My proposal, which the Dalai Lama accepts, is that for an emotion to be constructive it has to be of benefit both to the person experiencing—and showing—the emotion and the person who is the target of it. That is not a requirement for an evolutionary explanation of why an emotion has been conserved.

This commentary on contempt benefited from an exchange of ideas with Oliver Curry.[6]

❖ ❖ ❖

DALAI LAMA: (*Translated.*) Can you explain this a little more?

EKMAN: Yes. Helena Cronin is speaking as an evolutionary philosopher. From that viewpoint, anything is adaptive that causes you to have more offspring who survive. If the consequence of having a high testosterone level that makes a man so sexually active that he has many offspring is an early death, as long as he does not die before his children reach adulthood, then he has succeeded, from an evolutionary philosopher's point of view.

DALAI LAMA: (*Translated.*) I do not believe anyone wants to die.

EKMAN: From an evolutionary perspective, a person wants to propagate, and is motivated to beat competitors and have as much sex as possible, unaware of whether the consequence might be an early death.

DALAI LAMA: No one really likes to die. But one thing can be possible: that although you do not like dying, you feel that, "now, at least I do not regret dying. I do not regret." More or less accept it. "Now I have done something good, from an evolution point of view. I have good children. And they are settled." So, no regrets. So, accepted. But still, you see, I think still men [are] unhappy because of death.

EKMAN: I agree. A person might only be happy about death if he is in terrible pain. If he is not talking to his children, his wife hates him, and all he did was accumulate material wealth, then he may have many regrets about what he did with his life.

What I say to my children is to lead your life in such a way that when you get to be my age, you will look back and say, I tried to make the world a little bit better than I found it; I may not have succeeded, but I did as best I could. Then you may be able to accept your death. Otherwise, you are going to think, Oh, I wasted my time. Death does not, in my view, have to be something that we fear. It is part of life.

DALAI LAMA: I think, according to our common, general public sense, I agree.

EKMAN: Is there more? Or should I move on?

DALAI LAMA: (*Translated.*) Yes. When you look at emotions and try to understand what kinds are destructive (afflictive) and what kinds are not, it is not so much the nature of the emotions themselves but more a question of the extent to which these emotions are realistic and appropriate to the given conditions, and to what extent they are unrealistic. When an emotion becomes unrealistic, it tends to be afflictive, which is destructive.

EKMAN: I completely agree that each emotion can be enacted constructively or destructively. To have a choice about how you are going to enact an emotion you must be aware of the emotion as it is arising, of "the spark before the flame," or, in Western terms, the impulse before the action. Then, if you are aware in your consciousness that an emotion is arising, you should be able to adjust the level and the way in which you respond.

DALAI LAMA: (*Translated.*) This is very true, because in the meditation texts there is the role of the two main faculties that are being constantly applied—one is mindfulness and the other one Alan Wallace calls "meta-attention," a form of self-awareness.[7]

The role of self-awareness, this meta-attention, is to train the practitioner to the point where the person is able to detect, even before the actual emotion has arisen, a proneness to this emotion. So the more advanced you are, the earlier you will be able to detect the potential for the arising of that emotion.

EKMAN: We agree that emotions can be afflictive or nonafflictive. If they are afflictive, there is a distortion; they are not in tune with reality. Do you agree with that?

DALAI LAMA: Yes.

EKMAN: And if they are nonafflictive, they are appropriate to reality; no distortion.

DALAI LAMA: Yes. That's right.

EKMAN: What is responsible for whether the emotion occurs as afflictive or not? What I propose is that in the first instance of an emotion, a narrowing of attention occurs, and vital information that does not appear to be relevant to the emotion that has arisen is omitted from the person's perception. In a person who is emotionally skilled, that narrowing of attention lasts only a few fractions of a second. In most people, it lasts throughout the emotion, so they experience a distorted, afflictive emotion.

You are acting on insufficient information, only part of what is going on. The key, in Western terms, is "awareness," to be aware of what you are aware of.

DALAI LAMA: From my viewpoint, emotion is not necessarily something destructive.

EKMAN: That is a crucial issue.

DALAI LAMA: Yes.

EKMAN: Because there is a widespread misunderstanding of the Buddhist view, which is that you believe emotions are bad for people. We further agree that self-observation is the key to emotions being nonafflictive.

DALAI LAMA: Good.

EKMAN: And it is not that emotions are always afflictive or always nonafflictive. It depends on the skill of the person who is experiencing an emotion, and the person's previous mental state, whether it is enacted afflictively or nonafflictively.

DALAI LAMA: Okay.

ON NIRVANA

by Geshe Dorji Damdul

Westerners often misunderstand the Buddhist view of *nirvana*—the goal of becoming free of all emotions, the goal of enlightenment in Buddhism—and confuse it with a Buddhist view of how people should lead their lives, that they should never feel an emotion. Essentially, nirvana is a state of mind, in which one achieves freedom from pain and unsatisfactory nature and states (*samsara*).

Buddhism points to ignorance as the ultimate cause of all *samsara*. Of all ignorances, the worst ignorance is to conceive of the self and others as independent entities rather than understanding that we are all interdependent—in other terms, we all arise from "dependent origination." It is this ignorance that triggers the evolution of all afflictive, or disturbing, emotions, which in turn give rises to negative actions, known as *karma*, and then ripens into manifest pain and agony. Thus, nirvana is not to be thought of as some external divine place, but the purified state of mind in which you are free of all negative emotions.*

Nirvana has four characteristic features: (1) a state of cessation of disturbing emotions from one's mind; (2) absolute peace, a state of total tranquility of disturbing emotions; (3) exuberant satisfaction, which is free of all forms of dissatisfaction; and (4) definite emergence, when one will no longer relapse to an unenlightened state.

Geshe Dorji Damdul is a monk who serves as a translator and consultant on Tibetan scholarship for the Dalai Lama. He lives in Dharamsala, India.

✦　✦　✦

---

* From a Western viewpoint, I would say that this state of mind allows you to be free of enacting emotions in a way that is harmful to yourself and others and that interferes with building cooperative relationships.

EKMAN: Let me be certain that you have agreed that every emotion—let us just take a handful, the ones that every scientist agrees exist: anger, fear, anguish, disgust, surprise, contempt, enjoyment—can be, in a particular episode, either afflictive or non-afflictive? That each of them can be constructively or destructively enacted?

DALAI LAMA: (*Translated.*) In the standard Buddhist taxonomy of mental states (or mental factors), there is a specific class of emotions referred to as the afflictive class. These are aversion, attachment, and—although the terms are problematic—delusion; these are thought to be, by their very nature, afflictive. Then you have what is called the variable mental factors, such as sleep, regret, and so on. These can be either afflictive or nonafflictive, depending upon the circumstances and the state of mind the person is in. This is how in the standard Buddhist psychology the mental factors are parsed.

My own view is that a strong, forceful state of mind, say, a sense of outrage, motivated by compassion, can be positive—nonafflictive and constructive. But then, from the Buddhist psychology point of view, whether we would class that emotion as part of aversion and hatred or not—that is another question.

EKMAN: So you are using different words for the constructive and destructive version of each emotion. From a Western point of view, attachment and grasping are not emotions. What were the others that you mentioned?

JINPA: Aversion or anger—it's the same family—aversion, anger, and hatred. They belong to the same family. There are also the afflictions of attachment or craving.

EKMAN: Attachment and craving from the Western view are not considered emotions. Not that they do not exist, but they are just not considered to be emotions.

JINPA: A large part of the Buddhist position seems to be based upon the premise that any mental states and mental factors that contribute toward the attainment of liberation from an unenlightened existence are referred to as constructive, in the ultimate, final sense. Any mental factors or mental states that some-how prevent that—you know, harms this project—are referred to as afflictive. But His Holiness is taking issue with this. (*Laughs.*)

EKMAN: I want to propose a different definition of what is af-flictive or nonafflictive. Actually, I prefer constructive and destruc-tive because it is not simply that it's not afflictive, it is constructive. It is good for you on the one side, or bad for you on the other. In Tibetan, are the terms more like constructive and destructive, or are they more like afflictive and nonafflictive? Nonafflictive is neu-tral. You need something on the other side of it.

DALAI LAMA: (*Translated.*) It's a bit more complicated. We have this afflictive class defined in terms of those mental factors: When they arise in you, they create disequilibrium and a sense of unhappiness, a sense of unease—basically, a lack of peace; distur-bance. When you inquire further, what kind of disturbance is here? Then, the idea of destructiveness comes in. The factors are destructive to yourself and others.

EKMAN: I want to present another way of defining construc-tive and destructive. In our ancestral life, as best we can figure it out, nearly all of the time that human beings have been on this planet we were living in small villages, in which cooperation was required to deal with predators and prey. The development of traits that foster cooperation is constructive; if an emotion is enacted in a way that fosters cooperation, it is constructive.

Now, in industrial society, at least in the West, we have had pressure for being individualistic, not collective. "If it's good for me, why should I care about anyone else, because I do not need them to protect me. I do not need them to deal with the threats." But what I think has happened in the last ten or fifteen years is that we have come to see that we cannot live on this planet if we have a completely individualistic philosophy or if we have merely a tribal view. It has to be global. So, what is constructive are things that foster our global cooperation; what's destructive is what does not. I think one can look at emotion and emotion episodes in these terms.

Certainly, in terms of anger it is clear that it is destructive if it does harm. How are you going to create cooperation if you do harm? It is constructive when it enlarges your perspective to realize the need to get along with everyone. That does not mean that you let someone run over you; you can stop things that are harmful to you without harming the source of the harm. If you harm the source of your harm, that person will retaliate, a fight will escalate—and that is destructive. That may be very simpleminded, but it seems to me to provide a basis for distinguishing between constructive and destructive emotional episodes.

DALAI LAMA: (*Translated.*) This is an interesting way of defining the concept of constructiveness and destructiveness. If you observe the natural world, you see the biological organisms, especially the plants: By their very nature, for their own survival there is a kind of a mechanism in these organisms that allows them to seek those conditions that are necessary for their survival. And somehow, there is another mechanism that allows them to avoid those conditions and environments that are destructive for their survival. If the simple biological organism has that kind of natural mechanism, then of course we human beings must. And in addition to this natural mechanism, we also have intelligence. I am using "intelligence" in a broad sense.

From that perspective, attachment is part of a mechanism that allows you to seek the conditions that are necessary, that are conducive, for your survival and sustenance. Anger is part of that mechanism; it helps you get rid of and avoid those conditions and circumstances that are not conducive to your survival and sustenance. The problem is when you go to excess, the unrealistic level. Then they become distorted emotions, and destructive.

From that point of view, we can see that emotions that contribute toward this sustenance and cooperation can be said to be constructive. So it is in tune with what you are suggesting.

(*Switching to English.*) But also, whether there is cooperation, whether it is constructive or destructive—I think depends on motivation and aim. The war effort, war mobilization—of course, full cooperation in navy, air force, army. There is full cooperation, but the main aim is destruction, violence.

EKMAN: I was talking about cooperation on the level of one person.

DALAI LAMA: Yes. I think in a general sense, yes.

EKMAN: Now, if your army is going to be successful, then you cannot have afflictive emotions between the members of the army team. They have to have constructive emotions toward one another in order to work together and trust one another with their lives.

DALAI LAMA: That is right. From that viewpoint, it is constructive.

ATTACHMENT AND CONTROL

EKMAN: In the West, there is a lot of misunderstanding of what the Buddhists mean by attachment. I think what you mean by attachment is an over-possessiveness, or control, that inhibits the welfare of whomever a person is attached to.

DALAI LAMA: (*Translated.*) Part of the problem here is the usage of terms like "attachment." In the Buddhist taxonomy, attachment is grouped as part of the afflictive mental factors. However, that does not mean that in the sense of the English term "attachment" there could not be mental factors that are constructive—for example, someone with a true attachment to others as a basis for compassion. In that kind of mental state, you are not willing to simply disregard the other person, ignore that other person. There is an element of embracing the other person. So there is an attachment there, in the general sense of the term. From the Buddhist psychology point of view, this would not be an afflictive mental state.

Afflictive, by definition, presupposes an element of distortion, a superimposition of qualities that are not there, and is also accompanied by what Buddhists refer to as ignorance, or misconception or misunderstanding. Again, the problem of terminology here.

(*Switching to English.*) We have to make a distinction—*desire* and *attachment*. Without desire: no movement, no effort. Desire is very, very necessary. Unreasonable, unrealistic desire is attachment. According to our literature—I found there is some background, you see—the goal of desire is within the ordinary realm. The extreme things—killing, stealing, sexual misconduct, lying, hatred, and covetousness—that is a kind of attachment.

DORJI: If you have attachment, if you have a sense of attachment to one's own belongings, then this is not the covetousness. When you exceed that level of possession—you think about possessing something else, which belongs to others—then it becomes covetousness.

DALAI LAMA: That leads to stealing and, also, I think, to sexual misconduct.

DORJI: His Holiness is wondering, from the Western point of view, is covetousness destructive?

EKMAN: Yes.

DALAI LAMA: Attachment, up to a certain level, is positive. No? Then, when attachment goes beyond, then it is destructive. That is covetousness.

ON PARENTAL ATTACHMENT

by Paul Ekman

As we were reviewing this discussion in June 2007, the Dalai Lama's brother, Tenzin Lodoe Choegyal, made an interesting point: "From my observations, I think attachment has a strong sense of ownership." This fits with the general structure of most parent-child relationships.

Initially, in many senses, you own that child; the child cannot live without you. He or she is *your* child. But as the child grows up, you no longer own the child. As Tenzin said, "you cannot"—unless, in the Buddhist sense, you are over-attached, possessive, and controlling of your child.

When I suggested this, Tenzin's immediate response was, "The bottom line is that ownership means control." I agree. And control is not easy to relinquish. It is especially difficult when you watch your children put themselves in danger or make decisions that you know will be unwise and have negative consequences. But you do not own them anymore, and you must weaken your attachment.

In the 2000 Mind and Life meetings on destructive emotions, His Holiness asked me, "What is destructive compassion?" My response then, which I continue to believe, was, "Destructive compassion is controlling your children, not allowing them autonomy."

✦ ✦ ✦

THE POVERTY OF EMOTIONAL LANGUAGE

DALAI LAMA: (*Translated.*) In relation to the emotion pride, the normal view is a sense of self-importance. You can see an evolutionary purpose for this: Without a sense of self-confidence, a sense of self-importance and pride, often you will not initiate anything. You will feel discouraged and you will feel demoralized. When you confront a challenge, your immediate response will be, No, I cannot do this. Whereas, if you have a stronger sense of self, it can perform a function: to give you more energy and boldness. Is contempt better viewed as a kind of distorted form of pride, or is it a different class of emotion?

If a sense of confidence or self-confidence is grounded in reality, you have a certain basis for that confidence and drive; it is appropriate because it can be beneficial. But if your sense of pride and self-confidence is ungrounded in reality and does not suit your challenge, then it leads to distortion—although it is *still* being beneficial to you.

EKMAN: Pride is a term that has a long history, and in English at least, covers too many things. I distinguish the pleasure that you take in the accomplishments of your offspring, whether they are your biological offspring or your intellectual offspring. When they can stand on your shoulders, and when they can achieve things, it makes you feel very good. The only language that I know of that has a specific word for that is Yiddish. It is called *naches,* which means the uniquely different pleasure you feel, not when *you* have achieved something, but when your child or your student has. You have no sense of competition with your child when you feel *naches.* Unfortunately, when their students get a lot of attention, many professors think, Why not me? Why are you paying attention to my students? I was the one who started it. That is a sickness. I believe that *naches* is fundamental to why we parent. Why we take care of our children is built into us: It is this joy in what they can do. I think it is important to distinguish this emotion from what is usually called pride.

DALAI LAMA: There is still a self-reference: It is *my* student.

EKMAN: That is true. The self is still there.

DALAI LAMA: Because one would not experience the same joy if someone else's student achieves! (*Laughs.*)

EKMAN: Well, not necessarily so.

DALAI LAMA: For example, if you develop a sense of rejoicing and admiration in the achievement of others unrelated to your self—including, even, your enemies.

EKMAN: You always take things so far. (*All are laughing.*)

DALAI LAMA: That would be a truly impartial sense of rejoicing.

EKMAN: I do believe that this capacity can apply to others. When you see another student who is not yours, when you see them really achieve something, it warms your heart.

DALAI LAMA: Yes. Yes.

EKMAN: Just like when you see another child, not yours, really do something. They are up on a stage and they sing wonderfully. You feel for all children, you feel for all offspring, unless you are twisted.

JINPA: Paul's point is that the word "pride" is problematic, because it covers so many different emotions.

EKMAN: There is another emotional state that gets confused with pride, and that is the way we feel when we meet a difficult challenge that stretches us to our limit. That feels very good, and that has great benefit for everyone. It motivates us to do the best we can do with the abilities we have. We do not need to go around and tell everyone else that we are doing that. It is a totally internal experience, and that often gets called pride too.

DALAI LAMA: In Tibetan, we have two different terms. That state is called *popa*, which I suppose in English is "pride." And then the more negative, self-importance, that's called *ngagyal*, which literally means "self-victory."

EKMAN: I do not know other languages well enough to say, but English seems to me rather impoverished in its labeling of the different emotions. If we do not have words to describe different states, like these two in Tibetan, then we cannot think about them and anticipate them. We cannot discipline ourselves as much *because* we do not have the words to refer to these emotions. Without words, we cannot reflect on what has or could occur.

We are, in some sense, animals who do not have, at least in English, enough words to describe the varieties of our emotional experience, particularly when they are destructive versus constructive. Without different labels for each mental state it is hard to be able to reflect on their nature and consider how we want to enact them in future emotional episodes.

In the fall of 2000, B. Alan Wallace, Matthieu Ricard, Richie Davidson, and I spent five days at a cabin in the country, writing an article entitled "Buddhist and Psychological Perspectives on Emotions and Well-Being."[8] One of the first points in this paper is the concept of *sukha*. In Buddhist literature, *sukha* is defined as a state of flourishing that arises from mental balance and insight into the nature of reality. Rather than a fleeting emotion or mood aroused by sensory and conceptual stimuli, *sukha* is an enduring trait that arises from a mind in a state of equilibrium and entails a conceptually unstructured and unfiltered awareness of the true nature of reality. We do not have anything like that concept in English. That does not mean it does not exist, but we do not have a name for it.

We need to expand our vocabulary for describing our emotions, particularly the constructive and destructive aspects of each of them. I am hoping we can get help from Tibetan scholars in this. When I said this to Davidson a few days ago, he said, "Paul, the field of psychology will be shocked to hear you say this," because people think all I'm interested in is facial expression. No; I am interested in all emotional experience.

Expression is one way of being able to tell how someone feels, but it does not tell us whether it is afflictive or nonafflictive. I might be wrong; there might be a recognizable difference in the look on the face when anger is constructive, not intended to harm but to use force to prevent harm, versus when the anger is destructive, directed to harm, psychologically or physically, the target of the anger. That remains to be determined.

Words can get in our way, so we always have to keep clarifying what we mean by a term. An English word, used by Buddhist scholars to refer to a Buddhist concept, may have quite different meanings in Western and Buddhist contexts, yet it is the same word.[9]

Even within the English language, as it is used by psychologists, there is disagreement about a term such as "love." I do not consider parental love to be an emotion; it is a commitment. In a normal person, it is a lifelong commitment. You have many different emotions when you feel parental love. I feel joy. My two children are in an airplane at the moment, on their way here. I can be afraid of what will happen to them. If they miss the plane, I will be angry with them. I can have many different emotions, but the commitment is enduring, it is lifelong. It causes a parent to act in a self-sacrificing fashion, if need be, without thought, without consideration.

DALAI LAMA: *(Translated.)* It is becoming quite clear that you have quite a different take on the definition of emotions—what constitutes an emotion and what does not. So how would you define an emotion?

EKMAN: I am so glad you asked that question.

⋅ 2 ⋅

EXPERIENCING EMOTION

My own definition of an emotion comes out of decades observing the situations in which people show various facial expressions and implies several obstacles to experiencing emotion in a constructive fashion. By its very nature, the way in which the emotion system has evolved biases us toward having destructive emotional episodes.

As if that were not enough, a fundamental feature of *all* life that is required for natural selection to operate—*variation*—is manifest in the robust differences among people in how they experience emotion, and that can create another obstacle to harmonious relationships. Each person has a different emotional *profile*. Some of us become emotional very quickly, and when we become emotional it is very intense, endures for a long time, and fades very slowly; others have the opposite profile. It appears that those who have the first profile will find it much harder to guide whether and how to enact their emotions. In our research, we have not yet learned if it is possible to change your emotional profile, but we have discovered the essential first step—a means of examining what your profile is and how it differs from the profile of others with whom you have continued an intimate contact.

WHAT ARE EMOTIONS?

EKMAN: Thank you very much for asking me to define emotions. (*Laughs.*) As you might expect, I have written about this, proposing that there are a number of characteristics that distinguish emotions from other mental states.[1] One is that most emotions have a signal. That is, they let others know what's happening *inside us,* unlike thoughts, for which there is not a distinctive signal for the various thoughts people have. You do not know whether I just thought about my mother, who has been dead for more than fifty years, or what I am thinking now.

When people find out that I study facial expression, they often get very uncomfortable, saying, "You are reading my mind." I say, "No, I can only read your emotions." I cannot tell from the signal what caused the emotion. If I see a fear expression, I know that you perceive a threat. But the fear of being disbelieved looks just like the fear of being caught. Recognizing that is important in police work. If a suspect looks afraid, that does not tell you that he or she committed the crime. Maybe, but maybe not. That was Othello's error. He thought his wife Desdemona's look of fear was the fear of a woman caught in infidelity. But it was a wife's fear of her jealous husband, who had just killed someone he thought was her lover: She should have been afraid.

Emotions have a signal—this is one characteristic—unlike thoughts, unlike ideas. But there are exceptions.

Embarrassment is an emotion, but it does not seem to have a universal signal. Some people, but not everyone, blush. Very dark-skinned people blush, but you cannot see it. So, no signal.*

---

* My former postdoctoral fellow Dacher Keltner, now a professor of psychology at the University of California-Berkeley, maintains that embarrassment has a

Guilt and shame are very important, and different, emotions. Guilt is about an action; shame is about who you are. They do not have facial signals of their own; they pretty much look like sadness. Maybe there is no signal because you do not want people to know that you're guilty or ashamed. However, most emotions have a signal, so that is one characteristic.

A second characteristic is that emotions can be triggered automatically in under a quarter of a second—very fast—totally opaque to consciousness. And yet the appraisal that so quickly triggers an emotion can be very complex. When you are driving a car and another car starts to veer in your direction, in a fraction of a second, you not only recognize the danger, but you evaluate how fast it is moving and make adjustments to your speed and the steering wheel, and you do that all without conscious consideration.

We have evolved a mechanism for dealing with sudden threats and yet now we live in a world where the threats are not always so sudden. We may, therefore, overreact, because most of the time it is not a near-miss car accident, but we have a mechanism that can respond (*hitting hands together*) that fast. So, automatic appraisal is the second characteristic. Signal is the first.

ON EMOTIONAL TRIGGERS

by Paul Ekman

It is important to recognize that events do not literally trigger emotions. I used the term "trigger" as a shorthand for what actually occurs, in that it is a person's appraisal of an event that triggers an emotion, not the event itself. In my

---

signal, but it is only expressed through a sequence of actions over time. Facial signals, such as the ones for anger, fear, disgust, enjoyment, surprise, and sadness, do not require a sequence of expressions. They are what I call snapshot signals, which can be conveyed in an instant rather than a sequence.

view, there are some innate triggers that bring forth an emotional response with very little cognitive appraisal, such as a sudden loss of gravity, triggering fear: A person senses falling before, and possibly without, any appraisal process. But most of the events that trigger emotional responses are cognitively appraised as, say, threatening or repulsive, though the appraisal is typically so quick and automatic that the person is usually not conscious of making the appraisal.[2]

✦ ✦ ✦

EKMAN: The third defining characteristic is the most controversial, and that is our typical lack of awareness about emotion. Consciousness does not play much of a role in emotion. That is regrettable. We have to work hard to become conscious of the fact that we are getting emotional. Much of the time, we first learn that we are emotional when someone else tells us, "You're being emotional."

Let me use an example. You are reading a book and you are turning the pages. And then you notice that you're thinking about the movie you saw last night, but you are still turning the pages. So it was not that you were unconscious. You were thinking about the movie. But no part of yourself was conscious of the fact that that is what you were doing. Why turn the pages if you are not reading them?[3] That is what happens in our emotions. We are totally conscious, but there is no part of our self that is *watching* what we do, what Alan Wallace calls meta-attentiveness.

The notion that there is a part of us that can monitor, that can watch what we are experiencing, is very important. But we do not usually have that with emotion. It is in the nature of emotions to keep consciousness out. If we are going to become a balanced person, we are going to have to work to give ourselves what nature did not want us to have, which is a role for consciousness. I say that nature did not want us to have it because if we had to think consciously about whether to be afraid or not, we might not survive in some situations. It seems, however, that the emotion system is not fear specific, in that we can become angry in an instant, without thought or consideration, just as we can become afraid in an instant. So that is my third defining characteristic of an emotion: the initial lack of consciousness when experiencing it.

Another characteristic is that if it is an emotion, it is not unique to humans. Other animals have emotions. If it is something that is unique to humans, it is probably not an emotion. The only emotion that I thought was unique to humans was contempt, but it turns out that if you have a juvenile chimpanzee make a threat toward an alpha male, the alpha male shows the contempt expression.[4]

Still another characteristic of emotions is that an emotion can be as short as a few seconds. Sometimes it lasts minutes or even an hour, but an emotion never lasts a whole day. If it does, it is actually a mood. Emotions come and go.

People differ in terms of how fast they recover from an emotional episode. Matthieu Ricard, as you know, has now been studied in different laboratories, I think four—my collaboration with Bob Levenson; Richie Davidson's lab in Wisconsin; Steve Kosslyn's lab at Harvard; Jonathan Cohen's lab in Princeton; and Tania Singer's lab in Maastricht. Matthieu has a very fast recovery from emotion. That is not a surprise; you would expect that would be so after his many years of meditation. There are some humans who have never meditated in their life who also have a fast recovery, and we need to find out more about why they are like that.

To summarize, the characteristics of an emotion are: There is a signal; an automatic, very quick appraisal of what is happening that gives rise to the impulse to become emotional; you have to develop a skill to get consciousness involved; and, it is not unique to humans.

Still another characteristic is that emotions have a set of sensations. We are not always aware of those sensations. I have developed exercises for developing conscious awareness that you are becoming or are emotional. These are to be used not in place of, but in addition to, meditation. One of them is an exercise to increase your sensitivity to the sensations in your body so that those sensations will ring a little bell, so you will be aware of "getting"—you know the phrase?—"hot under the collar." The most dramatic difference in the sensations is anger versus fear. In anger, blood goes to your hands. It is preparing you to hit. In fear, it goes to the large muscles in your legs.[5]

DALAI LAMA: So, preparing to run.

EKMAN: Yes, right. That does not mean you will run, or that you will hit. But evolution has prepared you in this way. And you can learn to be sensitive to the difference in how your body feels when you are afraid as compared to angry.

DALAI LAMA: But you can kick someone.

EKMAN: (*Laughs.*) You could kick someone, instead of running. Absolutely. But it is more likely that you will run. The reason why these differences were conserved is because those people who ran were more likely to survive—

DALAI LAMA: (*Translated.*) So it clearly demonstrates that it is really part of the mechanism for survival.

EKMAN: Yes. I suppose I should add one more characteristic: that emotion can get us into trouble and lead us to act in a way that we subsequently regret. We have an English phrase, "I lost my head." "Why did you do that?" "Ach, I lost my head." What that phrase means is that my intelligence, my consciousness, was not there. Please accept my apology, because I "lost" my head. Well, what we have to do is give people back their heads.

DALAI LAMA: (*Translated.*) So, can you give me an example of a constructive positive anger?

EKMAN: Anger that stops interference, but is done in a way that helps the person who is blocking you achieve his or her goal without interfering with you. That is very positive. All of these emotions can be harmful or helpful, either one. And the question, in part, is how to develop the monitoring to know that you are becoming emotional so that you can choose how you enact it.

That brings to mind when I first encountered in Buddhist writings (in the English language) the idea of recognizing the spark before the flame. It reminded me of when I was trained to be a psychotherapist, in 1957; my supervisor said, "If you can increase the gap between impulse and action, you will have helped your patient." What he should have added was, "And, boy, that is hard to do!" But that is the area where we need to have consciousness, if we are to choose whether to be emotional or to simply let it pass—and, if we are going to be emotional, we need to know how we can do that in a constructive fashion. What I believe—this is strictly my opinion, this is not fact—is that we evolved in such a way as to make it very difficult to become aware of that, and to broaden that gap so that awareness can enter.

DALAI LAMA: Between the impulse and the action?

EKMAN: Yes. Or a spark before the flame. The same terms.

DALAI LAMA: (*Translated.*) In your mind, emotions are, by their very nature, ephemeral? They do not last very long.

EKMAN: Usually. But you can be angry for an hour. However, when you actually look at what people do, you find that emotions come and go. You get angry, and you yell and scream, or whatever you do. Then it recedes. Then you may think about it again, Oh my, what she did or what he did, and you get angry again. When we say, "I was angry all day," it may actually be a number of angry episodes.

DALAI LAMA: (*Translated.*) In Buddhist psychology we make distinctions between the sensory level of conscious experience and what is referred to as the mental level—the level of thought, emotions, and so on. Emotions like fear are the emotions that are much more immediate and spontaneous, whether they are operating at the sensory level or whether there is a role for the mental level of consciousness involved.

For example, the tactile sensation is thought to be the underlying basis for the experience of the other senses. But, even there, it is really thought to be on the sensory level, with no thought, with no consciousness, as you define it—no awareness by the person.

EKMAN: The near-miss car accident is the perfect example. The whole episode is over, if you've survived, before you are conscious of what you just did. But you continue to feel it in your body, because it takes about fifteen seconds for your heart rate and blood pressure to return to normal. You realize, I feel afraid, but there's no longer a danger.

In contrast consider the situation in which you have had a biopsy on a tumor, and you are waiting to find out whether it is malignant, whether you have a serious cancer, and they will not know for three days. It is not that you are afraid the whole three days, but it keeps coming back. And then you are conscious of your fear—the same emotion—and we will see the same expression pop onto the face in those moments of fear—the same sensations—but *consciousness* is there.

In the example I gave of fear, it is a *thought* that returns to your mind about the tumor. The fact that it is a thought that activates it, rather than an event or an action, facilitates consciousness. By contrast, when you get into an argument with your wife, she is right there and it keeps going, so consciousness may not be there at all.

DALAI LAMA: (*Translated.*) In the case of this person who had a biopsy—is it the case that the person is remembering the fear that he experienced in the examination room, or is the memory of that triggering another instance of fear?

EKMAN: Well, the person I'm referring to is me. (*Laughs.*) Francisco Varela would have liked this first-person use of information.*

It was the thought that life might be interrupted, that there might be great pain. I was thinking of the possible consequences and the helplessness, so it got worse.

Earlier I said that consciousness typically is not present during an emotion, but now I am explaining an exception, in which the remembrance of a frightening possibility triggers the emotion. It

---

* Varela, a biologist and neuroscientist who began practicing Tibetan Buddhism in 1974, emphasized the importance of examining first-person experience in the study of consciousness and of the information that trained meditators could provide about momentary changes in emotional experience. Varela's collaboration was instrumental in the first Mind and Life conference between the Dalai Lama and Western scientists in 1987 and in the creation of the Mind and Life Institute and subsequent conferences that followed. He died in 2001.

is a reiterated thought, but not a continuous thought process. In contrast, if you are in the middle of an argument it is continuous, but you may not be at all conscious of the fact that you are being very unreasonable. You do not even know that you have raised your voice. (*Raises his voice, to illustrate.*) Someone says, "Why are you shouting at me?" "Was I shouting?"

JINPA: (*After a long discussion in Tibetan.*) That's an automatic example that you are giving. His Holiness was saying that we ought to teach some of these in the debating courts.

OBSTACLES TO CONSTRUCTIVE EMOTIONAL EXPERIENCES

EKMAN: My definition of emotion implied two obstacles to experiencing emotions constructively.

The first obstacle is that what triggers the emotion is usually opaque, that is, we do not know what triggers it. The appraisal that triggers an emotion can be very complex, but it often involves very fast mental processes that are operating in a way that consciousness cannot enter. We do not choose when to become emotional unless we seek entertainment. When we rent a video, we are choosing to experience certain emotions, but most of the time the emotions that we experience, and when those emotions occur, is not by our choice. It happens to us, and this is the way we experience it; we are gripped by that emotion. In your writings you have expressed a view very similar in terms of what triggers emotion.

The second obstacle is the gap between the spark, or impulse to become emotional, and the flame, the actual emotional behavior. Most people, unless they engage in a lot of meditative practice, are not aware of what is happening during that gap; they have no conscious recognition that an impulse or spark has arisen before they engage in emotional behavior, the flame. They are not able to say, "I will not engage in that emotion" or "The way to engage in that emotion is to empathize with the other person."

To achieve an awareness of the impulse before the action takes work. Nature did not provide us with that tool as a fundamental part of our emotions.

I want to add to these a third. The third obstacle to experiencing emotions constructively is due to individual differences in how we each experience the very same emotion. Let me first tell you about a colleague's research that suggested there might be genetically based differences in how emotions are experienced, and then my own recent research on individual differences in emotional profiles.

This research was done forty years ago by Daniel G. Freedman.[6] He looked at Navajo, Japanese, and European-American babies in the first hour of life. He closed the nose and covered the mouth so the infant could not breathe. This is a standard test that is always done at birth because you have to be careful with infants who do not struggle: They might smother from a blanket blocking their air passages. Freedman did this in the first hour of life, so the infants would not have had a chance to learn much. Maybe they learned things in the womb, but not with people directly.

The Navajo were the least responsive; they did not do much. The Japanese showed more movement to get free. The European-Americans exhibited the most movement to get free. My point is that a fundamental truth about human beings is that although we are all the same, we are also different. We are different both in what we inherit and we learn. This was, of course, one of Charles Darwin's main points, that in order for natural selection to work, we have to have variations. Depending on the particulars of the situation, one or another of the variations will be the most successful in dealing with that situation.

In the field of emotion I am known for my work obtaining evidence that there are *universal* facial expressions, but for the last ten years I have been looking at how individuals differ in how they experience the very same emotion—not just in knowledge, but in sensitivity to a trigger—and in how they will respond.

DALAI LAMA: (*Translated.*) These differences between the

Navajo, Japanese, and European-Americans seem to be genetic, because it has been only an hour after birth.

EKMAN: Right. That experiment is almost never cited by anyone because it has been very unpopular until the last decade to recognize that genes play a role in behavior. In science, there are fashions, as in everything else.

Let us consider the following situation. You are standing in line at the post office to buy stamps. They have just raised the price from thirty-nine cents to forty-one cents. You have a lot of thirty-nine-cent stamps, so you have to buy a roll of two-cent stamps. You are standing in a long line. Someone comes in and pushes to the front of the line, right in front of you. You have been waiting for many minutes, but this person does not want to wait. We call it "cutting in." It is nice that we use the word "cut" because it is telling us that we are describing this as if it is a physical injury. How individuals respond to that very same event can be quite different. It is an emotional response. Let us suppose no one likes it and everyone is in some sense angered.

And now I have an illustration to consider.

These drawings are from research I recently did on what I am calling an *emotional profile*. The person on the left very quickly gets angry compared to the person on the right, where the onset of anger is more gradual. The person on the left gets very intensely angry, and his or her anger is stronger than that of the person on the right. The anger of the person on the right does not last very long, and it rapidly disappears. The person on the left's anger lasts longer, and it goes away more slowly. These two people are both angry, but their profiles show they experience anger in quite different ways.

Our research suggests that the strength of your emotional profile—depicted as the height of the volcano figure—is similar for anger, fear, and anguish. We also found that people know about the strength of their responses; we do not know if they understand other aspects of their profiles. I suspect most people are at least aware of how quickly they become angry. I suspect that

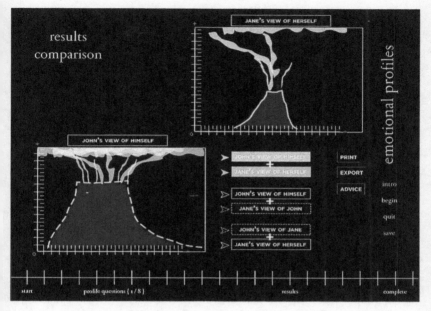

Emotional profiles showing differing experiences of the onset and dissipation of anger. © 2006 by Paul Ekman

the people they live with know about how quickly the person becomes angry and how intense it usually is.

I strongly suspect that the person who gets very angry very quickly is going to have much more difficulty in becoming aware of the impulse before the action, and may even have more difficulty becoming aware of acting emotionally. This is the third obstacle to experiencing emotion constructively: having an emotional profile with a steep onset and strong experience of emotion (the person on the left side of the drawing). These people are especially in need of mindfulness training and meta-attention training, but it is not going to be as easy for them. The person on the right does not need mindfulness meditation and meta-consciousness as much and, paradoxically, can acquire it more easily.

We do not know what creates these emotional profiles, but it would be extremely unlikely if it was not a combination of experience and genetic inheritance, the two working together.

What we want to achieve is to help people with profiles like the person on the left become more like the person on the right.

DALAI LAMA: (*Translated.*) In the profile of a person whose anger takes longer to rise, it might also take longer to subside. Would that suggest a mood difference—that an angry mood would last longer in such a person? There is a general recognition that short-tempered people may easily get very angry but the anger does not last very long, whereas you have to watch out for those who are slow to get angry, because they can hold grudges! (*Everyone laughs.*)

EKMAN: I have theorized that these features are independent of one another. You can have a profile where you are slow to become emotional but the emotion is very intense, then it disappears completely and quickly. All the possible combinations of speed of onset, intensity, duration, and recovery time can occur. These are all ways in which human beings differ one from another. The people (*pointing to left side of the figure*) who have a very fast onset and very intense emotions are much more difficult to get along with. They are the attack dogs. They are very good for protection. You can put them out as sentinels, because they respond . . . fast! But they would be terrible negotiators. (*All laugh.*)

ON EMOTIONAL PROFILES

by Paul Ekman

I first suggested the existence of these profiles twenty-five years ago at a National Institute of Mental Health conference organized by Richard Davidson, but only in 1992 did I begin to study the question. I developed a self-report questionnaire in which people described their own profiles and found that individuals' answers to questions about how strongly they experienced specific emotions predicted the strength of both facial muscular contractions and changes in autonomic activity when they watched emotionally arousing film clips two weeks later.

Based on this research, I developed an interactive online tool that allows people to explore not only the strength of their emotional responses, but the speed, duration, and recovery from emotional responses. The emotional profile tool asks a person to evaluate him- or herself and an intimate partner and then reveals how they differ and the extent to which the people share the perception of each other's emotional profiles.[7]

♦ ♦ ♦

EKMAN: In a sense, there is a role for everyone, but these days we do not need many attack dogs. The problem that I wish to raise is how do we transform the attack dog profile? What exercises can we use to do that? It is not that they do not know what they experience, they know it. And it is not that they do not want to change it. People who have this profile get into a lot of trouble with others, and they know that. The issue is: Do the people who learn meta-awareness, are they already people who have the slow onset/moderate intensity emotional profile (the person on the right side of the figure), and that is why they are attracted to it? What can we do for these people with the fast onset/very intense emotional profile (the person on the left side of the figure)?

DALAI LAMA: (*Translated.*) There are famous stories of rival scholars who keep their grudges throughout their lives. Whenever a rival is defending in a debate, his opponent is certain to attack. (*Jinpa and the Dalai Lama laugh heartily.*)

EKMAN: All too frequent.

JINPA: This is very true in academia.

EKMAN: Actually, people come to enjoy this. Not that they enjoy being attacked, but the counterattack is engaging. It can become similar to an addiction; they crave the opportunity to trade insults.

DALAI LAMA: (*Translated.*) In a sense, there is a kind of an addiction, too, for the debaters, after so many years of debating in the courtyard. Right from the beginning, the model is, if the opponent says something, you *have* to disprove it. (*All laugh.*) You *have* to try. There is even a saying that elementary debate students learn: The mark of achievement that you have mastered the technique is if you can turn what the other person says from "yes" into "no" and "no" into "yes."

The main purpose of the debate is to try to make more precise the position. So that one sees the other side, you see, the answer, precisely. Then, finished: The purpose of this debate is fulfilled. When the defender becomes unable to answer precisely, the debater comes up with all the arguments that point to those loopholes to let him get to the precise answer. It is not just a matter of defeating the person, in relation to a counterpoint. It is to discern the precise truth.

EKMAN: Jointly.

DALAI LAMA: Jointly, jointly.

EKMAN: Is there a winner? Or no winner?

DALAI LAMA: Joint winner. Then both are satisfied. Both get some sort of benefit. The main purpose is simply to let the monks or the students learn how to debate well. If the student is able to disprove what it should be, then it is said, "Oh, this person is qualified, to have understood this."

ON BUDDHIST DEBATE

by Geshe Dorji Damdul

The subject matter of debate consists of five major treatises: epistemology; the study of the six perfections of generosity, morality, patience, enthusiastic perseverance, concentration, and wisdom; the view of the middle way, that is, nonextremism; metaphysics; and *vinaya* (ethics).

The debates, driven by the use of logic, can be comprehensive, precise, and decisive. The monk-students in the major Tibetan monasteries spend about five to seven hours in debates, in both the morning and the evening, each day.

◆ ◆ ◆

CALMING DIFFICULT PEOPLE

EKMAN: Another study we did with Matthieu Ricard is relevant to our discussion. Matthieu came to our laboratory three different times, separated over a two-year period. In one session we asked him to have a conversation, with two different people, about reincarnation, which is not accepted by most Western intellectuals or academics. One person I chose is the most gentle academic I know—very interesting to talk to, very developed ideas. There is no element of this characteristic you talk about: He does not enjoy debate or insult. He and Matthieu conversed while we were measuring their bodily responses—their blood pressures, heart rates, skin temperatures, and facial expressions. They had a lively, interesting discussion. They were both annoyed with me when I told them, "You now have to stop." They wanted to continue. There was a lot of mutual smiling, and their physiology showed a very low level of arousal.

Then I had Matthieu talk with a very difficult person, actually the most difficult professor I could find on the Berkeley campus. He was so difficult that as the time got closer, he kept laying down new conditions for me as the scientist. Finally, I could not use him at all because he was being true to form: impossible.

I got a substitute who, while still difficult, was more cooperative. He conversed with Matthieu, and there was no mutual smiling. Matthieu remained very calm physiologically, but this other fellow showed a very fast heart rate and high blood pressure. Over the course of fifteen minutes his blood pressure and heart rate went down, he began to smile, and he said to me afterward, "There is just something about him—I could not fight with him."

ON ONE-ON-ONE INTERACTIONS

by Robert W. Levenson

In our studies of dyadic interactions in intimate relationships, we have found that discussing areas of disagreement are wonderful stages for studying how people express and regulate their emotions. After all, it is really because humans are a social species that they have this profound need not to let their emotions run amok, but rather to adjust them to fit the demands of the situation and the comfort level of others.

We have found that married couples who are able to maintain physiological calm while discussing problems in their relationship are much more likely to have satisfying marriages and to stay together over time. Often in marriages, one partner assumes the role of the "thermostat," monitoring the temperature of the interaction and applying corrections as needed. These corrections take the form of helping the partner regulate his or her emotions (typically the woman assumes the role of thermostat in male-female relationships) and stay in an emotional comfort zone where issues can be discussed productively without things getting too hot (intense) or too cold (withdrawn).

Matthieu played the thermostat role in these interactions. Even when dealing with a very hostile and difficult partner, he had a calming effect that allowed the discussion to proceed in a constructive way.

Robert W. Levenson is a professor of psychology at the University of California-Berkeley and the director of the Institute of Personality and Social Research.

◆ ◆ ◆

EKMAN: What do you make of that? Could it be that when you encounter someone who has a highly cultivated emotional balance, and Matthieu is very well balanced emotionally, you feel a lot of goodness about him or her as a person? You feel that you have encountered someone unlike anyone you have known, and they have a calming influence on you? How do you explain that?

DALAI LAMA: (*Translated.*) One factor here is the well-known cliché that you cannot clap with only one hand. There is also a recognition in the Buddhist tradition—in fact, it is a quality that is attributable to the Buddha—that without using weapons or powerful instruments, through the weapon of loving-kindness alone, he was able to subdue his foes. Loving-kindness and compassion has this natural capacity to subdue and tame. It would also depend upon the actual content of the conversation, as well as the topic.

In the early 1970s, there was a British gentleman by the name of Felix Green. He was one of the very few Westerners who was able to visit Tibet and China—China, many times, several times.

JINPA: Green had a large amount of motion picture film footage of Tibet. He was a friend of Chou En-lai, the Chinese prime minister at the time. He was convinced that life under the Communist rule in Tibet was perfect, the people inside Tibet were happy, and everything was fine. He wanted to come and show the footage to His Holiness. Before he met His Holiness, he was received by the Tibetan officials. The officials warned His Holiness that this person had believed the Communist view of Tibet, with only limited personal knowledge, with one-sided information about the situation. "Please be careful" and "He is dangerous," they said. His Holiness met him over a period of three days. They started talking and looked at the footage, and by the time he left, Green had completely changed!

His Holiness's understanding of this phenomenon was that this was the power of truth. Green had incorporated a foregone conclusion, a particular perception, but as he came to recognize the actual situation, it changed him.

DALAI LAMA: So the truth seems to also matter.

EKMAN: If I were to apply this to the situation I described, I would have to say that in the first interaction with the gentle person, that person did not change Matthieu's mind, but they did not have a very long time to talk.

Another way that people differ is in their susceptibility to changing a belief. There are people who are fanatical or zealous who are highly resistant to change.

DALAI LAMA: True.

EKMAN: I am reading from your book *The Universe in a Single Atom:*

> A key characteristic of these mental states is their effect in creating disturbance and a loss of self control. When they arise, we tend to lose our freedom to act in accordance with our aspirations and become caught in a distorted mind set. Given that they are ultimately rooted in a deeply self-centered way of relating to others and to the world at large, when these afflictions arise, our perspective tends to become narrow.[8]

MINDFULNESS

DALAI LAMA: (*Translated.*) The more skilled you are in being attentive, the greater you are able to watch out and catch it.

EKMAN: Yes.

DALAI LAMA: (*Translated.*) In the Buddhist meditation practices, one key method for cultivating this awareness is the development of mindfulness. The second one, which is thought to be more specific to the cultivation of this monitoring, is applying constant awareness to the actual processes of thought, just observing your mind and the thoughts as they arise, and being aware of what arises in the present.

EKMAN: Let me be certain I understand the distinction. One practice deals with knowledge. Knowledge would be to understand that you should focus on the act, not the actor. Knowledge would be that it is dangerous to you and to the other person if you shift from *removing* the obstacle to *punishing* the person for having put the obstacle there. This is all knowledge. Now, a lot of people do not have that knowledge. We can teach knowledge much more easily than we can teach the second practice, which develops the skill of being aware of momentary experience.

DALAI LAMA: (*Translated.*) True. Similarly, knowledge about the benefits of compassion can be taught.

EKMAN: The knowledge can be taught. But learning the skill of monitoring awareness—of being in the moment, to be aware of the spark before the flame—is not easy. You need both. You need knowledge and you need skill. Knowledge you can even get just from reading a book.* Skill you cannot get from a book—you need to practice again and again. They are two different, but related, matters that are essential for a balanced life.

DALAI LAMA: (*Translated.*) Very true. The way the term "mindfulness" is used in modern Buddhist literature is slightly different. The way in which it is used in the Tibetan tradition is the mindfulness of *that knowledge,* not the monitoring of awareness.

EKMAN: Just knowledge?

DALAI LAMA: (*Translated.*) Yes. The Sanskrit term is *sati* and the Tibetan term is *drenpa,* which literally mean "memory, recollection." Mindfulness is bringing to the present the awareness of things that you have learned.

EKMAN: But in order to do that, you have to have self-monitoring, a meta-consciousness. You need to be aware of the present. What is the term for developing that skill?

JINPA: That is what Alan Wallace calls "meta-attention," or monitoring awareness.

---

* I came to realize later in our discussion that although you can learn about this type of knowledge from a book, if that knowledge is to become so ingrained as to form the mental framework from which you see the world, it requires many, many hours of meditative practice.

ON THE MEANING OF MINDFULNESS

by B. Alan Wallace

While mindfulness (*sati*) is often equated with bare attention [that is not correct; instead] bare attention corresponds much more closely to the Pali term *manasikara*, which is commonly translated as "attention" or "mental engagement." This refers to the initial split seconds of the bare cognizing of an object, before one begins to recognize, identify, and conceptualize, and in Buddhist accounts it is not regarded as a wholesome mental factor. It is ethically neutral. The primary meaning of *sati*, on the other hand, is recollection, non-forgetfulness. This includes *retrospective* memory of things in the past, *prospectively* remembering to do something in the future, and present-centered recollection in the sense of maintaining unwavering attention to a present reality. The opposite of mindfulness is forgetfulness, so mindfulness applied to the breath, for instance, involves continuous, unwavering attention to the respiration. Mindfulness may be used to *sustain* bare attention (*manasikara*), but nowhere do traditional Buddhist sources *equate* mindfulness with such attention. . . .

When mindfulness is equated with "bare attention," it can easily lead to the misconception that the cultivation of mindfulness has nothing to do with ethics or with the cultivation of wholesome states of mind and the attenuation of unwholesome states. Nothing could be farther from the truth. In the *Pali Abhidhamma*, where mindfulness is listed as a wholesome mental factor, it is not depicted as bare attention, but as a mental factor that clearly distinguishes wholesome from unwholesome mental states and behavior. And it is used to support wholesome states and counteract unwholesome states.

The cultivation of bare attention is valuable in many ways, and there's a rapidly growing body of research on its benefits for both psychological and physiological disorders. But it's incorrect to equate that with mindfulness, and an even greater error to think that's all there is to *vipassana* (insight meditation designed to experientially realize key features of reality that liberate the mind from its afflictive tendencies). If that were the case, all the Buddha's teachings on ethics, *samadhi* (focused, sustained attention and the meditative practices that are designed to develop attentional skills), and wisdom would be irrelevant. All too often, people who naively assume that bare attention is all there is to meditation reject the rest of Buddhism as "claptrap" and "mumbo-jumbo." The essential teachings are dismissed rather than one's own preconceptions. . . .

Bare awareness as calm, nonreactive awareness of one's meditative object plays a crucial role in *shamatha* practice, which alleviates such afflictive mental states as craving, aversion, dullness, agitation, and doubt. . . . Bare attention is not a complete practice, and by itself, it can be helpful and yet very limiting.

A Buddhist monk for many years, B. Alan Wallace, PhD, is the founding director of the nonprofit Santa Barbara Institute for Consciousness Studies and the author of numerous books on Buddhism.

✦ ✦ ✦

EKMAN: I want to raise the technical question of why it is that sitting every day and focusing your attention on your breath going in and out of your nose, why in the world should that help you with your emotions?

I am accepting the idea that it does. In 2006 I went on a seven-day silent retreat led by Joseph Goldstein and Sharon Salzberg. I was sitting eight hours a day, focusing on my breath. Very hard to do! Very hard. (*Dalai Lama and Jinpa laugh warmly.*) And doing walking meditation, which is not as hard, but still very hard, and eating meditation.* Each of these meditative exercises have a common theme, which is that you are focusing consciousness on something that in ordinary life we do not need to focus consciousness on.

When you are a child, you have to learn how to use the fork. Once you learn how to use the fork, you never think about putting the fork into a piece of food and bringing it up to your mouth. You do not miss; it goes right into your mouth. No thought at all! The same with walking. It is only when you are walking on cobblestones or suddenly trip that you then have to think about each step. Breathing we never think about. What we are doing with these meditative practices, such as focusing on the breath, is creating skills that in some sense we do not need. It is very hard to focus attention on our breath because it is automatic. We are not equipped by nature to focus on it: It is unnecessary. But if we learn how to do so, then we are more generally acquiring the ability to monitor automatic mental processes and that means we are building new neural connections for monitoring what occurs without consciousness.

If you create these new connections, which are unnecessary to breathe, walk, or eat, I postulate that it will allow you to monitor the automatic nature of emotion. If you develop the skill to focus on your breath for longer and longer periods of time, then that very skill that you have developed will benefit your emotions because your emotions are automatic also. I made this suggestion in the afterword to the paperback edition of my last book, *Emotions Revealed*. No one has responded to it, so I do not know if it makes

---

* Goldstein and Salzberg are well-known meditation teachers who direct the Insight Meditation Society, in Barre, Massachusetts. In breathing meditation, conscious attention is focused on the breath going in and out of the nostrils. In walking meditation, conscious attention is focused on lifting the foot, moving it forward, placing it down, and so on, with these movements done very slowly. In eating meditation, conscious attention is focused on using the fork to grasp a piece of food, lifting the fork, and raising it to the mouth, again with these movements conducted very slowly.[9]

sense to Westerners. I would like to know what you think about this idea. Does it make sense that that is why focusing on the breath would help increase this gap between impulse and action?

ON ATTENTION

by Clifford Saron

We do not yet know the way in which this quality of careful attention to the breath and other aspects of physical behavior should provide someone with more awareness of the beginnings of an emotional response. We do know that precise sensorimotor skill doesn't necessarily generalize to other untrained actions. However, one of the prime instructions in mindfulness meditation is to cultivate awareness of intention—trying to catch the moment before one reaches for a glass or inhales the next breath or takes the next step. Awareness of intentions trains one to catch very subtle moments of experience as they evolve in elaborated behaviors.

In turn, the subcomponents of elaborated behaviors, including a course that might lead to destructive behavior, consist of additional strings of intentions. Having this "attention to intention" skill handy means more opportunities to break the chain of events that leads to harmful actions. Likewise, the cultivation of metacognitive awareness (attention to the quality of attention) during meditation practice importantly contributes to the general ability to detect the flux of feeling states "off the cushion." This breeds a kind of friendly knowledge of oneself that persists during strong emotion and can itself mitigate the enacting of destructive acts. The neural basis for this skill will be represented, like learning of all kinds, in changes in the patterns of connectivity in the brain, but the precise brain regions involved are not yet understood and may be different for different individuals.

*Clifford Saron is a research scientist at the Mind and Brain Center at
the University of California-Davis. He is directing an investigation
of the impact of three months of meditation training on subjects.*

+ + +

DALAI LAMA: (*Translated.*) The basic idea behind the mindfulness meditation, and applying it on a daily basis, particularly with
relation to what, in Buddhist language we refer to as the everyday
activities—walking, eating, and so on—is to maintain the sharp-
ness of your mindfulness, so that the mindfulness is always alert
and present. It is a cultivation of the skill of mindfulness, which
can then be applied.

(*Switching to English.*)

When your thoughts focus on some matter, it may create agitation in your mind: disturbances. At that moment, forget everything. Just think about breathing—breath in, breath out, counting
for each cycle, breathing one, two, three, four, five, up to twenty,
thirty, like that. That is the taught way. Then your disturbing
thoughts get relieved.

EKMAN: Brings you to a calmer state.

DALAI LAMA: Yes. So, that, we usually do that when fully occupied at work, preoccupied. Some rest and calm mind. That is a
temporary method—not a real changing of your mind. The problems are still there. Now, to cultivate compassion is really dealing
with basic problems. This is only a temporary method. Relief or
forgetting all those you dislike, the craziness or disturbances of
mind. So then, the mind becomes calm.

EKMAN: That is very helpful.

DALAI LAMA: Burmese Buddhists, Thai Buddhists, they have a
long tradition of this practice. This is actually the beginning or
one method to train mindfulness. During that period, hold your
mind and concentrate on the breath: outgoing, coming, in, out,
in, out. That is one method of increasing mindfulness. Then, you
see, these Buddhist monks, the Buddhist tradition, walking the
whole day, the whole day, walking.

EKMAN: Yes.

DALAI LAMA: Walking mindfulness. Now the right leg, the left leg. Try that. Or eating. Yes? So, that is mindfulness. This practice changes your mindfulness.*

(*Translated.*) In the meditation manuals, mindfulness focused on breathing is thought to be one of the most effective antidotes to dissipation of thoughts, where your mind wanders everywhere. With that kind of unfocused mind, breathing mindfulness meditation is thought to be very helpful.

We have to make a distinction, however, between mindfulness meditation focused on breathing and more advanced yoga meditations that are aimed at manipulation of certain energies. These are two different things. Here we are talking about simple mindfulness focused on breathing. This other, more advanced form of meditation which is not focused on breathing, seems to suggest you can bring about physiological effects as a result.

ON MINDFULNESS

by Margaret Cullen

Mindfulness has become an increasingly popular term in the West due to the influence of several prominent meditation teachers and authors, including Thich Nhat Hanh, Jon Kabat-Zinn, and Jack Kornfield. Thich Nhat Hanh, the

---

* Clifford Saron brought to my attention a discussion by Ruth Baer and James Carmody of the five meanings of mindfulness that have emerged in academic psychology: "These include observing (attending to or noticing internal and external stimuli, such as sensations, emotions, cognitions, sights, sounds, and smells), describing (noting or mentally labeling these stimuli with words), acting with awareness (attending to one's current actions, as opposed to behaving automatically or absentmindedly), non-judging of inner experience (refraining from evaluation of one's sensations, cognitions, and emotions), and non-reactivity to inner experience (allowing thoughts and feelings to come and go, without attention getting caught up in them)."[10]

world-renowned Vietnamese Zen master, poet, and peace activist, defines mindfulness as "the miracle which can call back in a flash our dispersed mind and restore it to wholeness so that we can live each minute of life."[11] Jon Kabat-Zinn, an author and the founder of mindfulness-based stress reduction, widely taught in secular settings including health care, education, and business worldwide, writes, "Mindfulness can be thought of as moment-to-moment, nonjudgmental awareness, cultivated by paying attention in a specific way, that is, in the present moment, as non-reactively, and as openheartedly as possible."[12] Jack Kornfield, the cofounder of two primary mindfulness meditation centers in the United States, has described mindfulness as "an innate human capacity to deliberately pay full attention to where we are, to our actual experience, and to learn from it."[13] Nyanaponika Thera, a Buddhist monk, teacher, and scholar in the mid-twentieth century, wrote a book in which he named mindfulness as the heart of Buddhist meditation.[14] All these definitions refer to a quality of mind or way of being that is not only aware in the present, but wholesome insofar as it is "open-hearted," "restores wholeness," and permits learning.

Historically, the Pali word *sati* has been translated as mindfulness but, according to Alan Wallace, the root meaning of *sati* is simply that of recollection, of memory.[15] In the Theravada Abhidhamma [Buddhist psychology], *sati* is precisely defined as one of nineteen "beautiful" mental factors whose function is the "absence of confusion or non-forgetfulness."[16] In the context of the Nikaya [Buddha's discourse], *sati* is referred to as a "kind of attentiveness that . . . is good, skillful, or right"[17] and can become a shorthand for *satipatthana*, which is usually translated as the establishment of *sati* but also refers to the complete methodology in which this establishment is accomplished.[18] Bhikkhu Bodhi, the Buddhist monk, scholar, and student of Nyanaponika Thera, writes, "we have no word in English that precisely captures what *sati* refers to when it is used in relation to meditation practice."[19] Here, then, are at least three contexts in which *sati* is used a little differently, though the English translation remains fixed as "mindfulness."

Many contemporary Buddhist teachers use the term "mindfulness" in a more comprehensive way than simply "remembering" or "lacking confusion." According to John Dunne, a Buddhist scholar at Emory University, the components of mindfulness as it is more broadly construed might include not only *sati,* but also *sampajanna* (clear comprehension) and *appamada* (heedfulness). Clear comprehension includes both the ability to perceive phenomena unclouded by distorting mental states (such as moods and emotions) and the meta-cognitive capacity to monitor the quality of attention. Heedfulness in this context can be understood as bringing to bear, during meditation, what has been learned in the past about which thoughts, choices, and actions lead to happiness and which lead to suffering.

Though the contexts and interpretations of these terms may vary, scholars and meditation teachers would probably agree on the factors of *sati, sampajanna,* and *appamada* as foundational to the development of mind. Moreover, as both Buddhist and secular mindfulness programs proliferate in the West, this broader use of mindfulness has become a culturally meaningful and accessible "umbrella" term for the vast majority of practitioners unversed in the intricacies of translating Sanskrit or Pali.

Margaret Cullen is a licensed marriage and family therapist and a certified Mindfulness-Based Stress Reduction (MBSR) teacher. In 2004, she helped develop and write, and then coteach, with Alan Wallace, the curriculum for the research project "Cultivating Emotional Balance."

✦ ✦ ✦

EKMAN: It is a good example of how complex it is. Let me add to that by drawing on my second research area. In addition to my work on emotion, I have been studying lying for many years.[20]

A feature of lying that I have identified is relevant to our discussion of emotion. When someone for the first time considers lying about something important to another person, he or she thinks, Should I do this? Shouldn't I? Will I get caught doing it? Is there another way? But once he or she lies and succeeds, then the next time they do not think about it, the person just does it. It becomes a habit. What we mean by a habit is that it becomes automatic, so no longer does the person weigh and consider the choices. We could not live without habits; they allow us to do many things without thinking. But without thinking, we can get into a lot of trouble.

With emotion, it is even worse, because we never start out thinking. We start out *not* thinking. We have to learn to be aware and consider how we are acting when we are emotional. In terms of the skill of being aware of moment-to-moment experience, one of the most interesting findings in our study of Matthieu Ricard came when we asked him to use a joystick to register how he was feeling while he watched an emotionally arousing film. The more he moved it to the left, the more unpleasant he was feeling, and the more he moved it to the right, the more pleasant he was feeling. Matthieu did this continuously as he watched the film. How he moved the stick related to changes in his blood pressure more than one finds with other people, or at least most other people. My friend and colleague Richie Davidson has found the same thing with a different measure of physiology. It is a very dramatic demonstration.[21]

The tragedy is that I did not know Matthieu thirty years ago, before all of his Buddhist training, because what we need to know is, was he always like this or is this the result of meditation? I met his mother recently and asked her what Matthieu was like when he was an adolescent, before he became a monk. She said he was very difficult. Matthieu overheard her and said, "I was quite a typical Parisian student. The word *happiness* did not mean much to me. I had some feeling that there was a potential to develop deep within but had no idea what it was or how to proceed. Now, looking in retrospect, I believe any progress that I might have made is the result of spending so many years with remarkable spiritual teachers who were living examples of practicing to the best of my limited capacity."

DALAI LAMA: (*Translated.*) What is the time lapse in the different states that is being monitored in this experiment?

EKMAN: Very small, very small. As he moved the joystick, his blood pressure was changing in coordination. It is not that we think he was aware of his blood pressure, just that he was *so* aware of his momentary emotions. He was doing this as he watched a film we selected because it aroused emotions.

After the film is over, we ask people, "What did you feel when you watched the film?" Most people say, "Upset." So, we ask, "Can you tell me more?" "Well, I felt badly about this person, that he seemed to be very unhappy." "Anything else?" "That is it." When we asked Matthieu, he produced about eight hundred words, describing moment by moment each feeling he had. This, too, would make Francisco Varela very happy.

ON THE MATTHIEU RICARD STUDY

by Robert W. Levenson

The question of how close the relationships are among autonomic, subjective, and behavioral aspects of emotion has a long history in emotion theory and research. I have written about emotions as the master choreographers, imposing order on these normally independent systems, making them dance together, even if only briefly, in the service of important goals. There is a related question about how aware we are of our visceral sensations, for example, the pulsing of the blood through our arteries and veins. Many classic theories of emotion (as well as newer ones that come from the realm of modern neuroscience) emphasize the important role that visceral awareness plays in shaping our emotions. Matthieu's emotions may well be more tightly choreographed and his visceral awareness more acute than most. Currently, stimulated by our work with Matthieu, my students and I have launched a study of these issues in a group of experienced meditators, comparing them with dancers (who may gain heightened bodily awareness through another route) and normal controls.

Robert W. Levenson collaborated on the study of Matthieu Ricard's emotional responses.

✦ ✦ ✦

EKMAN: I would like to return to an earlier topic, to explore further the reasons why people might respond to a coiled rope as if it were a snake, more often than the reverse.

From a Darwinian perspective, those who respond to a coiled rope as if it were a snake were more likely to survive and therefore be able to put more offspring into the next generation than those who responded to the snake as if it were a coiled rope.

DALAI LAMA: (*Translated.*) It seems the more suspicious you are, the better your practice of survival. (*Laughs heartily with Jinpa.*)

EKMAN: That is right! In a sense, it means that we are biased as a result of our evolutionary history to respond as if there is danger, seeing snakes more often than coiled ropes. We use the term "false positive" for when you think the rope is a snake. It is a *false* positive because it really is not a snake. Still, you have responded; you jumped away. When you respond to the snake as if it were a rope, that is a false negative. It is not a rope—it is a snake, and you should have jumped back. You get bitten, or you could get bitten. The history of humans has biased us toward such false positives; it has biased us to see danger when it is not there, and to have developed a mechanism to respond instantly to threats, to dangers, without thoughtful consideration.

DALAI LAMA: (*Translated.*) Are suspicions and doubts learned, or are they part of a basic emotion?

EKMAN: Well, suspicion and doubt are more complex than hypersensitivity and a fast response, particularly to dangers and threats. They may have been very useful when there were leopards and lions and cheetahs in the places where humans were living, when suddenly there could be a threat and you had to respond instantly. Most of us no longer live with such threats.

DALAI LAMA: (*Translated.*) Can fear be seen as a learned emotion?

EKMAN: Fear is a biological given; avoiding a perceived threat is widespread in the animal world. As I mentioned earlier, I have proposed that a few threats—an object moving very close into your visual field that appears likely to hit you if you don't duck or a sudden loss of gravity—are unlearned triggers, perceived as threats without learning. But most of the fears we have are learned as a result of correctly or incorrectly evaluating the dangers we encounter in our environment.

DALAI LAMA: I think young children are much less suspicious. They do not care about the background or things like that, or the family situation.

JINPA: And not race.

DALAI LAMA: And then we grow up. (*Translated.*) Once our knowledge expands, we want to know, Who is that person? Where does he come from? What is his religious thought? What is his ethnicity? Should we trust him or should we suspect him?

EKMAN: Once again, I think we have to acknowledge that individuals differ in such attitudes. Some people are very trusting, like Candide, to the point of being gullible, while others are suspicious. I have written in one of my books that we have a choice about what risk we want to take. If we are suspicious, we risk disbelieving a truthful person, while if we are trusting we risk being deceived. I believe that in family life and in friendship we are better off if we can operate on the basis of trust.

DALAI LAMA: (*Translated.*) Is it all attributable to the difference in the environment where you grew up?

EKMAN: It is probably both the environment and the genes.

THE REFRACTORY PERIOD

EKMAN: I first explained the idea of a refractory period when we met in 2000, and I later elaborated upon it for the first time in my book *Emotions Revealed*.[22]

When an emotion is triggered, a set of impulses arise that are translated into thoughts, actions, words, and bodily movement. Once the emotional behavior is set off, a refractory period begins in which we are not only *not* monitoring, we cannot reconsider. We cannot perceive anything in the external world that is inconsistent with the emotion we are feeling. We cannot access the knowledge we have that would disconfirm the emotion. That struck me as being exactly the same concept you wrote about in your book, *The Universe in a Single Atom*.

How do we shorten the refractory period? I am not focusing now on the gap between impulse and action, but the period after an emotional action has begun, when all of the information available to us is filtered to just what supports the emotion. How do we shorten this refractory period so that, in Buddhist terms, the person does not continue to be deluded?

After an emotional episode is over, a person may think about why it happened, especially if regret is felt regarding what he or she said or did during the episode. Such after-the-fact consideration can provide the basis for learning how to respond better or avoid such situations in the future. When we last met, you used an education metaphor, saying that this was the kindergarten level. The next step—high school, maybe—is when the refractory period ends during the emotional episode and the person can then reconsider the situation, and perhaps modify how he or she is acting. The PhD level is recognizing the impulse before the action is taken and considering whether to engage and if so, how. The person can *see* the impulse before the action. Is that correct?

DALAI LAMA: Yes.

EKMAN: To carry this a step further, would it be the

postdoctoral—after the PhD—to reach a point at which a person does not even experience the impulse to act in a harmful way?

DALAI LAMA: (*Translated.*) Yes. In the case of the kindergarten level, the emotional episode has already occurred. The person may have also expressed it in action. But the fact that he or she recognizes the destructiveness of what has happened will help prevent future occurrences. In itself, it is beneficial. Insofar as the actual episode is concerned, it has already occurred. The harmful action has already been done.

EKMAN: My experience, both when I was a psychotherapist and when I was a patient in psychotherapy, was that I learned to be extremely good at understanding afterward why I had acted in a way I regretted, but it did not help me stop behaving that way again when I encountered a similar provocation.

There is some evidence that children and adolescents can overcome early problems, particularly early bad experiences with parents, through subsequent healthy peer relations. Most of the findings are with animals other than humans, but consistent with those findings is the work in the 1950s of a psychoanalyst, Harry Stack Sullivan, who wrote about how a strong friendship in preadolescence could overcome many distortions of personality that had arisen earlier.[23] What it raises—this sounds very soft-minded—is the healing power of a loving and appropriately challenging relationship.

Probably not everyone is susceptible to such change. There may be some people who are totally intractable to any change agent, who are going to lead miserable lives and make other people miserable. But they should be a small number compared to people who are amenable to influence.

I think of emotions as like a fish trap, where it is very easy for things to enter, as fish can easily enter a trap, but once they are in, the fish cannot swim out. It is very easy for us to learn new emotion triggers or new ways to respond when we are emotional. But once we have learned a new trigger for the emotion, it operates automatically, as if it were inborn. Unlearning triggers is very difficult, if not impossible.

It is such a common complaint: "Why did I get upset about that? I should not get upset about that," and then, again, the person gets upset about the very same thing. It is not that everything that triggers our emotions is inborn—no—much, even most, is learned, built on a foundation, a foundation that people inherit.

JINPA: Your point is that we learn to respond in a particular emotional way to a specific trigger.

EKMAN: Yes. And once we learn it, it is very difficult to unlearn.

DALAI LAMA: (*Translated.*) One basic point is that, generally, the majority of people do not really think about the destructiveness of many of the emotions. I mean that the awareness simply is not there. That is partly because the emotions are a very natural part of humans. In general, society's perspective is that it is only the emotional manifestations in murder or rape or stealing that are thought to be very destructive. There is not much thought given to the underlying mental states that motivate them, partly because they are innate, a natural part of the human mind. If an individual has learned, either through cultural exposure or another means, that these emotions can be destructive and can lead to undesirable consequences, he or she would have a different attitude and reaction. For example, in Tibetan society, children learn from a very early age about the undesirability of harming any living being, including small insects. They are culturally exposed to this idea from a very early stage, so it becomes part of their basic habit. You immediately resist from harming.

EKMAN: In the West and also in Japan (I do not know China at all), self-help books are very popular, which shows that there is a widespread desire for changing our emotional lives. Certainly, not everyone wants to do so; it is more evident in women than in men. But they want help with their personal emotional lives. I am not a historian to know how far back this goes, but this has certainly emerged in the twentieth century, and there are industries devoted to it. Just like people who want to be slim and read one diet book after another to lose weight, people read one self-help book after another to try to attain better emotional balance.

DALAI LAMA: (*Translated.*) This is true. This is very true. It is obvious that there is a growing appreciation of the importance of understanding one's emotions, how they operate, and how to manage them.

Just as in modern society, if you look at the idea behind the establishment of the legal system, rightness and wrongness, legality and illegality, it is based upon physical actions. Similarly in the Buddhist context, the monastic discipline deals with physical and verbal actions, whereas the Bodhisattva ethics pertain primarily to the underlying mental states, not the specific actions themselves.[24]

EKMAN: Would you elaborate on the difference between emphasizing actions and emphasizing motivations that lead to actions? I think there is a tendency in the West to focus on the action and not on the motivation. Do I understand you correctly that it is necessary to deal with and be conscious of the motivation, if the action is to change?

DALAI LAMA: It seems as if, obviously, according to our concepts, the real harm comes from action, not by motivation. On the mental level, that is, just what is happening inside the person's mind, the motivation for the action for example, no harmful effects on others. Therefore, even within the Buddhist tradition, in monastic systems, the emphasis is on the action, verbal as well as physical action, for it is actions that harm others, not thoughts or motivations, the mental level. Also, obviously, you see, it is very easy to judge actions. The motivation level, like in the courts, it is difficult to judge. Action or reaction there, some witnesses there, so much easier to decide. But motivation level is difficult to judge. Perhaps we need more people like you in the courts, to try to read their motivation.

On a practical level, there is more emphasis on the action, rather than motivation. However, when we think, when we take more serious concern, particularly for the preventive measures, then we have to deal with the mental level, the emotional level, because the emotion is the mover of our action.

EKMAN: And what I have learned from you is that it is not just the emotion; it is the motivation that guides how that emotion will be enacted.

DALAI LAMA: Therefore, I think, on a more deeper level, or particularly in the case of preventive measures, you have to deal with the motivation level. Once you stop, or once you deal with the old motivation—and you use that new motivation—then automatically you use a new action.

EKMAN: Yes. Or *change* the action. Because if we combine emotion and motivation so that the underlying structure is compassion, then the action is going to be different. It could be the same emotion, but the action is going to be different.

DALAI LAMA: That is right. I think, usually. I describe violence and nonviolence: Essentially, you have to judge on the basis of motivation, rather than action.

EKMAN: Explain that a little more.

DALAI LAMA: A smile, and praising, nice words, and with some gifts. But motivation: to cheat that person, and to exploit that person. Could it not be?

EKMAN: Yes.

DALAI LAMA: Now that is as far as the action is concerned. The direction: You say very nice words, and efficiently. If that person is really trained, then, I think they can deceive you. You see, it looks like a genuine smile.

EKMAN: Yes.

DALAI LAMA: Very friendly, very respectful. On the level of action, it is nonviolent. But all these actions, verbal actions as well as the visible actions, can be a motivation to try to harm other people. That worsen. So, therefore, essentially, this is violence.

EKMAN: So nonviolence that is motivated by a desire to harm is violence.

DALAI LAMA: That is right.

EKMAN: Interesting.

DALAI LAMA: Now, the other side. The other side is out of a sense of concern, you say some harsh words. For instance, from a teacher who really is carrying a sense of responsibility toward the long future of the student, and a sense of balance. Out of a sense of concern and a sense of their own interest. Sometimes, there is no other way except harsh words.

In my own case, my senior tutor, when I was young, smiled, like that—(*Demonstrates the smile.*)—always very stern. Certainly not out of hatred or anger, but mainly out of genuine concern about me. Later, my junior tutors told me that; my junior tutors, you see, they tended to help me with my lessons. Then another monk acting as a tutor, one monk who actually visited my own village as the head of the search party to find me [the 14th incarnation of the Dalai Lama], later he became my semi-tutor, or acted like a tutor. Since I know him from childhood—and he also as a person is very nice, very, very playful and very nice—when lessons, you see, go, sometimes I would ride on the shoulder of the teacher. "Then, you should read." And, "I am a student, so I have to read." So I rode on his shoulders. (*Laughs warmly, and Ekman joins him.*)

You see, like this: "You read." So the senior, semi-tutor told my junior tutor, "It is easy, you see, to defeat the errors of the mind. You should be stern." So at an early age, the senior, semi-tutor never smiled. Always—(*Acts out a frown.*). Occasionally the senior tutor also scolded me. I think I mentioned to you, he always, he kept a stick.

EKMAN: Did he ever use it?

DALAI LAMA: Never. So, action, emotional action, as well as physical action, and facial expressions, also, you see, a bit violent. But that comes out of a sense of concern. Deliberately.

EKMAN: Yes.

DALAI LAMA: Essentially, nonviolence.

EKMAN: Let me tell you about a more extreme example. You know how committed I am to my daughter, Eve, whom you have met twice. When she was three years old, she had learned a game to tease me, which was to run out into the street when cars were coming. I would go running after her, grab her, and pull her back!

DALAI LAMA: Hmm.

EKMAN: For her, as a three-year-old, this was enormous fun. Every time, I would say, "Don't run out to the street! You'll get hit!" That is not what she understood. She understood: What a fun way to get Daddy to play with me. So, she would run out again. (*Dalai Lama laughs.*) The third time she ran out within five minutes, and there were cars coming, without thought, I grabbed her and I slapped her.

DALAI LAMA: Ooo-oo.

EKMAN: The only time in my life I have ever slapped her. It was a violent act. But she never ran out again. Never.

DALAI LAMA: So it is good—it brought out a positive self, yes.

EKMAN: I did not think before I acted.

DALAI LAMA: Oh. Oh.

EKMAN: It was not that I thought, well, now is the time: Use physical force. It just happened. In retrospect, I believe this was compassionate, loving violence.

DALAI LAMA: Yes. That is right.

EKMAN: You agree.

DALAI LAMA: Yes. Totally. So, now, therefore, without consideration of the emotional or motivational level, you cannot judge right or wrong purely on the basis of physical or emotional actions.

EKMAN: The problem, of course, for the courts is that it is only actions that you can see.

DALAI LAMA: That is right.

EKMAN: Facial expression you can see, but facial expression tells you the emotion. Motivations are totally inside. We cannot know people's motivations from their facial expressions. Even *they* may not know their motivations. And so it is very hard.

EMOTIONAL SCRIPTS

EKMAN: I want to introduce another concept, another complication—or, if you like, another obstacle—to achieving emotional balance. My hope is that by recognizing the obstacles, we can overcome them.

I learned the concept of an emotional script—that our emotions follow often a repetitive script—from my mentor, Silvan Tomkins, many years ago.[25] It is as if many of us carry around the script for a play, a drama that we continually impose on situations when they give us any opportunity to do so. We are casting—like a film director would—people we encounter into the different roles that we need in order to replay the same script again and again and again. Like moods, emotional scripts cause us to misperceive the world.

She (*He points to his wife, seated at the other end of the room.*) is not my mother. My mother died very early in my life. There are things that I never settled with my mother, such as her continual invasion of my privacy and attempts to micromanage my life. I have caught myself replaying that script, misinterpreting what my wife is doing as micromanaging me, as my mother did, then responding in terms of that script, which allows me to relive the same play again and again.

Emotions often, but not always, occur in scripts that distort reality. Uncovering a person's script can be helpful, alerting him or her not to continually play that same dull script again and again.

DALAI LAMA: (*Translated.*) In a way, there is a similar idea, not exactly the same, in the Buddhist meditation on compassion. One of the elements suggested is to cultivate a view, a perception, of all beings as someone very dear to you. One model that is used is to view all of them as your teachers, or as your mother.

EKMAN: If they have been very dear to you, that is one thing, but in the script I am referring to, you are reenacting the script because they have not have been very dear to you.

DALAI LAMA: (*Translated.*) The general Indo-Tibetan cultural assumption—of mother as a primary symbol of affection and endearment—may not necessarily work in another cultural context. In the last year, I visited a rally and gave a big public talk, and there were a lot of children there. I talked about the importance of appreciating one's parents, particularly a mother's role in one's life, and how a mother can act as a symbol of compassion and love, unconditional love. I received a letter from one child saying, "You are wrong. My mother was never such a symbol of compassion!" (*All laugh heartily.*)

This is a suggestion; because generally, culturally, the mother is seen as a symbol of compassion and affection. The point is that you can condition yourself to view other people in a different light. This suggests that you can deliberately cultivate a perspective to view others in a light that you want—in a positive, constructive light.

Similarly, there is a Buddhist practice of deliberately preferring to use the term "poison" to describe delusion, aversion, and attachment or craving in order to disturb the person, to make the person become aware of the destructive nature of these states of mind. These methods suggest that you can deliberately cultivate certain perspectives.

EKMAN: It strikes me that another way to say this is that you can write your own script; you can choose the script that you want to guide your dealings with the world.

In my personal life, it would be hard for me to think of two worse parents than the ones I had, in terms of destructive impact. For many years I was afraid to have children, afraid that I would be as bad a parent. One of my father's curses was "I hope that your children will make you as miserable as you have made me." But I am very impressed with the healing power of being a parent, and as a parent being able to be the parent you never had, in a sense freeing yourself of that script. I had not anticipated that. Of course, I had a very good partner, my wife, Mary Ann Mason.

DALAI LAMA: (*Translated.*) I wonder if there are similar experiences among Tibetans of having a difficult relationship with their parents and then becoming apprehensive about being parents themselves. In your case, you were probably very self-aware.

EKMAN: When I could feel my father emerge in myself, I was very aware of it and struggled with it. Then, over time, it is as if that disappeared. There was certainly no lack of awareness. That is, of course, always the key issue. Two central issues have come up repeatedly in what we have talked about so far: consciousness and compassion.

DALAI LAMA: (*Translated.*) In the monastic community, the monks live with their teachers. If a student happens to have a teacher who is very harsh, then sometimes the student repeats that pattern when he becomes a teacher.

EKMAN: Those who study parents who abuse their children report that often those parents were abused when they were children. I have to believe it, because it has been reported so many times, but it does not fit my experience. My father would hit me and knock me to the ground, but it is an impossibility that I would ever hit my children. I could never do that.

DALAI LAMA: (*Translated.*) It would be better to ask the children directly, rather than get it from you. (*Laughter.*)

· 3 ·

EMOTIONAL BALANCE

In the 2000 Mind and Life meeting between the Dalai Lama and Western scientists, I had focused the attention of the participants on initiating a study to meet the Dalai Lama's request that the meeting not just be good talk, but actually move toward an evaluation of the benefits of meditation. I felt that meditation training should be combined with techniques for improving emotional life that were drawn from scientific research. The Dalai Lama argued that it was important to conduct a rigorous study, which I interpreted as meaning that we include random assignment of participants to training or control groups, with more than paper and pencil measures of the outcomes.

With initial support from the Mind and Life Institute, I formulated the research design and treatment plan. A year later, the Dalai Lama provided the first fifty thousand dollars to fund the initial project; his donation made it much easier for me to raise the rest of the money needed for the study. John Cleese, whom I had met when he asked for my assistance with a BBC series on faces, provided narration for a fund-raising video for the project; the video included footage of the Dalai Lama pledging, unsolicited, the initial funding for the research. With the funds raised, I recruited Professor Margaret Kemeny of the University of California-San Francisco, who has extensive research expertise in clinical trials, to take over the leadership of the project. I report several of the early results to the Dalai Lama in this chapter.

MEDITATIVE PRACTICE

EKMAN: Let's return to the question of how to help people who are very quick to experience very strong emotions. What can we do so that their emotions arise more gradually and less intensely? What practices would help accomplish that? What exercises, bearing in mind that in most people's lives in industrial societies, twenty or thirty minutes a day is about as much time as can be expended? Since it seems that these practices require continued effort, what can you suggest? What are the best practices for the beginner? What would you introduce after a year to someone who is continuing a particular meditative practice?

DALAI LAMA: (*Translated.*) I wonder if we can really speak of one effective method since we are talking about the transformation of mental states and thought processes. To make any impact, these require approaches from many different angles. That is why in Buddhist terminology we speak of the "union" of method and wisdom, of skillful means and wisdom. Is it the right way, to look for one effective method, like a medicine?

EKMAN: Where would you start?

DALAI LAMA: (*Translated.*) It became clear in your own definition of emotion how complex that phenomenon is, and that there are many components to it—which suggests that the antidote will also need to incorporate that kind of complexity. There are so many components contained in it.

DALAI LAMA: (*Translated after a long exchange in Tibetan.*) A recent experience with a very great monk, a scholar who is one of the main teachers at a monastery is relevant here. The monk was suffering from what we call an imbalance of the winds, something like the beginning of a nervous breakdown, a form of anxiety and depression. I wondered whether the imbalance had been because the kitchen of the monastery had been completely vegetarian for over seven years. The monk said, "No, that is okay," that the more immediate trigger was a very intense meditation on death and impermanence. I felt that perhaps the monk's approach was not comprehensive enough, and that he should not narrow his focus to death and impermanence alone. By complementing it with many other factors, such as the preciousness and opportunities of human existence, he would have probably avoided that imbalance.

This suggests that even in spiritual practice, if you focus narrowly on one aspect at the expense of others, it can have harmful consequences.

EKMAN: This is a very practical question. Do you remember that at our first meeting at the conference in Dharamsala in 2000, I asked you if the governor of the state of California were to say, "I will give you a certain amount of time to provide meditation training for all the prison guards or all the teachers, what is the minimum time needed to produce a noticeable difference?" You said, "Forty-five hours."*

We took your response very literally. In the scientific study of how meditation training might improve emotional life, we have given participants between forty and fifty hours of training. It combines a secular version of meditative practices with training based on recent Western research on emotion.

DALAI LAMA: (Translated.) How did you spread out the hours of training? Was it over a period of one week?

---

* Clifford Saron noted, "Conditions may exist where either contemplative practice is contraindicated or exceedingly onerous, even for a short time. Meditation is not a substitute for appropriate psychological or psychiatric treatment, although it is likely an important adjunctive intervention and a component of promising and recently established treatment modalities such as Mindfulness-based Stress Reduction and Mindfulness-based Cognitive Therapy."

EKMAN: No; it was spread over eight weeks. Most sessions were three hours over an evening, but there was also a full day on one weekend. We asked the participants to practice every day for twenty minutes. We do not know whether they did so: Many of them were relieved when Alan Wallace said, "You do not have to do twenty minutes all at once. If you can do five minutes, do five minutes, then later another five minutes."

DALAI LAMA: (*Translated.*) From your point of view, can you explain how it benefited them?

EKMAN: How or why? Those are different questions.

DALAI LAMA: (*Translated.*) How? In what way is it benefiting them? Am I right in understanding that in the case of people who are, for example, irritable, that they get immediately triggered by something and remain in an agitated state of being, but as a result of breathing mindfulness meditation, they became less disturbed?

EKMAN: Let me be more specific. In one of the measures taken before and after training, each person had to give a short, spontaneous talk in front of two people who did not look very interested. It is well known that this is a stressful situation for most people, and that is why we used it. We measured a stress hormone in their blood, cortisol, hoping to find a change in either the level or in the recovery back to a normal state in those who were changed. In this same situation, their autonomic nervous system activities, such as heart rate, blood pressure, and sweating, were also measured. Some of the measures did show that those who received the training, which as I said had combined meditation and emotional skills, dealt better with this stressful situation than those who were in the control group.[1]

Another measure was how these women handled conflict with their husbands. When I was planning this research, Ann Harrington [a professor of history at Harvard] said, "If you cannot change how they get along with their spouses, it is not worth anything." Although we were not providing training to the husbands—all the subjects in the training and control group were female schoolteachers—we brought their husbands in, and we had the couples talk about a conflict in their marriage. Their discussions were video-taped, and the emotional behavior they showed was measured. The analysis focused on a constellation of behaviors that has been found to be predictive of divorce, including contempt and a domineering stance.

There was an increase in these negative behaviors in the couples who did not receive the training. By contrast, those couples in which the wives had received the training showed no change after training. Of course, it would have been a more resounding finding if they had showed a decline in their negative behaviors.

On further reflection about this study, I have come to think that expecting to change how the participants in a long-term marriage deal with conflict when only one of the partners received treatment was not very realistic. If it occurs, it would be great, but because the spouses were left out of the treatment process, I suspect we won't find it.

DALAI LAMA: (*Translated.*) The spousal conflict, generally speaking, takes place within a framework of shared affection and love. There is no antagonism and animosity—as opposed to a conflict you would have with, say, one of your colleagues, which takes place within the framework of competition and rivalry. Of course, when the conflict in a family moves outside the perimeter of affection, it ends up leading to separation and divorce. The conflict that you see in the family between spouses is different from normal conflict.

EKMAN: It is, but I think you have too rosy a picture of what most marriages are like.

JINPA: Yes, that is true. Maybe as a monk—His Holiness was saying—he is admiring the married life. (*Everyone laughs.*)

EKMAN: In 2000, my daughter, Eve, was an observer at the meeting in Dharamsala. In the breaks each day, you kindly allowed observers to ask you a question. She asked, "Why is it that we get the angriest at those we love?" And you said to her, "Because you are not seeing them realistically. Focus on their clay feet. If you will accept their imperfections, then you will not be so disappointed and angry." Those who can hurt you the most are those who love you the most.

In very good marriages, those that work well, each person has a commitment to the marriage, even when you look at the words they use. One of the best predictors of whether a marriage is going to endure is how often each spouse says "we" versus how often they say "I."[2]

In our research project I am not certain we used the best meditation training for improving how marital conflict is handled, even if we were able to work with both husband and wife. We had only three hours a week. What do you recommend, when we try this research again?

DALAI LAMA: (*Translated.*) I am not sure what would be most appropriate in this particular context or practice. One of the things that is most effective in my own dealings with others is reflecting deeply upon the interdependent nature of interests. Of course, in dealings with people that you do not know, initially it does not really matter; the people are not going to affect you. But the people that you do know, and that you have relations with, are part of your life and their interrelations with you matter—part of the community—and you are part of that community. If you can deeply meditate and reflect upon this—and nature—on the interdependent nature of your well-being and interests, that could be helpful.

One of the most important factors would be to reflect deeply upon the destructiveness of the emotions that get in the way, such as anger. There is also a particular approach suggested in Shantideva's text [*A Guide to the Bodhisattva Way of Life*], where, when dealing with a problem in which there is no solution, you should not be overwhelmed by depression or by being discouraged.[3] There is no need. If there is no solution, then there is no point in being so overwhelmed. That approach may also be helpful. Reflecting deeply upon the destructive nature and the consequences may, in fact, be helpful. This general approach promotes peace of mind.

EKMAN: When you reflect on that, do you reflect on it in an abstract fashion, or on a specific incident of anger?

DALAI LAMA: More in abstract terms. Because the more you have a conviction regarding the destructiveness of intense anger, and the more you have an appreciation of the value and advantages of loving-kindness and emotions of that kind, it will have more of an impact upon the actual experience of the emotions.

HOW HIGH THE BAR

JINPA: This just reminded His Holiness of a story that he brings up often in his public talks, the story of one of his colleagues who was held in a Chinese prison for a long time. After many years in prison, he was released, came to India, and then met with His Holiness, and they spent many hours together. During this time he had mentioned to His Holiness that occasionally he experienced deep fear.

DALAI LAMA: He was in the Chinese gulag. A few occasions.

JINPA: On a few occasions, he experienced a deep sense of fear.

DALAI LAMA: Of danger.

JINPA: His Holiness asked him, "What kind of danger?" And he said, "The danger of losing my compassion . . . for the Chinese prison guards." What this suggests is that when a person has that kind of mind-set and perspective and appreciation of the value of compassion, then such a person is never going to willingly embrace any kind of hateful emotion. The basic outlook on life that you have probably makes a big difference in how you respond to emotions.

EKMAN: There is a side to the story of the man in the Chinese prison that I think for some can cause a problem: When you hear this story and you might think, I could never be like that. It is as if you were to hear a spectacular violinist playing and think, How could I ever play that well? My question is, Should we all be aiming for the level that this man in the Chinese prison reached? Or is that too high a goal for most of us? If we hear about something that is so elevated, will that discourage us from even trying?

DALAI LAMA: (*Translated.*) Not everyone should try to reach that level. This colleague was not a well-known, intense meditator; he was an ordinary monk, not even a highly learned scholar. I told you this story to underline that your outlook on these emotions, whether or not you are deeply convinced of their destructive nature, or whether or not you are deeply convinced of the value of positive mental states, will make a big difference in how you respond to triggers, how you respond to situations, and so on. The goal is to develop an outlook in which you fully realize the interdependent nature of your well-being with that of others, and of your interests with others' interests.

Human beings are part of the social animal world, and we share the world of emotions with animals. If you look at the animal world, the basic emotions that they display are really part of their survival mechanism. And that level of emotion need not lead to long-term negative or destructive consequences. The problem with the human being is that our emotions are then complemented with human intelligence, the faculty of intelligence, with memories. Given that human emotion is in some sense textured by memory and so on, the antidote to our destructive emotions would also need to come from that same world—of thought, intelligence, mindfulness. That is the point.

EKMAN: I like the point. I also like the use of the word "outlook." It is very general. I have thought of this before in terms of the platform that one stands on to greet the world; "outlook" is a way of putting that in one word. Cultivating that outlook is a preparation.

DALAI LAMA: (*Translated.*) Many of the practices that you find in the Buddhist texts relate to the spiritual project of attaining enlightenment, such as cultivation of faith and a high level of compassion, so it may not be relevant to your focus on improving emotional life.

EKMAN: (*Shares with the Dalai Lama a cartoon from* The New Yorker.) The joke is that the Dalai Lama may be able to have such loving-kindness, because he does not have to deal with such nasty people like this wife.

DALAI LAMA: Ohh.

EKMAN: This relates to the story of the man who fears losing his compassion for the guards. That is an amazing level of achievement. Is that the level that we should all seek? Or is that like Mozart—something that just a few people can reach, though we can all seek to go in that direction? What is your answer when people say, "How can we all be like the Dalai Lama? Is that asking too much? We cannot; we have families, we have children."

DALAI LAMA: Oh, that is right. So, that means possibility—only *possible*. This simply tells us that there are people who can reach that level of accomplishment. It does not mean that everyone has to do that.

EKMAN: When I asked Matthieu [Ricard] about it, he said to me, "Very few of us could ever be an Olympic javelin thrower. But all of us, if we practice, can learn to throw the javelin farther." We will not all be the Dalai Lama. But his example points a direction, and we can all, to differing extents, try to move in that direction. It shows us that it is something that humans can do, not that every human should expect to reach the same level.

DALAI LAMA: That is right.

EKMAN: But we can all move in that direction.

DALAI LAMA: That is right.

EKMAN: It is inspirational. But it also marks out a direction for how to lead our lives.

DALAI LAMA: That is right.

EKMAN: If I may restate my understanding of your position, the goal is to develop an outlook in which you fully realize the interdependent nature of life. If you realize interdependence and impermanence, then your life is different. In your view, this is most important: You focus on these important wisdoms until they become ingrained in you. So, it is no longer just a superficial

"Yeah, well, the Dalai Lama never had to deal with your whining."

thought. It has become like an intellectual habit: It has reorganized your value system. You now have a different outlook on the world. Without achieving that, everything else does not go very far. That is the hardest part because it seems so simple. That outlook has to become the core of your being. That is what I understand to be your view, which I find very compatible with my personal view of the nature of human life.

DALAI LAMA: Right, right!

EKMAN: It seems to me the issue of outlook is separate from the issue of developing in-the-moment self-monitoring. Those two are different. One is more of a skill, and the other seems to me to be more of a perspective. Although we can distinguish the skills from the perspective, they typically become interwoven and benefit each other.

There are skills that, once you learn them, you have them for life. If you have learned to type, even if you have not typed for a month or two, you could still type very quickly. I went for a period of ten years without riding a bicycle, and then I got right back on and rode one. I never forgot how to do it. But being in the moment, monitoring in the moment, seems to be a totally different skill. It is more like a concert pianist. You have to practice it; it is not maintained without practice. Would you agree with that?

DALAI LAMA: (*Translated.*) Maybe slightly different, because in the case of the other skills that you described—typing or bicycle riding—they are really much more contingent upon the actual physical activity, whereas the mindfulness is more a mental activity. Perhaps they are different kinds of skills. Although mindfulness needs sustained practice there is recognition in the Buddhist texts that after a certain point it will become effortless.

EKMAN: Is this a goal that one is seeking? Is this something that everyone achieves?

DALAI LAMA: (*Translated.*) There are people who have developed their focused attention to such an advanced stage that when they are in meditation they are totally oblivious to what is happening around them—that kind of focused attention. There are people who have that kind of skill.

EKMAN: Two things—or three. First, this is occurring during their meditation, but not during their interaction with others?

DALAI LAMA: (*Translated.*) Of course, yes, your point is well taken. An eighteenth-century master was said to be able to continue with his daily meditation practice while engaged fully in everyday activities, such as having a conversation. In a sense he was doing two things at the same time. He would be counting his beads, but at the same time he focused his attention on the conversation that was taking place.

EKMAN: A multitasker.

JINPA: A multitasker—yes. You can bring mindfulness into an everyday interaction as well.

EKMAN: I generally object to multitasking; I want someone's full attention.

DALAI LAMA: (*Translated.*) In Buddhist epistemological and

psychology texts, there is an understanding that human beings are able to focus on only one thing at a time. You cannot have two distinct mental thoughts focused at the same moment. The question is, How does this not contradict the experience of this master? The way in which you can understand this is that the statement that one can focus attention only on one point at any given moment is applied in a much smaller temporal sequence. Basically, two streams of thought are happening. While one stream is going on, the other is going, making it possible to flow in and out of each stream within an instant. In a sense, what you are seeing is the transition from different thought processes happening much faster.

EKMAN: My wife reads the newspaper and watches the news on television at the same moment. I feel that she cheats each one, that neither gets her full thought. But that is the way she likes to do it.

JINPA: His Holiness was saying there is a Tibetan epistemological term for this—"inattentive perception." (*All laugh.*) To some extent, His Holiness does this multitasking as well, because often he has to attend these long meetings. While he is listening, he has some part of his daily practice to be done at the same time.

EKMAN: He does that?

JINPA: He quietly does it. But he says that he can do it only up to a point. If there is serious discussion, he cannot multitask.

EKMAN: I said I had three thoughts. The first was that this person who maintains attention is doing so during meditation; it may not be as easy to not be distracted when one is not meditating.

The second thought was that maybe what this person is able to do is highly unusual. Maybe he is like Mozart, who we know had a highly unusual ability. If we all thought we had to become Mozart, we would be very unhappy. Just as there are gifted composers and gifted athletes, there are gifted athletes of the mind, whose mind has more plasticity, more capability for what we are talking about. We can learn from it, but it should not be our goal. We will be disappointed if we think we will all reach that. Our goal should be to cultivate our own minds to the maximum we can reach, not to reach the state of achievement of any other specific person.

THE STARTLE AND THE BUFFER

EKMAN: The third point was about Matthieu Ricard. I told you about two of the studies we did with him: the discussions with the difficult person, and his tracking his own blood pressure. The third study we did most systematically. We used a very loud noise, as loud as a firecracker, just below the threshold for doing damage to hearing—115 decibels of white noise—to produce what we call a "startle," which is a reflex, not an emotion, activated by a very old part of the brain. Infants that are born without a cortex, who are not able to survive more than a few hours, will still startle when exposed to a very loud noise. You do not need any cortex at all. This reflex can be observed in many animal species.

The startle is interesting because it is so primitive. It is also fixed. The startle reaction begins exactly 250 milliseconds after the noise, and it is over at 500 milliseconds—never shorter, never longer. It is a very fixed reflex.

JINPA: Across the species?

EKMAN: I only know about the timing for humans, but I suspect the timing of the startle reaction would be fixed in other species.

The pattern of response in the face and body is also fixed. There are five movements that occur, and they occur simultaneously. However, the size of those responses is quite varied; some people are literally knocked out of the chair, while others show a very small response. We asked Matthieu to use a meditative practice to interfere with or diminish the startle. We began each experimental series with him not knowing exactly when the loud noise would occur. He has a small startle reaction in that unanticipated condition.

After the condition in which he did not know when the noise would occur, there were three more conditions: (1) to be distracted by thinking about something, a particular event; (2) to be in what he said was fixed-point meditation; and (3) to be in open meditation. In fixed-point meditation there was a specific object on which he focused his attention, while in the open meditation there was a kind of empty space, his attention focused on nothing.

We repeated this again and again, all day long, varying the order. One time, open meditation went first, and another time open went last, another time open was in the middle, and fixed was first, etc.

JINPA: Were you registering some signature for each of these states?

EKMAN: We were. We measured the autonomic nervous system [ANS] physiology and his face and body responses. The results were extremely consistent: The biggest responses, both in his physiology and his muscles, were with distraction. The next were with fixed-point meditation. And the smallest, so small that sometimes—not always, but sometimes—we could not measure it, were with open meditation. Different types of meditation were achieving different effects, at least for him.

We have not tried this same exact routine with other individuals who are not meditators. I expect if we were to see a few thousand, we could find one or two who would be like this without training. What we still do not know with Matthieu, and we will not know, is if he was like this to begin with, before he spent decades meditating. But clearly he is able to direct his attention in a way that basically reduces the outside world while he is in this open, vast state.

DALAI LAMA: (*Translated.*) In the open-space meditation, would Matthieu's response suggest that all sensory levels of experience ceased?

EKMAN: Matthieu reported that in his state of open presence he heard everything, but his perceptions did not cause waves and perturbations as when your mind is tense and narrow. Our measurements revealed that despite the sound being overwhelming to the typical person, Matthieu's responses reduced to the point of being on the edge of undetectable. It was always detectable with his change in heart rate, but it got extremely tiny. And sometimes there were no observable muscle movements at all. None. He did say that he always heard the sound, even in the open state. It was not that he did not hear it.

JINPA: Interesting.

KERZIN*: Sometimes it is described as hearing, or if your eyes are open, seeing, but not focusing.

DALAI LAMA: That is it.

KERZIN: It is much more of a global focus than a focus on a specific sound or on a particular image.

EKMAN: Yes. I asked Matthieu to give a complete description of his state; you are describing it quite well. Matthieu described "open presence" as a case where sensory input flows over you. It barely results in formation of knowledgeable perceptions—as if the activation in sensory regions of the brain tapers out without much further processing. It appears that the part of the brain that can monitor, be the watcher of our consciousness, is an area called the prefrontal cortex.

DALAI LAMA: (*Translated*.) Perhaps meditators have gained the power of concentration, which allows them more awareness and memory of their momentary experiences.

EKMAN: Yes.

DALAI LAMA: (*Translated*.) So even if that moment is brief, because of the power of meditative concentration we can actually pick up those things. Has any research been done in relation to showing objects quite quickly on a screen, one after another, and then have the different subjects identify these things, and see if meditators display something more skilled as compared to the ordinary layperson?[4]

---

* Barry Kerzin, an American physician who was ordained as a Buddhist monk in 2003, resides in Dharamsala and was traveling with the Dalai Lama at the time of the April 2006 dialogue. He primarily attended the sessions as an observer of our dialogue; this exchange is one of the few times he commented.

EKMAN: Good experiment. Another study that needs to be done, in my view, is to examine someone like Matthieu when he is dealing with a difficult person—so now he is not in isolation, but dealing with difficulty. Do we still see that high level of momentary awareness? My guess is yes. One of the criticisms that we get for this research is: It is all very well and good, they are sitting in a quiet room by themselves, not having to deal with anything, so why does it matter?

ON THE BUFFER

by Richard J. Davidson

The notion here is that the content of our buffer is always changing. In this sense, it is very akin to the Buddhist notion of *anicca* (impermanence), which means that all things change. The prefrontal cortex provides a short-term buffer, or it at least guides other parts of the brain to provide such a buffer, but the contents of the buffer are always changing. Most of us may not be acutely aware of this constant change. This is one of the important experiential insights that can be gleaned from meditation practice. The practitioner literally becomes more familiar with the nature of his or her own mind.

I do not think the issue of why an individual needs to practice continually is directly tied to the buffering quality of the prefrontal cortex and the fact that the contents of our working memory (that part of memory that is easily accessible to consciousness) are always changing. I believe that the need for practice comes from other factors. Why does a musician need to practice continually despite already being very good at what he or she does? Why do athletes need to continuously practice their sport despite also being outstanding at what he or she does? And why does a bridge or chess player need to continually practice to remain excellent at his or her game?

I believe that the situation is the same for the skills that are cultivated by meditation.

I believe there are two fundamental reasons why continual practice in each of these domains is necessary. The first has to do with the fact that in each of these cases, the practitioner involved has the aspiration to improve. Merely stabilizing the status quo is insufficient. In meditation practice, it is similar. The practitioner has the intuition that there is always further development that can occur, and this motivates him or her to continue to practice.

The second reason is that there are factors and forces that operate in the world to reverse the gains that we make in these domains. This is particularly true for the skills that are cultivated in meditation. There are many sources of destructive emotions in our culture, and there is the constant barrage of stimuli that can impair attentional stability. Thus to simply maintain whatever levels of attentional stability and emotional balance that might have been cultivated by meditation practice, the person would need to keep practicing to effectively maintain the gains achieved.

I do believe, based upon both personal experience and new data, that meditation can produce enduring changes in certain parts of the brain that are important for emotion regulation and attentional control. However, it is very difficult to know if such changes would persist if a practitioner were to stop practicing since most continue. Moreover, as practice develops, the boundaries between formal practice and everyday life become increasingly blurred and ultimately become obliterated.

Richard J. Davidson is a professor of psychology and psychiatry at the University of Wisconsin. His research, which involves such technologies as positron emission tomography (PET) and functional magnetic resonance imaging (fMRI), focuses on cortical and subcortical substrates of emotion and affective disorders, including depression and anxiety.

✦ ✦ ✦

FORGIVENESS AND RESPONSIBILITY

EKMAN: May I change the topic by reading a story from your and Victor Chan's book *The Wisdom of Forgiveness*?

DALAI LAMA: Yes.

EKMAN: This is a story in which Victor quotes you. I want to ask you a question about the story.

> When I heard from one Tibetan who was put in a Chinese prison (he is still alive, now living in Nepal), who told me in his prison there was a Tibetan boy. The boy was at that time sixteen years old—according to Chinese constitution not yet having reached the age of punishment. But he was in prison and about to be executed because his father fought the Chinese. One day, Chinese soldiers came with guns. One officer looked around, found an iron rod, picked it up, and beat that boy, whose father had killed some of the officer's soldiers. In revenge, to satisfy himself, the officer beat the young boy, who was going to die in any case, with that iron rod. When I heard that, tears came into my eyes. First I was angry. Then, I felt sorry for the officer. The officer's action depends on his motivation. His motivation depends on propaganda. Because of propaganda, the counter-revolutionary father is seen as evil. Elimination of evil is something positive. That kind of faith—wrong faith. You cannot blame that person. Under circumstances like that, even I myself may act like that.

I found that part of your story to be not believable, but I will continue reading.

> So, thinking along this line, instead of anger, forgiveness and compassion came. Interdependence gives you the whole picture. This happens because of that, and that happens because of this—clear? The essence of Buddhism—one side compassion, one side points to interdependence. And I always tell people it is very important to make the distinction between actor and act. We have to oppose bad action, but that does not mean we are against the person, the actor. But

if I was on the spot, and met the Chinese soldier, the officer who beat that boy, if I was there and I have a gun, then I do not know. Such a moment, I may shoot the Chinese.[5]

Victor wrote, "I asked the Dalai Lama, 'Even with your Buddhist training?'" and you replied, "Possible. Under such tense circumstances, possible. Sometimes thinking comes later, action comes first."

There are many parts of that story that I would like to discuss. Because it is a very rich story, yet it is a terrible story. It brings tears to my eyes to read this story—when I first read it, and now when I read it aloud—because it is such a terrible event, executing a boy for what his father did.

JINPA: Recently, His Holiness met a relative of this boy.

EKMAN: And then beating the boy. Bad enough they were going to execute him.

DALAI LAMA: Yes!

EKMAN: Beating him before you execute him. It is so outrageous.

JINPA: Yes.

EKMAN: The first question I want to raise with you is the high likelihood that not everyone subjected to the propaganda would beat the boy. Not every German became an enthusiastic Nazi. Think, for example, of Oskar Schindler. Some Germans tried to stop Hitler, even at the cost of their own lives.

Your forgiving and being compassionate with this man seems to me to be based on the idea that everyone would do this, but not everyone *would* do this. Some people would, and some people would not. And that is one of the problems I have with the concept of forgiveness, because it seems to me to ignore choice. We have the choice even when subject to propaganda. We have the choice. Are we going to yield and engage in terrible acts, or not? So, how can I excuse it?

DALAI LAMA: (*Translated.*) It is true that there will be people who are not as susceptible to propaganda. But it is also true that a large number of people will become susceptible to propaganda. That is why in the Communist system it is considered so important, political indoctrination. That is the reason why they suppress outside information; because it is very important, this information from their own side.

EKMAN: I spent time in the Soviet Union, twice, in 1979 and 1990.

DALAI LAMA: 1990, different.

EKMAN: 1990 *was* different, but still there were political prisoners in jail. Gorbachev had not let them all out. I was working to try to get one prisoner free—Mikhail Kazachkov—who had been in the gulag for seventeen years. There were people in this communist country, like there were in Germany during the Nazi regime, who enthusiastically responded to the propaganda. There were also people who tried to have nothing to do with it. And there were people who actively opposed the regime. It is easier for me to forgive the people who tried to have nothing to do with it than the people who enthusiastically embraced what the propaganda preached. This Chinese officer, to me, sounds like an enthusiastic embracer. I have not reached that state of being able to think that I could forgive.

DALAI LAMA: (*Laughs.*) (*Translated.*) From a Buddhist point of view, of course, there is another consideration, which is that the Chinese officer who is committing this cruel act against this young boy is in a sense initiating a new cycle of negative karma. The negative consequences he has to face in his next incarnation or in the future. From that point of view, from the Buddhist perspective, in the case of the child, there is a closure of a particular karma that the child is experiencing. It is from that angle the Buddhists would say that the perpetrator of the crime is in fact an object of more compassion and mercy, rather than the child.

EKMAN: Because he is in some sense punishing himself?

JINPA: Yes.

Ekman: From a non-Buddhist viewpoint, that is very hard. Going back to this example, you could say, "Okay, he was carrying out the law by executing." He was not carrying out the law; the law says you cannot execute someone that young, yet he is going to execute him. Then executing is not enough, he is going to make him experience a lot of pain beforehand!

Jinpa: It is because of this outrageousness that His Holiness mentioned that if he were there, he probably would have shot him.

Ekman: Okay, okay. That I can empathize with. (*Dalai Lama laughs freely.*)

Although it raises another question. People who have read this in Victor's book said to me, "Even His Holiness? With all of his wisdom, with all of his enlightenment, he would shoot him?" That is not a problem for me. The question that I want to pose to you is: Suppose you were there and you were told you are going to walk into this prison where this officer is beating this boy, and here is a gun. How would you prepare yourself, if you believe it is wrong? Do you believe it would be wrong to shoot him? And, if you do, how would you prepare yourself before you entered?

Jinpa: Of course, these are two completely different situations. Because His Holiness has not seen the actual beating taking place, but has only heard of it.

Ekman: Right.

Jinpa: So, the emotional response would be very different from physically seeing it. When you actually see the event, you will have a much more intense, immediate emotional reaction.

Ekman: In my example he is going to see it. He knows he is about to see it.

Jinpa: I know, but his Holiness was saying that when he has heard it, of course, given his background, he will consider it is wrong to even kill the officer. The general Buddhist advice is that for practitioners, there are two ways in which you can deal with a problem. One is to avoid circumstances that would put you where you will have a negative emotional outburst and indulge in negative action. The other one is to confront and actually immediately apply the antidote. In many cases, the first approach—avoidance—is much more effective. In the second case, you confront it, but then you will have to apply an antidote. His Holiness was saying that in the final analysis, what he might actually do in this scenario is unpredictable.

DALAI LAMA: (*Translated.*) Individuals will differ in how they respond to a given situation, and especially in more adverse circumstances. In the case of this young boy who was being beaten up and was going to be executed, as he was being dragged to the execution place, on the way he showed a tremendous amount of outrage and anger and shouted.

EKMAN: The boy?

JINPA: The boy, yes. The Chinese had to gag him so that he could not scream and shout. His Holiness heard this from a relative of this boy, whom he met recently. But contrast that with another situation, which happened in 1958, when the Chinese were carrying out military suppression where uprisings occurred in Tibet. This happened at a monastery that had about three thousand monks at the time. All of a sudden, Chinese soldiers came and arrested about a thousand monks, out of whom about a hundred were selected for execution. In this number was one senior monk who was actually the tutor to an important lama.

DALAI LAMA: Great scholar.

JINPA: They were all taken to the execution grounds, and when his turn came, he asked the Chinese officer to give him a little moment to pray. Then he did his Tonglen meditation, which is giving out happiness and joy to others and taking on the suffering and pain of others. And he was killed. Of course, at that moment, as a human being he probably experienced fear, but it seems that he had no hostility or animosity toward the Chinese who were shooting him.

DALAI LAMA: So, through training, through practice, one can transform that attitude to a better attitude.

EKMAN: One interpretation I have heard of this story in Victor's book is that you say that, if you were there you might shoot him, out of modesty. That you would really not do it; that you are being characteristically very modest. I need to ask you, were you being modest? Or are you saying that the action could come before the thought, even for as experienced a practitioner as you?

DALAI LAMA: Possibly. The stories in the book were part of a conversation with Victor Chan. Often the conversations had a slightly lighthearted humor. But the fact remains that as a human being, the possibility is there, and the susceptibility as a human being is there.

EKMAN: Let me now make it a more general point. If we know we are about to enter a difficult situation—

DALAI LAMA: (*Translated.*) The point is that human beings in desperation can act in all sorts of ways. There is a monastic college, a country college, where they are known for their disciplined approach to practice. Compared to other monks at other monasteries, they are much more orderly, very disciplined, and tame. There was a story that one monk was being robbed. The monks of this particular college carry with them a kind of pen knife, very small; the blade is less than two inches. The monk managed to get hold of the thief and took out this tiny pen knife and started stabbing. (*Laughs.*) Even this monk, part of this very disciplined order.

Similarly there was a meditator who had a meditation hut. One night, a robber came and he could not get in, so he was banging on the door. The meditator said to him (*Laughing.*), "Okay, now, why do not you stretch your hand underneath the door? There's a gap. I will give you something." So the thief stretched his arm in, and the meditator grabbed it, tied it, and opened the door and hit him really badly three times, saying, "I take refuge in the Buddha! I take refuge in the dharma! I take refuge in the sangha!" Then he let him go. The thief ran away. Later the thief told someone, "Thank God there are only three refuges. If there were four, I would have been killed!" Even a meditator who is meditating in the wilderness can do this.

EKMAN: In your book, and in your discussion, choice is very important. Human beings are not simply machines operating for reproduction. You said something almost like that. Clearly, free will or choice is very important in your thinking.

DALAI LAMA: Oh, yes.

EKMAN: If I have choice, then if I act in a way that harms others, why do you forgive me for doing so? I could have chosen not to.

DALAI LAMA: *Forgive.* If you keep that sort of grudge, then you'll get more suffering.

EKMAN: Yes. That is good.

DALAI LAMA: If you give forgiveness, then you feel more relieved.

EKMAN: Oh. So it's good for *you.*

DALAI LAMA: Yes!

EKMAN: It is good for the person who forgives. But does it not remove responsibility?

DALAI LAMA: No, no. For example, now, we mentally give forgiveness to the Chinese. That means we try not to keep negative feeling toward them because of their wrong deeds. But that does not mean we accept it, what they have done. So we have little forgiveness against them, as far as their action is concerned.*

EKMAN: Explain a little more. I am just on the edge of understanding.

DALAI LAMA: Forgiveness means not to forget what they have done. But forgiveness means do not keep your negative feeling toward them. As far as their action is concerned, you use your intelligence. You totally have to take countermeasures, but without negative feeling.

EKMAN: Can you take it away from the Chinese for a moment? Because, whoever it is, if they act in a harmful fashion, and they

---

* Matthieu Ricard commented: "We can forgive them as persons but have no forgiveness for their actions."

had free choice and they chose to act in that way, nevertheless you forgive them. But do you also condemn their actions?

DALAI LAMA: Oh, yes.

EKMAN: Yes?

DALAI LAMA: Yes!

EKMAN: It is a wrong action.

DALAI LAMA: Yes!

EKMAN: An unethical, immoral action.

DALAI LAMA: Yes—if your side is honest! Then, must criticize.

EKMAN: This, I think, is what is in the West misunderstood about the Buddhist view. They believe that the forgiving means you do not hold them responsible for having acted wrongly. If you do not hold them responsible, how will they learn and change?

DALAI LAMA: That's right. Oh, that's right. Usually, you see, I make the distinction, "after an action."

EKMAN: Yes.

DALAI LAMA: Where action is concerned, you have to oppose. You have to stop; you have to try to stop. Even use a bit harsh method. But as far as actor is concerned, you should not develop negative feeling, and should keep a more compassionate attitude. We ourselves often do that. If I made a mistake how I act to you, then later, I have to, later I will say—

JINPA: Confess.

DALAI LAMA: Oh, confession, right.

EKMAN: Yes.

DALAI LAMA: Sorry. I apologize. I myself now feel that my action was wrong, wrong action.

EKMAN: Okay. Very important.

DALAI LAMA: Wrong—so, I recognized that action is wrong, but then I make a distinction between my previous action and myself.

EKMAN: If I accept your apology, then I am recognizing that you and your action are not identical.

DALAI LAMA: Yes, that's right.

ON THE POWER OF FORGIVENESS

by Paul Ekman

A few months after our last meetings in 2007, the Dalai Lama's office asked me to meet Richard Moore, whom the Dalai Lama regarded as his "hero"; the Dalai Lama said that he only talked about forgiveness, while Richard lived it.

When he was ten years old, during the time of what has been called "the troubles" in Northern Ireland, Richard had been shot with a rubber bullet by a British officer and blinded. As an adult he founded an organization to help others, Children in Crossfire. On the tenth anniversary of the founding of that organization, Moore met the Dalai Lama for the first time.

I found Moore to be a very cheerful fellow, talkative, charming, and totally without any sign of resentment. In some sense he considered his misfortune a gift that enabled him to lead a life of compassion for others who suffer misfortunes. Of course, he regrets that he cannot see his wife or children, but forgiveness was not a choice, not a deliberate or sought-after state: he *felt* it, immediately. He realized that his reaction—no bitterness, resentment, disappointment, frustration, not even sadness at his loss—is unusual.

In our meeting, Moore ascribed his reactions to the way in which he had been brought up, in a family filled with love. It is his mother's influence, her example, that he believed enabled his forgiveness. Yet he also acknowledged that his brothers still do not forgive the soldier for what he did, even though they were brought up by the same mother.

Moore located the officer who had shot him, and met with him a few times. Most recently, the now retired British officer, Moore, and the Dalai Lama met and spoke at a public meeting about forgiveness. The Dalai Lama asked the officer who had shot Richard to join them onstage. The three embraced. The officer said, "Thirty-five years ago, I took a tragic action that resulted in Richard being blinded. I was appalled and devastated by it and upset for many years. But completely out of the blue I received a letter from him, one of the most inspiring letters I have ever received. If Richard and I can do this, then there's hope for this country and everyone in it."

Moore obviously is exceptional, as are those who without prior thought act heroically at the risk of their own lives to save others in danger. We do not know why some people have such a nature, only that they are few in number. They represent ideals, which the rest of us have to work at, strive to become. Most of us do not start out with their gift, but these people serve as a beacon for us, of what we wish to become.

✦ ✦ ✦

EKMAN: In the West when we consider forgiveness, our focus is on the person who is forgiven, so he or she is no longer in difficulty. I hear you saying if you could stop that person's bad action you will, but you will not harbor within yourself negative feelings of resentment.

DALAI LAMA: Yes. That is right.

EKMAN: My forgiveness is an antidote to any negative feelings in myself.

DALAI LAMA: The Buddhist texts also mention that if I let him or let her engage in negative actions continuously, he or she faces more negative consequences. Then, there are certain reasons to take appropriate measures to stop that.

EKMAN: There is a reason to stop bad actions.

DALAI LAMA: Yes, there is a reason!

EKMAN: What you are saying is that stopping the bad action is motivated by your compassion for that actor.

DALAI LAMA: That is right.

EKMAN: So that they do no more harm, which would later cause *them* harm.

DALAI LAMA: That is right.

EKMAN: Years ago, in our first meeting you said, "When I engage in and feel compassion, it does more good for me than the person I am compassionate to."

DALAI LAMA: Mmm. That is right.

EKMAN: It sounds like forgiveness is the same. Forgiveness is aimed at your mental life.

DALAI LAMA: Yes.

EKMAN: It is not the person you are forgiving. It is for you—you will not allow yourself to develop hatred.

DALAI LAMA: Yes, that is right.

EKMAN: So, your forgiveness is a hatred antidote.

DALAI LAMA: That is right. Plus—

EKMAN: Plus?

DALAI LAMA: With consideration that the perpetrator of the actual crime, if I do not stop him from this action, then he is going to produce suffering.

EKMAN: (*Chuckles.*) So interesting, so interesting. In the Tibetan community, if someone does a terrible thing, kidnaps a child, some terrible thing, will you punish the person for this action?

DALAI LAMA: Now, that, I have to judge. Punishment, in order to prevent future mistakes, then necessity, punishment. But then, punishment, in a sense, is revenge. It is not good. Not necessary. So when somebody has killed, I think, Okay, he has already . . . so better to keep life, a life imprisonment. Out of revenge, it is injustice.

EKMAN: Retribution. Are you talking about retribution?

DALAI LAMA: Then, punishment. According to that concept, if someone, if he kills someone, is a simple individual, now, in any case, no danger to carry further crimes. See, this is not a preventative measure; it is simply revenge. That is not justice—it is unjust.

EKMAN: There are three principal justifications given for punishment. One is retribution, or revenge—you are opposed to that. The second is prevention. I punish you in a way that prevents you from doing more harmful action—and you approve that, if that is the case.

DALAI LAMA: Yes, and not only preventing him; or some other people.

EKMAN: Ah, well, that is the third one. Now, the third is, I punish you so that others will see, If I try to do that, I am going to get punished.

DALAI LAMA: Yes.

EKMAN: We do not know that that actually ever works. Much of the research on criminals suggests that knowing others have been punished for committing a crime does not stop them from committing the very same kind of crime. But those are the three different justifications for punishment. If I understand your position, if you believed that by punishing this person, it will prevent many others from doing it, by example, then you would approve. But you do not approve of punishment when it is simply for revenge. Or when the person cannot do harm. So why punish them?

DALAI LAMA: Yes, I totally oppose the death penalty.

EKMAN: You oppose under any circumstances.

DALAI LAMA: That is what I think.

EKMAN: Certainly, there are other ways to prevent further harmful acts—there is life imprisonment.

DALAI LAMA: Yes, life imprisonment.

EKMAN: But life imprisonment does not give the revenge. It is not, "you killed, I get to kill."

DALAI LAMA: I think we are negligent about the effort to improve that person. There are always possibilities to change, to transform. The worst kind of murderer, with effort, with kindness, there is always possibility to change.

EKMAN: I am much more an optimist since I have gotten to know you than I used to be. However, whether you can rehabilitate people who enjoy killing—and there are such people—I have not seen any evidence.

DALAI LAMA: Then, put in prison.

EKMAN: That is right—until we can release them with safety.

DALAI LAMA: Yes. Unless we can be sure that now he not re-do, commit this negative thing again. On few occasions, I asked some lawyers to imagine one family, the mother no longer alive, passed away, and three very young children there. The father is the only one person taking care of these children. There is no other relative. No one else in the world is caring. Then giving the father who committed serious crime punishment, these three young children will suffer. So, under that circumstance, then how do we get rid of this: whether to kill this father or let him be alive. The holistic view is you have to take serious consideration about him, and about these three children. But if you are without this ho-listic view, just this person, he murders, so he has to go to prison.

EKMAN: If this was an accident where he has never been vio-lent before—he either got drunk or his girlfriend betrayed him, it was one action—that would be one thing. I would be in favor of not imprisoning him, but keeping track, continual monitoring.

DALAI LAMA: Yes.

EKMAN: But if he is someone who always gets into fights and kills people, then I would think that is not the best person to be bringing up those three children. I have to look at: can he be a good parent and good model? Killing once raises the question. It depends why he killed and has he killed before. Suppose there is an aunt, who has a wonderful family and she wants to take care of the children? There are many things to consider. I think the basic issue is you have to be fully considerate. Unfortunately, in my country, the judges used to have the power to take all of these fac-tors into consideration. Now, in some states, they have taken that power away from the judge.

ANGER, RESENTMENT,
AND HATRED

The 2000 meeting in Dharamsala at which I first met the Dalai Lama centered on a discussion of destructive emotions and became the basis of Daniel Goleman's book *Destructive Emotions*, which was published in 2003. At the meeting, I had argued that if emotions were truly destructive to us, they would not have been conserved over the course of human evolution. The Dalai Lama objected to this Darwinian view of emotion. Meeting six years later, we found common ground.

Nearly everyone would agree that anger, resentment, and hatred are destructive emotions, but a far more complex picture emerges from our conversation. Anger is the emotion that most often is implicated in regrettable emotional episodes, including instances in which violence or irreparable harm occurs. Yet without the capacity for anger, people would be defenseless when attacked. As we consider the core of anger and whether the impulse to harm is intrinsic to it, we decide that resentment and hatred should be considered on their own terms, looking at how each obstructs us from moving beyond a short-term emotional experience and holds long-term consequences.

PREPARING FOR ANGER

EKMAN: When I read your book *Ethics for a New Millennium*, I noted that you said that we should use force to stop *the action* and maintain compassion for *the actor*. That, I believe, is the description of constructive anger. If we accept your view of that, we then have to say anger can be constructive.

DALAI LAMA: Yes.

EKMAN: You agree?

DALAI LAMA: Now, hear, see that anger toward that action—not the person.

EKMAN: It does not try to hurt the person.

DALAI LAMA: Yes, yes, that is right.

EKMAN: But stops the action.

DALAI LAMA: Toward person, toward actor: compassion. Toward action: anger.

EKMAN: Even from a practical viewpoint, leaving aside everything else, people will never change if you try to hurt them. Only if you have compassion for them, will they stop acting—

DALAI LAMA: Oh, yes, that's right!

EKMAN: —in a harmful way.

DALAI LAMA: That's right!

EKMAN: So even if you did not have any concern for ethics, just for practical consequences, this is the right tack to take.

DALAI LAMA: Yes. Very good.

EKMAN: I want to come back to the question, If you *know* you are going to enter an emotionally challenging situation, a situation that may terrify you or infuriate you, is there preparation you can do before you enter it to better ensure that you will respond constructively?

DALAI LAMA: In my own case, one of the approaches that I find beneficial is not to take things too seriously. A touch of lightheartedness makes a big difference. (*Translated.*) The heavier you feel the burden and the responsibility, the more vulnerable you become to emotional situations. The late 1950s was a very challenging time. I had to take the responsibilities and the burden very heavily when I was dealing with China and our own people. Less experienced. Those were decades when I was much more tense, and felt the burden much more heavily.

About a decade ago, there was quite a big earthquake in Dharamsala. One meditator, who died a couple of years ago, told me later that he did not really feel the earthquake because he was in the middle of a meditation on cultivating forbearance. He did not actually physically feel the tremors that much.

JINPA: Similarly, in His Holiness's own case, there was another quite strong tremor a few years ago in Dharamsala. His Holiness did not feel it that much because he was in a meditation session. It seems that the state of mind you are in also affects the way you respond to external situations.

The meditation he was doing was on altruistic intention, the basic Buddhist meditation. It is the Bodhisattva's vow, dedicated to the altruistic life. When he later found out that there had been a big tremor and he did not feel it, the thought occurred to him: "At the point of death, if I were to meditate on the Bodhisattva vow, the fear will not come." Of course, this is related to many other elements of the daily practice, which are reflecting upon the possibility of perfection that exists in the human mind, and upon overcoming afflictions, and so on.

THE BODHISATTVA VOW

In its most essential form, the Bodhisattva vow states:

Beings are numberless, I vow to awaken with them.
Delusions are inexhaustible, I vow to end them.
Dharma gates are boundless, I vow to enter them.
Buddha's Way is unsurpassable, I vow to become it.[1]

The Tibetan form encompasses many more vows. In addition, many scholars have written extensively on these vows and their complementary aspirations of compassion, loving-kindness, empathetic joy, and equanimity. For example, in a passage related to the idea of forbearance and altruism, Geshe Sonam Rinchen writes:

> At present the affection we have for friends and loved ones is mixed with clinging attachment. Our aim is to develop an unbiased affection for all beings which is not tainted by such attachment. If a single being is excluded from this affection, what we do will not be a Mahayana practice. It is difficult for us even to think in this way, let alone embody it in our actions. Only Buddhas and Bodhisattvas possess this attitude. How worthwhile to try to arouse such thoughts and feelings for even a moment!
>
> The first prerequisite, then, is the cultivation of boundless equanimity. Living beings are born again and again in cyclic existence because of their clinging attachment towards some and hostility towards others. Wouldn't it be wonderful if they could all remain in a state of equanimity? Why shouldn't they do so? May they do so! Thinking in this way is called the practice of boundless equanimity.[2]

✦ ✦ ✦

EKMAN: Let me give you an example of what I mean by preparation. It is something that my wife and I do. We do not argue about too many things. A few things we may disagree about, yet we must settle our disagreement, or at least find a compromise. We have the practice of saying to the other person, "I have something controversial I want to discuss with you." Then the other person can first do a mental scan and might say, "Now is not a good time. Let's do that tomorrow"—but we rarely do that. Instead, if she says that to me, I then "set" myself: I focus on my mental state, both to calm myself and to try to be certain that I will not respond impulsively.

I have been warned; I know that what she is going to tell me about is something she thinks is going to be very difficult for me to deal with. Actually, she is wrong about what truly will be difficult for me a good part of the time, but sometimes she will raise something that is very difficult. By knowing, by being warned ahead of time, I am able to focus all of my consciousness on responding constructively. It works very well, for both of us. That is what I meant by preparation—that if you anticipate, "I am going into a difficult situation," even if you are not someone who is self-monitoring all the time, you can use what capability you have in those moments.

DALAI LAMA: (*Translated*.) This is very true. Because, as I said earlier, where human beings differ from animals in their experience of emotions is when the emotion no longer stays at the level of spontaneous experience; but additionally, there is the dimension of intelligence, memory, and thought processes. Given this, the method of dealing with emotion also involves application of thought processes, in differentiating the actual sequence of experiences. When you are warned ahead, you prepare.

EKMAN: You can use all of your intelligence.

JINPA: Exactly, exactly.

EKMAN: One more step, in the practice that my wife and I use, is that when we begin to talk about this controversial topic, if we find that it is getting hot, metaphorically—but not just metaphorically, because in anger you do get warm—then we will say, "Write me a letter" and one of us will write a letter to the other. Now when you write a letter—if you do not do it by e-mail, which we do not—you are able to think carefully about what you say. And how you say it. Then, after you have written it, you can look at it the next day. (We never send it the same day.) You look at it and reconsider if this is the best way to put it. You try to express the other person's view, as you see it, and your view. After you have considered it, you share it. The other person is not supposed to respond that day. He or she should read it and write a reply the next day, and then the day after that, review the reply.

It sounds like we have terrible problems—we do not. This has happened maybe three times in twenty-seven years, but each time it was very helpful. To me, it exemplifies using all of our mental faculties to keep from responding in a mindless fashion and is applicable to someone who is not necessarily a meditator.

DALAI LAMA: This is very true. The moment the intensity of the anger decreases, already you will be in a different state of mind.

EKMAN: It can escalate quickly if you are not highly mindful, first to be aware that this is a danger and second to maintain your commitment to not letting that happen, and to not hurting.

EXPRESSING ANGER

DALAI LAMA: In an intense state of anger, sometimes you use words that are very harsh and hurtful. There is a Tibetan master who wrote a beautiful poem in which he says that even a dearest friend who is close to you today, as a result of one or two wrong words that you use, may turn into the worst enemy tomorrow.

EKMAN: Yes. Let me tell another story. This is not about me, it is about a friend, and it raises the question of whether anger is always hurtful. This person travels a lot, as many of us do. Often he gets home from a trip very late at night. He takes out his key to open the door, but his wife has put the bolt across from the inside, so he cannot get in. He has to knock on the door. He gets irritated because time and again, four or five times a year, when he goes on a trip, she always puts the bolt on and forgets to unlock the door from the inside so that he can get in. He thinks, if she really considered my feelings, she would remember to slide back the bolt so that I can open the door with my key.

When she comes down and opens the bolt, he simply says to her, "I wish you would remember not to put the bolt on when you know I am coming home." Now, those are not terrible, hurtful words. What he said was directed at her action, not to hurting her, the actor. When he said it, she heard the anger in his voice and saw it in his face, even though he did not use angry words; and those signals that he was angry hurt her. My question is: Even when you do not say angry words, and you do not engage in an angry act, is the fact that you are angry itself hurtful to the other person?

I could argue that most of the time when you see an angry expression, or hear one, people are hurting you, and by that means we all learn the association. Once this connection has been established, even if you are not being hurt, you are hurt, for the feeling of being hurt is a conditioned response to another person's angry voice or facial expression. Following this reasoning, the only way not to harm the other person is to not be angry or, if you are, prevent any sign of that anger in face or voice. That is a strict requirement.

DALAI LAMA: (*Translated*.) There are a couple of things happening here. One is that so far as the husband is concerned, it is the wife's fault because she has bolted the door, and he has asked her not to. So she might recognize that it is her fault. That is different from him pointing it out and feeling angry. The second is him pointing it out to her, that it is her fault. Another is her being hurt. In this situation, the fact that he got angry is actually wrong, because, regardless of whether he expresses it verbally or not, it will be registered by his wife. At the same time, if he is angry, it is probably more honest if he expresses it.*

EKMAN: Well, he is expressing it in his face and the sound of his voice, but not in his words. He is trying to use his words in a way that will not be hurtful.

DALAI LAMA: (*Translated*.) What exactly is the question you are asking?

---

* When I read the Dalai Lama's comment to the person described, he replied, "She did know by the tone of my voice that I was angry, so I do not think I was being dishonest by pretending not to be upset." I learned that after this episode, the person's wife never again forgot to leave the door unbolted when he returned from a trip: His anger had a beneficiary effect; it showed her that it mattered to him, and this led her to change her behavior. Another interpretation is that she had to change her behavior in order not to be hurt again by his look of anger.

EKMAN: The question that I am asking is: Even if I take it to its most extreme form, if he says nothing to her, but she sees an angry expression pass across his face, if that hurts her, and it may do so, must he not even *feel* angry? Is it a realistic expectation for any married couple that neither would ever become angry? I think it more sensible to seek not to ever *say* anything that is intended to harm the other person.

Overall, then, how should we evaluate this episode: the momentary hurt she felt on one side, which is regrettable, versus his anger communicating to her how important this was to him, which motivated her to be more thoughtful and not bolt the door when he was due home. Given that his anger was directed at her actions and not an attack on her, and that it led to a good outcome in their relationship, I think it should be regarded as constructive anger.

I have thought about this incident many times, wondering if there might be other ways to deal with it. My friend could put a note on his wife's calendar about the night he is arriving, reminding her not to use the deadbolt on the door. He could also call her before he takes his flight home, reminding her to leave the door unbolted. Or when he discovered she had locked him out once again and felt the anger rise within him, he could have waited until it subsided before he knocked on the door, so she would neither hear nor see anger when he asked her to try to remember.[3]

Our discussion of the incident raises many questions for which I do not believe there is a categorical answer. Should our goal be *never* to experience anger? I think that is not only impossible for most people, but as this incident shows, anger does signal that there is something important to deal with. I strongly believe that once the anger is sensed, hopefully as in this incident very early in the unfolding of the experience, the conflict that triggered the anger should not be dealt with until the anger subsides. Anger is a message that there is a problem to be dealt with . . . later.

DALAI LAMA: (*Translated.*) There is a story of a Tibetan official, who was already quite senior and old when I was growing up. It was apparently well known that when this official got really annoyed and angry, he would respond in a very gentle, almost smiling way and pat his own knees. (*Laughs.*) He would say, "Wow, wow," as if he were surprised. So, is that a good response, or a bad one, to show anger?

EKMAN: Well, it is probably less hurtful.

DALAI LAMA: Yes.

THE VARIETIES OF ANGER

EKMAN: I think of anger as having many varieties. In English, we name some of them. We use "annoyance" for a very low state, and "rage" for a very high state; those are variations in the strength or intensity of the anger. "Indignation" refers to a self-righteous anger—"I am right. I have the right to disapprove of what you have done." "Sulking" is a passive anger—"I am going to make you sorry for how much you are bothering me, but I will not talk to you." "Exasperation"—"My patience is tried." "Seething" refers to barely restrained, intense anger. The nice aspect of the term "mad" is that it has dual meaning—of being angry, or insane—and, of course, in an uncontrolled rage we have lost our senses. That is different from indignation or sulking.

Do you use the word "rancor"?

DALAI LAMA: Sorry? What is "rancor"?

EKMAN: It is another angry word. It is like bitterness. It is anger that has a *history,* and that brings in a kind of bitter twist to the anger. It gives a sour taste. The angry person who is feeling rancor does not feel good about the feeling of anger. Some people, incidentally, love to feel angry. It is very enjoyable.

DALAI LAMA: Hmm.

EKMAN: In fact, for some people, that is the prelude to intimacy. "We had a terrible fight, to the point of beating each other up! But, oh, I love you!"

DALAI LAMA: Yes.

EKMAN: Amazing. Other people who have a terrible fight—"I can't talk to you. I can't go near you." People are so different in this regard.

"Vengeful" is still another type of anger and usually requires a period of ruminating about the offense. It is different from the others in that it is not immediate.

DALAI LAMA: (*Translated.*) Could there be a vengeful anger that is immediate, that would not require ruminating? Of course, there will be instances in which you will ruminate upon what was just done to you, and then as a result, your vengefulness increases and you want to hurt the other person. But could there be more immediate vengeful anger? In some parts of Tibet, there was a culture in which revenge was very important, like in the Italian, Sicilian culture, so much so that if a son of a family was not able to avenge a death, the family lost respect. In these cases, the vengeful anger is more immediate.

EKMAN: I am not convinced that that is a correct use of the concept of revenge. To properly get revenge, you need to plan the level of punishment. But there is always an exception.

DALAI LAMA: (*Translated.*) Part of the problem here is, again, the use of the term "anger" and its correspondence in the Tibetan language. The Tibetan term is *shay dang*. The etymology of the term conveys more than simply a wrathful state of mind; there is also an element of wanting to harm. Some kind of harmful intention is there that the English term "anger" does not probably or necessarily connote.[4]

EKMAN: There is no definitive scientific evidence as to whether or not the wish to harm is intrinsic to anger.

DALAI LAMA: (*Translated.*) In Buddhist psychology, there is an understanding of a correlation between two strong emotions—attachment on the one hand, and what is translated as anger or aversion on the other. They are perceived to be expressions of two different modes of engagement with a particular object or person. Attachment is primarily an expression of an attraction to an object or person. It is a way of connecting, whereas aversion or anger is the opposite side of the relationship.

In the experience of attachment, there is even a sense of somehow merging with the object, a kind of fusion. There is an attraction, while aversion is the repulsion from that object. In the case of anger motivated by compassion, what is happening is not really a repulsion, because you are still engaged with the object. You are not repulsed by that object, because the compassion is involved. However, the way in which you are helping that object is through a more wrathful, fierce state of mind.

EKMAN: (Sighs.) There are so many issues involved in this.

DALAI LAMA: (Translated.) In Buddhist literature, there are various discussions on the possibility of whether such afflictions *can* be constructively used in a spiritual context. But in many texts, somehow this aversion, anger, is considered to always have a component of harmful intent.

EKMAN: Let us discuss the issue of "harmful." A colleague, Joseph Campos, a professor of psychology at the University of California at Berkeley, is studying emotion in infants in different cultures. In order to do this, he had to find something that would bring forth anger in any culture. What he did was to take infants early in life after they have learned to crawl, and put in front of them a very enticing-looking object, a toy. As each infant began to crawl toward the toy, he held the infant, preventing the infant from getting to the toy, imposing an obstacle, blocking a desired goal. That brings forth anger in all the cultures that have so far been examined. It suggests that the fundamental issue of anger is to remove the obstacle to a goal. If that is true, that does not mean that the only way, or the best way, to respond is to hurt whoever is imposing the obstacle—which may only intensify the intention to maintain the obstacle.

DALAI LAMA: (Translated.) But even in the case of the infant, when the child becomes angry, there is a wish, not necessarily articulated, a wish to get rid of the obstacle and the person responsible for it, and also a certain hostility toward that obstacle.

EKMAN: Maybe.

DALAI LAMA: Maybe the harmful intention is the next step! For example, if the obstacle is not removed, then anger could—

EKMAN: In a young infant, when it is frustrated in this way, it does not engage in purposeful movements; it flails.

DALAI LAMA: That is because they are not capable of targeting. (*Laughs.*)

EKMAN: If the obstacle is close to the infant, then the flailing may hit the other person.

DALAI LAMA: (*Translated.*) Because even in the case of adults, sometimes you are so angry—and when you cannot do anything to stop the person, you beat your own hand.

EKMAN: Yes?

DALAI LAMA: (*Laughs heartily.*) This suggests that there is something in the very nature of anger, that you want to hit; a harming element there.

EKMAN: I see there being two possibilities. One is that most infants will learn that when you are flailing, you unintentionally strike the person who has put the obstacle in your way, and more often than not, that person then removes the obstacle. This would mean that you have learned the value of harming another person when you are angry because of an obstacle in your way. The other possibility is that the intention to harm is built into the very nature of anger. When I asked Joe Campos, he said it could be either. Practically, it makes no difference since it is highly likely that most human beings will have the experience that harming the other person can be helpful in the short term. If that is the case, then it must be unlearned.

DALAI LAMA: (*Translated.*) Even in the case of the scenario of getting rid of the obstacle by means of harming it, harm is a somewhat inseparable component of the anger itself; the basic emotion is more aimed at removing the obstacle. Once that objective has been fulfilled, then the harmful intention toward the person will no longer be there.

The difference with human beings is that we have a very long memory. We remember that the person put an obstacle in our path, and even though the person may have gone away, up to a thousand miles away, we still think about how to get back at him. (*Laughs.*)

EKMAN: It is a very dangerous matter, because it means that the wish to remove the obstacle can be subordinate to the wish to harm the person who placed that obstacle. "Why did you do this? Why do you want to injure me? Why are you preventing me?" Now the focus is no longer on removing the obstacle, but on the perception of the person's motivation and a wish to punish him or her for having caused trouble. That is the dangerous part.

DALAI LAMA: Then it becomes evil. And even animals, to some extent, have this capacity to remember something done to them. I had a small dog, ages ago, and at one time the dog was quite sick, and then my physician one day came and gave the dog a shot, which was obviously painful. After that, every time the physician came, this little dog would yell and yell and yell, bark. (*Laughs.*) He was always hostile.

EKMAN: We call that one-shot learning. And this case fits it perfectly! (*Laughs.*) He learned from one experience. Now, to unlearn that—very difficult, very difficult.

When we feel resentment toward what a person has done, even though the person has gone away, up to a thousand miles away as you say, we still think about how to get back at him. Your dog example is too easy. Suppose another dog comes in and steals a piece of meat and runs away. Will the dog who lost the food remember that, and think of how to get it back? I do not know the answer. Maybe a dog would act just as badly as a human.

DORJI: It depends on the size and the shape of the dog. If the dog that lost the food is bigger than the other one, he would probably chase it. There are different temperaments in different dogs.

EKMAN: That is true. Because we breed dogs to have different temperaments.

DALAI LAMA: (*Translated.*) When this dog sees the other dog the next time, he might feel a little bit of uneasiness or anger toward that dog. The determining factor for the human being is having such sophisticated thinking, the presence of sophisticated intelligence. (*Switching to English.*) So, longer memory. Also, I think, more desire, because of the intelligence thinks: now, how to hit back?

EKMAN: It is a very interesting point, because we think of having a good memory as only a positive attribute. You are pointing out the negative consequences that can occur with a good memory.

DALAI LAMA: (*Translated.*) My own personal feeling is that with an emotion like anger, the primary role really is to push away the obstacle. It may manifest in many different forms. But the primary role or purpose is to push it away.

EKMAN: We are in complete agreement on that.

THE ACTOR AND THE ACT

DALAI LAMA: (*Translated.*) The application of mindfulness to anger is to recall what you have learned about the destructive nature of anger and the destructive nature of certain behavior. From the Buddhist ethical point of view, you have physical actions, mental actions, and verbal actions.

Mindfulness applies to all three. The difference in the case of verbal and physical actions is that generally the time lapse between the state of mind and the manifestation in action is longer than the mental processes. If you become skilled in mindfulness, with knowledge of the destructive consequences of anger, applying monitoring awareness may be sufficient to prevent you from engaging in harmful physical and verbal actions because the time lapse is longer. With mindfulness of these destructive consequences, you are constantly watching the state of your mind, to the point where you might be able to detect early signals of anger arising. As to whether you will be successful in actually preventing anger from rising is another matter. Because here it may depend upon your own level of practice, your development of mind, and other factors.

ON MEDITATION TRAINING

by Clifford Saron and Marc Schwartz

The general discussion has thus far been concerned with optimizing personality tendencies and dealing with typical weaknesses of human character that we all share. In considering promoting meditation practice and training widely, it is important to realize that circumstances exist where contemplative practice, particularly intensive retreats, may be unwise and potentially damaging without proper psychological support. This is especially crucial when individuals have experienced abuse or other trauma, have been diagnosed with a psychopathology in which dissociative states are a problem, or have other brain-based vulnerabilities. While meditation is not a substitute for appropriate psychological or psychiatric treatment, it can be an important counterpart to those treatments. The cultivation of self-awareness, a basic human capacity, is fundamental to many forms of psychotherapy. Mindfulness facilitates receptive nonjudgmental awareness, spontaneous insight, and sensitivity to the minute movements of mind and emotion. It opens the space and time for a person to absorb his or her momentary reality and how the moment relates to other thoughts (and memory) as well as to see his or her possible intentions as they arise (and before acting). Mindfulness complements the spheres of psychological mindedness, emotional intelligence, and psychoanalytic mentalization, while meditation practices complement fields that promote healthy psychological function and, in this context, can find a natural home in the arena of positive psychology.

Clifford Saron is a research scientist at the Mind and Brain Center at the University of California at Davis. Marc Schwartz is a practicing psychiatrist.

✦ ✦ ✦

DALAI LAMA: (*Translated.*) In the case of mental actions, because the mental processes are so fast, it is not simply adequate to have the knowledge. You also need a very sharp and a quite advanced level of monitoring awareness to be able to "catch" the mental processes. You can catch before you act.

EKMAN: I believe these are very important distinctions that you have drawn our attention to. First is the issue of whether we can be aware of the impulse to become angry and not engage with it, so we do not become angry. The second issue you describe is that if we fail to recognize the impulse, if we have become angry, we may be better able to prevent a harmful action than harmful words because we can speak more quickly than we can move. Mindfulness may not catch the harmful words before they are spoken.

DALAI LAMA: (*Translated.*) Take an example of telling a lie: There is the object of the lie, the motivation, and the completion of the act itself. There is a time lapse between the motivation that leads you to lie and perpetrating the lie. A harmful mental action may arise because you believe someone has done something that wronged you. This is the motivation. Sometimes the gap between the motivation—the perception of being wronged, in this example—and the harmful intention it motivates is very small. For all practical purposes, when the harmful intention arises, the act is already done.

In this model, anger is thought to be the motivating emotion for a harmful intention. If this formulation is true, it already recognizes a distinction between anger and a harmful intention, suggesting that anger in the Buddhist definition need not necessarily have a harmful component.

EKMAN: I think that is a crucial issue for how people are educated about the way in which they can experience anger in a constructive fashion. You cannot get rid of anger, but you can learn how to use it in a way that is good for you. And the way that is good for you is not to hurt the other person. That almost always backfires. Unless you eliminate him or her, the person will come back and hurt you.

DALAI LAMA: (*Translated.*) There is a famous story in the Buddhist texts about a Bodhisattva. (*Laughs.*) This story seems to suggest an interesting take on the question, How can there be a compassion-motivated anger? The story is there is a Bodhisattva who is traveling on a boat. There is also a mass murderer on the boat and the Bodhisattva finds out that this person is going to kill all the other passengers. After failing to persuade the potential murderer to desist from what he is planning to do, he kills the mass murderer. The idea is that the Bodhisattva has full compassion for this potential murderer, but at the same time total disapproval of the act that he was about to commit. He has compassion for the mass murderer but anger against the act he is about to perform.

EKMAN: In the 2000 conference, a group of us met one night to plan the research project to respond to your challenge, "Is this going to be just talk, good karma, or is something going to happen?" There were about six of us sitting around, beginning to plan. One of the participants kept raising obstacles: "You should not do this," "you are reinventing the wheel," and "why do you think you need to do this?" Mark Greenberg* showed a beautiful example of constructive anger, because this person was putting an obstacle in our way. Mark said, "We really want to proceed, and if you want to participate, then we welcome you here. But if you do not want to participate, you should not stay in this meeting. You should let us do what we want to do." He said it with strength. I asked him afterward, "Were you angry?" and he said,

---

* Mark Greenberg is a professor of psychology at Pennsylvania State University.

"Yes." But it was a very constructive anger. There was no element of trying to harm. He did not say, "Why do you think you know more than we know?" That would be harmful, right? Mark's anger was totally focused on the action, removing the obstacle.

Focusing anger on the objectionable action, not the actor, appears also in the writings of an emotion theorist, the late Richard Lazarus, who was a professor at the University of California at Berkeley, in exactly the same terms.

What is needed, I think, is to give people practice in doing it. You could start with a situation in which anger was directed at the actor, and ask how you could instead direct the anger at the act. But that does not have as much life and vitality.

We need exercises for developing this skill. When I anticipate that I will need to discuss an issue with my wife about which there might be some conflict, ahead of time I plan in my mind how I am going to deal with it. I actually go through a rehearsal in my mind: how I will direct my disagreement only at the act and be careful not to criticize her. I do not let her know that that is what I am doing. I have found it to be useful, and often successful, in finding a solution to our disagreement. You have to practice focusing on the act that is causing difficulty, not the actor; you cannot just think about it. This practice is based on a realization of our interdependence, but it is a practice, in my example, rehearsed in the mind.

DALAI LAMA: So, anger by itself is negative. But because of the motivation—because of the agent that has triggered it, it is positive. So, it is positive.

EKMAN: I would not put it that way.

DALAI LAMA: Anger, for example, or any emotions that are considered harmful generally, in a special circumstance can be positive. Fear or anger or all emotions, to some extent, up to some degree, are usual. Beyond that, go extreme and then harmful. And that is the basis.

EKMAN: Let me add an elaboration. When they go to extremes, we lose control.

DALAI LAMA: That is right.

EKMAN: Disequilibrium. We distort—

DALAI LAMA: Yes, that is right.

EKMAN: We distort what is occurring. And then, instead of, let's say with anger, seeking just to stop the interference, we seek to hurt the person. That is going out of control.

I think a different—a minor, but an interesting—theoretical difference between your viewpoint and mine is that you believe that if you are a compassionate person, when you get angry, you will not get up to that higher level because your concern, from your compassion, is for the person who is getting you angry.

DALAI LAMA: That is right.

EKMAN: That is your view. My view is slightly different—I do not know if it makes a difference practically—that if you become skilled in observing yourself, if you have become skilled in being conscious of the impulses to become angry as they arise, then you will always enact it in a compassionate fashion. We are saying the same thing with slightly different emphasis.

DALAI LAMA: (*Translated.*) So, if you are very conscious, right?

EKMAN: Yes. And *understand* the nature of anger. Then you will know that because of interdependence, it is always harmful to try to harm the other person! This is just a different facet of the same phenomenon. I think we are in total agreement. People may be disappointed that we are not disagreeing enough. (*Laughs.*) Without that knowledge, if you do not understand the nature of interdependence, then the motivation will not be the same.

DALAI LAMA: Interdependence. (*Translated.*) What about this concept of interdependence? Does it come into science?

EKMAN: Well, it is starting to creep in. (*Both laugh heartily.*)

DALAI LAMA: Like a spy.

EKMAN: Like a spy. It has been there in other forms, in terms of studies of what facilitates cooperation rather than competition.

DALAI LAMA: The concept, I think, must be there.

EKMAN: I want to acknowledge that before I encountered you and your thinking, interdependence was not for me a central concept. My thoughts about this are in a continual state of change—influenced and reacting, trying to preserve the Western framework and bring into it things that are not and have not been as emphasized, at least in the area of work that I have done.

DALAI LAMA: (*Translated.*) So then at first, the spy, he just started creeping in. And now he has got to stay there.

EKMAN: Oh. Now, he is well recognized. (*Laughs.*)

THE RELATIVES OF ANGER

EKMAN: Let me talk about a relative of anger that I do not think is part of anger itself—*resentment*. Resentment is focused on a specific unjust or unfair act by a specific person. It can be harbored for a long time. You can be resentful for months or years, which does not mean that you always feel the resentment, but if anything reminds you of what someone did that was unfair, the emotion returns in full force. Resentment can motivate many different actions; one does not know what the resentful person will do when an opportunity arises. Unlike annoyance, rage, indignation, sulking, and exasperation, resentment is harbored. If it is not harbored, it is not resentment.

Resentment can fester. When it festers, it takes over your mind, and then it is never out of your mind. You think about it all the time, every day, every hour of the day. You try to think of something else, you read a book, and it invades your thoughts. That is festering resentment.

DALAI LAMA: (*Translated.*) In Buddhist psychological literature, there is a quite extensive analysis of the different types of pride and conceit, as an emotion, and the different degrees of it. But for more basic emotions like attachment and anger, there is not a complex division of the various degrees. In English, there seems to be a lot of words for these different degrees of anger— "outrage," "resentment," "indignation," and so on. Why are there such resources in the English language for anger?

ON BUDDHIST MENTAL FACTORS

by Geshe Dorji Damdul

Fifty-one mental factors are listed in Asanga's *Compendium of Higher Knowledge* (*Abhidharmasamuchaya*). Twenty-five of the mental factors are nonafflictive: five omnipresent mental factors (feeling; discrimination; intention; contact; and attention); eleven virtuous mental factors (faith; integrity; consideration for others; nonattachment; nonhostility; nonconfusion; joyous effort; pliancy; conscientiousness; nonharmfulness; and equanimity); five object-ascertaining mental factors (aspiration; appreciation; mindfulness; concentration; and wisdom); and four variable mental factors (sleep; regret; investigation; and analysis). In addition, the compendium lists twenty-six afflictive mental factors: six primary afflictions (attachment; anger; pride; ignorance [or confusion]; deluded pride; and view), and twenty auxiliary afflictions (wrath; vengeance; spite; jealousy; harmfulness; miserliness; complacency; excitement; concealment; dullness; laziness; lack of faith; forgetfulness; nonalertness; pretension; dissimulation; lack of integrity; inconsideration; unconscientiousness; and distraction). Only a few of these mental factors relate to attachment and anger.

❖ ❖ ❖

EKMAN: Although many mental states are distinguished, I was hoping that in Tibetan there would be more different words for different types of anger, because, as far as I am concerned, English is rather impoverished.

We can see and distinguish on the face more than a hundred different angry expressions. I believe I could write a different story for many of them—not all, because I expect some of them are synonyms. In English, we do not have a single word for many of the forms of anger shown in these expressions. The only ones we can distinguish with a single word are those I already mentioned, perhaps a few more.*

And now, hatred. That seems like a terrible statement—"and now, hatred"! (*Laughs.*) We have gone from annoyance to resentment to hatred. Hatred is different. It is not a form or variation of anger; it is instead an enduring, intense, focused wish to harm a person, not for a specific act. Resentment is about a specific act. Hatred is about that person as a person; if you hate that person you want to hurt that person, or if you do not yourself carry out a harmful act, you wish for a misfortune to occur in the hated person's life.

DALAI LAMA: (*Translated.*) Would you say that hatred would not require resentment as a basis?

EKMAN: The way in which I am using the term, resentment is about a specific thing that a person did. Hatred is about everything that the person represents.

Resentment can grow into hatred. But then it is about more than one offense. If it is just resentment, the person could make amends. "Oh, I am sorry I got a bigger piece of the cake or the pie, or that I got a raise and you did not and you deserved it." And you could get over the resentment. But it is very hard to get over hatred, because it is about that person. You want to hurt that person—they have to suffer. That is why hatred is so dangerous. Do you accept this as a definition?

DALAI LAMA: (*Translated.*) According to this definition, conceptually, will it make sense to speak of having hatred toward afflictions? Or is it really person-directed?

EKMAN: It is person-directed.

DALAI LAMA: (*Translated.*) In English, do you use the phrase— maybe it is a kind of a popular usage—"I hate the weather"?

EKMAN: Yes, but that is a bad use of language. The problem, of course, is that people do not use words as I would like them to. (*Laughs.*)

---

* Words such as "petulant," "testy," "cranky," "irritable," and "hostile" refer to moods or personality traits, not emotions.

DALAI LAMA: (*Translated.*) What about hatred toward a system? Hatred toward a country, a race?

EKMAN: I think hatred toward a people, or group, or a country, is possible, and very dangerous.

DALAI LAMA: What about toward animals, like ants? What about scorpions and snakes? For instance, "I hate snakes."

EKMAN: Some people are repulsed by snakes. Actually, there is some very interesting research that shows that humans are prepared to become fearful of a reptilian shape. It is not as preformed as a mouse's fear of a cat the first moment the mouse sees a cat. The research with humans suggests that a person needs at least one negative experience with a reptile to become afraid. But what is unusual, what I meant by "prepared," is that it only takes one exposure with a reptilian shape, while with other objects it takes repeated negative experiences. Guns and knives are the real threat, but it is very hard to get a good fear response to them without a lot of learning taking place.[5]

At the basis of hatred is the belief that a person has been more than unjust. He or she wanted to hurt you, has hurt you, and it is unforgivable. At least as long as the hatred continues, you cannot forgive the person for what he or she has done. You hate the person.

DALAI LAMA: (*Translated.*) On this planet we have more than six billion individuals, each with their own differences and unique features and mental states. It would be very difficult to try to come up with a comprehensive understanding of the nature of emotions that would be universally applicable and that would also somehow explain the individuality of each of us.

In the case of the Chinese soldier who hated the Tibetan boy, beating him before the execution, and in the case of Nazis who were indoctrinated, conditioned to hate Jewish people as a people, and who deeply believed in this hatred and the negativity of these people, when they were able to subjugate them, it is conceivable it did not poison their lives; they may have been able to enjoy a good sleep, have a better appetite, and so on. In a very perverted sense, it benefited them. Because of this, in the Buddhist

texts, there is a recognition that sometimes even a distorted understanding of the world can be beneficial in the short term. Yet
hatred is a poison.

EKMAN: Do you mean that hatred is a poison in the literal
sense, or metaphorically? Are you deliberately using this word to
command attention, or do you actually think it starts to destroy
the person, physically, like a poison does?

DALAI LAMA: (*Translated.*) This is actually a metaphor. But
there are important parallels. Some actual poisons may not kill
you immediately, but over time they will lead to your death. Similarly, hatred first will disturb your mind, the mental peace. Sec-
ondly, it will create mental suffering.

EKMAN: It is a pretty strong metaphor. It is not totally literal in
the sense that you are dead because you feel hatred immediately.
But it does destroy your life. It destroys your mental life. It makes
you a tortured person. But in the short run, it may be enjoyable to
hate someone. I encounter many people who hate a foreign or
domestic leader. They think about the hated person often, and
when they describe their intense hatred, not just anger but enjoyment shows on their face when they state especially nasty remarks. I suspect that in their minds, they are enjoying the
possibility that the hated person might hear their insults and suffer as a consequence.

If you look at the language used by Hitler and Goebbels in
talking about the Jews, it is the language of disgust. Jews were
"lice"; they were "vermin." You had to exterminate them because
they were a pollutant. It was not hatred. It was disgust. I believe
that disgust is the emotion that motivates holocausts. I was given
videotapes of Osama bin Laden taken over a five-year period. In
the early videotapes, he showed anger. After two or three years, it
is all disgust when he talks about Americans. Before I saw these
videotapes, I could not comprehend why he could approve of
killing women and children and old people. Once I saw the disgust on his face, I understood. When I see a cockroach, I do not
worry, Is it a baby cockroach? Is it a lady cockroach? I just want to

get rid of it, because it is vile, repulsive. When you feel that toward people, it is the most dangerous.

JINPA: In the case of, for example, the Nazi attitude toward the Jews, would not you say there is hatred in that?

EKMAN: No, I would say it was primarily disgust. [They thought] Jews were vile, a scourge on the earth, if you look at the language that was used.

DALAI LAMA: (*Translated.*) What about Mao's treatment toward what he called antirevolutionaries? Or Stalin's attitude toward what he called antirevolutionaries? Would that be disgust or hatred?

EKMAN: Well, Stalin I know a little more about because I think in the latter part of his life, the last twenty years, he was really a bit insane. He met a lot of the criteria for paranoia. He was seeing enemies everywhere. His closest associates, they were the most likely enemies. I actually know nothing about the Chinese. Two of my books have been translated into Chinese, but I have not visited there. I do not know enough about their propaganda; but I know the Nazi propaganda. Much of the Nazi propaganda used the language of disgust, not hatred. The Nazis hated the Communists, but the Jews did not deserve hatred—they were too repulsive. They were beneath contempt.

DALAI LAMA: Chinese Communists say that Tibetan Buddhism, because there is a lack of science knowledge, those foolish Tibetans, they were full of blind faith or superstition. So, that is their attitude in the early sixties, seventies, eighties. I think that from the beginning, they feel like that.

MOTIVATING ANGER

EKMAN: I want to raise the possibility that sometimes hatred can have a positive consequence. The example I will use is one I know very well, because it is from my own life.

For many years I hated my father. He was a cruel man—insulting, physically abusive. He was very competitive with me. He taught me to play chess when I was six years old. When I would give up, he would turn the board around and take the side I had just abandoned and beat me again. A little humiliation. He was a boxer in college. When I was about nine, he taught me how to box. Then, with one of his arms, which of course were longer than mine, he would hold me off and hit me with the other.

Unwittingly, I became competitive with him. I wanted to beat him, to get revenge. My hatred for him motivated me to seek achievements that I knew would—the term that comes to me spontaneously—"kill" him, a regrettable metaphor. Of course, I did not literally kill him, but I was determined to beat him at his own game.

He always wanted to be and never could be a medical school faculty member. So I did it, and earned the highest honors for research from my medical school. In part, at least, I was motivated by the wish to make him burn with envy. I wrote many books; he never got anything published. Every time I achieved something new that earned recognition, I would think, Oh is that going to make him mad, is that going to show him that I am better than he is.

Even when he had been dead for forty years, when I received some new recognition or award, I would immediately think, I wish he could know about this! He'd turn over in his grave! Now, I am a little ashamed of this. But the point is that hatred motivated good work.

In the last few years, for reasons I do not understand, I have forgiven him. I never thought I would be able to. With that forgiveness, my competition with him, my need to outdo him, also died.

I never once thought, If my father knew I was meeting with the Dalai Lama, how upset he would be! It never came to mind—but that is recent. My point is that hatred, although destructive, can motivate constructive action. Some of my research and writings have helped other people. I do not know whether I would have had as much drive to do all that I have done if it had not been motivated by this hatred.

When I finally discovered, "My God, I am doing all of these things because of my crazy dead father," it seemed stupid. But by then, I had already had twelve books published. It seems hatred can sometimes motivate good action, not bad action. So how can I consider hatred as the Buddhists do, a poison?

DALAI LAMA: (*Translated.*) In a way, what is happening here is really the role of an emotion like hatred in *motivating* people. We can see that also in the case of attachment, jealousy, anger, and so on. One of the things about these emotions is that they are very forceful, intense states of mind. This energy, this force, can motivate you in a very strong way. But can you attribute all of the good work to this underlying emotion, as a *cause*?

EKMAN: It was always a central concern of mine not to be like my father, yet in some ways I am. He was a physician. I was a professor in a medical school. He studied every night. I used to see him sitting at the kitchen table studying the medical journals. Well, I study; I write books. He helped children. His life was dedicated to relieving suffering. I do what I can to produce knowledge that will be helpful to people and reduce suffering. So, you could say we were on parallel tracks.

Very often, my actions were motivated by what I learned from him about what not to be. For example, I think for parents to compete with their children is a terrible distortion of parenting. I see that a lot in academia—professors competing with their intellectual offspring, as I mentioned before. But I learned that for a child to compete with his parent is also not good, yet it did motivate good action. It may not have been the only motivation—I am sure it was not. But it was a contributor, an important contributor. In that sense, the hatred did not poison me.

DALAI LAMA: (*Translated.*) We also know that from a meditation practitioner's point of view, you can enhance the capacity and the practice for forbearance, because of the action of an enemy. A cause-and-effect relationship is there. It is very diffi-cult to pinpoint one factor as the *key* factor because human be-ings are so varied, and some human beings are more capable of drawing lessons from every experience in their lives. In your ex-ample, certainly your relationship with your father was an im-portant part. What has happened here—in the Tibetan language, from the Tibetan perspective—is "turning adversities into fa-vorable conditions," conditions that are conducive to one's de-velopment.

But then to go on to generalize that hatred can be useful and constructive. . . . (*Laughs.*)

EKMAN: (*Also laughs.*) That is going into the morbidly bizarre.

There is one other point I want to make from the story of my hatred toward my father. Previously I talked about a *refractory pe-riod*, in which you cannot access memories that contradict the emotion that is being experienced.

After I forgave my father, I remembered positive things about him that I had forgotten for fifty years; they just came back to mind. For example, when a question about race came up, I re-membered for the first time that my father had been a founding member of the National Association for the Advancement of Colored People. (I was a founding member of the Congress of Racial Equality in San Francisco years ago.) It was a good thing about him, which I had totally forgotten. Hatred, like an emotion, blocks your access to your own memories.

DALAI LAMA: Yes!

EKMAN: It makes you stereotype the person.

DALAI LAMA: (*Translated.*) That is true.

EKMAN: You cannot see the good side. While hatred can be of benefit as a motivation for good actions, that is a benefit in the short term. In the long run, hatred is corrosive, distorting one's view of reality.

DALAI LAMA: That is true. Absolutely.

EKMAN: But in talking with you and thinking about your posi-tion, I have changed my view of hatred.[6] In my last book, *Emotions*

Revealed, I argued that hatred can have positive consequences, sometimes motivating good actions or helping a person deal with a severe trauma.[7] I now think that this is an incomplete view.

Although hatred can in the short term have a positive effect in motivating—as it did in my life—good actions, over time, hatred has a very negative effect, and in that sense is a poison. The change in my viewpoint was sudden; like a lightbulb turning on in my head, I saw my own life differently. As a child and adolescent, I was known as someone who rarely got angry. I recall my parents telling me not to let my older sister be so mean to me, to hit her back. But I never fought. My mother died when I was fourteen. I blamed my father, which was unfair; he contributed to her death but he did not kill her. My belief that it was his fault fired the development of hatred. Within three or four years, I became known not as someone who was always even-tempered but as someone who got angry easily. And that went on in my life for fifty years, until I met you ten years ago.

Hatred poisoned my overall character, facilitating anger whenever I was blocked by someone. My hatred for my father motivated me to make him suffer by achieving much more than he ever did, and knowing how competitive he was I knew this would hurt him. What I did had value in itself, so that was the short-term, positive benefit of the hatred. But the long-term poison was that it made me into a person easily angered toward anyone, about anything.

I want to speculate about how hatred actually poisons a person. It may be that if hatred develops and is maintained, that its maintenance reorganizes the brain in a way that facilitates anger. The consequence of sustained hatred is that you become, in general, *ready* to get angry. There must be a change in the brain generated by hatred. So we can now literally think of the brain having been poisoned in a way that makes you more likely to become angry than you would have been before. And that will last until the hatred goes away—if it goes away.

Do you agree with this account? Does this way of looking at hatred make sense to you?

DALAI LAMA: (*Translated.*) It seems agreeable.

Hatred, as you described it, seems to have two elements, which can, as well, be seen in compassion. For example, though the very nature of compassion is something virtuous and positive, if you have excessive compassion toward the wrong person, that may not give the adequate punishment to a person in order to stop that person from engaging in actions that are harmful to others. Even compassion can lead to a faulty side. It has its drawbacks. If you think carefully, it is not a form of compassion—there needs to be more intelligence.

To weigh the situation—to carefully give merit to the pros and cons of whether to give punishment or not—this has to be judged by the intelligence. It is not the compassion that is the problem; it is the fault of lacking intelligence. Similarly, if you go back to the hatred, it brings some positive things. But if you look very carefully, if you examine it closely, the positive quality may not be a direct result of the hatred. It could be because of some other element of intelligence, which makes you think, Oh, I must compete with this person, or I must try to do some harm to this person. So it may be not be the result of the hatred itself.

EKMAN: I think that is all possible. There are so many determinants of any action—an extended complex series of actions involved in many achievements.

DALAI LAMA: (*Translated.*) I have also observed hatred in animals.

A person who took me to a lake would go every morning. And he used to take his dog with him. Three other dogs would always appear at the right moment and attack this person's dog. Actually, they have claws. This happened again and again. They have the capacity to keep that anger. And another incident, at the Rhizong Gompa Monastery, in Ladakh: There was a fight between two bulls. The one bull killed the other. For the next seven years, when this bull, the winner, happened to be in that spot, he would get so outraged. Even, his enemy already passed away. Even then, next seven years.

EKMAN: A good memory.

What I want to talk about next is compassion and goodness.

JINPA: High time. (*Laughs.*)

· 5 ·

THE NATURE OF COMPASSION

While compassion has been a central issue in Buddhist thinking and is also emphasized in other world religions, it has only very recently become a particular topic of scientific study. This is remarkable, but given the hallowed place of compassion in the spiritual realm, it seems to have been considered off-limits to scientific examination. Yet compassion is clearly very amenable to objective examination: It is not simply a private unobservable set of thoughts or beliefs but sometimes manifest in a specific observable set of actions. Take for example a recent experiment that found that only some people act in a retaliatory fashion toward a partner who has acted unfairly; others act in a more compassionate fashion.[1] The question to be pursued is what accounts for this difference and if there is training that can increase the likelihood of the compassionate response. Not much is known about why some people, without any special training, are much more compassionate, feeling concern for the suffering of total strangers or why they act on that concern. There is not even consensus among scientists about how to define *compassion*. As we discussed compassion, I proposed a new set of scientific distinctions for the different types of empathy, including compassion, which the Dalai Lama considered useful.

DEFINING COMPASSION

DALAI LAMA: On one occasion, meeting with scientists, then I think, I remember Francisco Varela, we agreed, strong compassion, infinite compassion—it's a kind of emotion.

EKMAN: I do not agree that compassion is an emotion.

DALAI LAMA: (*Translated.*) It really depends upon how you define emotion. Compassion or loving-kindness does not develop spontaneously, but through training, through reasoning. It will depend on whether or not we would want to define this kind of compassion as an emotion or not. There is an understanding that repeatedly and intensely practicing Shamatha Bodhisattvas,* on a daily basis, cultivates compassion for all beings. Once the person experiences this heightened compassion, his or her compassion retains that kind of tone throughout the day, although the compassion itself may not remain as a "felt" state of emotion. Still, whatever the person does is affected by that tone; in that sense, it resembles a mood. However, because of that state of mind, the basic emotion is not thought to be harmful. Therefore, the mood or the state of mind that it creates is not thought to lead to a falsification of reality or a distortion of reality.

EKMAN: That is one of the reasons why I say compassion is neither an emotion nor a mood: It does not distort or selectively filter our view of reality. It makes us more sensitive to reality. It makes us care more about reality. We have emotions, we have moods, but compassion is different from either.

---

* The practice of *Shamatha* meditation has been crucial to the Buddhist tradition for over two millennia. Buddhist teachings provide detailed protocols for seeking and attaining *shamatha,* or meditative quiescence. The goal is to achieve a state of sustained voluntary attention, characterized by exceptional stability and vividness, free from distraction or wandering thoughts.

A second important difference between the emotions and compassion is that the emotions do not need to be cultivated; they are part of us, given by nature. But compassion, if it is to extend beyond the immediate family, needs to be cultivated. Nature only gives us a start. It only gives us compassion focused within the immediate family. If we wish to direct it at *all* human beings, we have to cultivate it.

We do not have to learn how to be angry. But we do have to learn how to be angry *with compassion*.

DALAI LAMA: (*Translated.*) But is not compassion like emotion or mood?

EKMAN: Not in my view. A mood may last for a day, but it does not last forever. Once you have cultivated compassion, it is then a permanent part of you. Whenever you encounter suffering, you respond compassionately. It is not something that you can turn off. If you have become a compassionate person, it is there all the time, whenever you confront a situation that calls upon relieving suffering. Things that are permanent are not moods and they are not emotions. This is a third way compassion differs from the emotions.

There is a fourth difference between the emotions and compassion, and that is the focus is more narrowly circumscribed in compassion than in any of the emotions. Compassion is focused just on relieving the suffering we witness—very important, crucial probably, to the survival of the world we now live in, but very specific.

So in my view, compassion differs in four ways from emotions: (1) compassion needs to be cultivated, while emotions do not; (2) compassion once cultivated is an enduring feature of the person, while emotions come and go; (3) compassion does not distort our perception of reality, while emotions do initially, during the refractory period; and (4) the focus of compassion is restricted to the relief of suffering.

But saying compassion is not an emotion does not make it less important.

DALAI LAMA: (*Translated.*) When you have an intense emotion of compassion, an intense state of compassion for someone, there is a disequilibrium. There is a sense of affliction. But the difference here is that in the case of afflictive mental states, there is an element of loss of self-control, loss of freedom. Whereas in the case of compassion, there is no such loss of freedom. We deliberately train in order to be concerned with the other's suffering. So strong emotion or feeling comes out through effort, voluntarily. The affliction that is experienced by the person who is having compassion is in some sense not out of control, because he or she chooses to be in that state. Voluntary.

Because of this, although on the surface there might be a sense of anxiety in that compassionate person's mind, deep down there is a strength.

EKMAN: What is voluntary is *cultivating* the compassion. But once compassion has been acquired, when you see someone wounded or suffering, you do not have the choice to ignore it. Your compassionate response is an involuntary desire to help relieve suffering.

DALAI LAMA: (*Translated.*) This is true, Paul. This is very true, because once you have experienced it, once you're in the height of compassion, then you have no choice—not in the sense of, I'm going to show compassion to this and not to that. It is more at the causal stage that it is voluntary.

EKMAN: In the development.

DALAI LAMA: In the development. Because Varela is no longer with us, we can change our definition of compassion.*

EKMAN: (*Laughs heartily.*) It will not bother him. (*All three laugh.*)

---

* Varela died in 2001.

COMPASSION FROM AN
EVOLUTIONARY PERSPECTIVE

EKMAN: Charles Darwin assigned ethics a central place in human evolution. I want to read to you a few short quotes from Darwin:

> Many animals, however, certainly sympathize with each other's distress or danger. This is the case even with birds. Captain Stansberry found on a salt lake in Utah an old and completely blind pelican, which was very fat. And must have been long- and well-fed by his companions.[2]

DALAI LAMA: (*Translated.*) One would not know how long it has been since the pelican was blind. It could have been eighty when he got blind. (*Laughs.*)

EKMAN: (*Laughs.*) I have learned how good you are in finding alternative explanations—and how much you delight in doing so!

Let me give you a few more examples:

> Mr. Blythe informs me he saw Indian crows feeding two or three of their companions, which are blind. We may, if we choose, call these actions instinctive. But such cases are much too rare for the development of any special instinct. I have, myself, seen a dog who never passed a great friend of his, a cat, *without* giving her a few licks with his tongue, a sure sign of a kind feeling in a dog.
>
> For with those animals which were benefited by living in close association, the individuals which took the greatest pleasure in society would best escape various dangers. Whilst those that cared least for their comrades and lived solitarily would perish in great numbers.

Darwin is pointing out why in social animals it is advantageous to your survival to be concerned about other animals. Of course, humans are social animals.

DALAI LAMA: Yes.

A chimpanzee offering consolation. *Photograph © Frans de Waal.*

EKMAN: Shortly I will get to his discussion of why this provides an ethics. It is not as elaborated as in your book, *Ethics for a New Millennium*, but it is in exactly the same spirit. Exactly.

These photographs come from an article written by the primatologist Frans de Waal, on empathy in animals.[3] What you see in the top picture, the large animal is a chimpanzee that has just been defeated in a fight with another chimpanzee. This juvenile comes over and puts its arm around the defeated chimpanzee.

JINPA: Seems nice.

EKMAN: "Consolation" is what this is now called in research on primates, when one animal appears to comfort or aid another. Ten years ago, scientists were not willing to use such terms about animals, not wishing to be anthropomorphic.[4]

Here you have a juvenile who has climbed a tree and does not know how to get down. Another chimp, who is not the mother, comes over to help it. We saw this same thing occur when my

A chimpanzee offering help to another chimp in distress. *Photograph © Frans de Waal.*

wife and I were in Africa in February 2006: A juvenile got so high up in a tree that it began to scream because it did not know how to get down. Another one climbed up, a large, older one. The juvenile grabbed hold of its back and it took him down.

Clearly, consoling, helping, and supporting does happen in animals. It is not unknown.

In order to console, you must recognize the emotion of the other animal: You must recognize the distress or fear. You must distinguish between yourself and the other animal. I would like to call this "emotion recognition," to know how the other animal—or human being—feels. Most people do not need aids to do this. It is something that either is innate or we all learn very early in life.

There is a second step after emotion recognition that I call "emotional resonance," to feel what the other person is feeling.

You feel in your body and mind what the other person is experiencing. Darwin said: "The sight of another person enduring hunger, cold, fatigue revives in us some recollection of these states, which are painful even in the idea. And we are thus impelled to relieve the suffering of another in order that our own painful feelings may be at the same time relieved."[5]

Darwin is giving an explanation for compassion. That is, when you see another person suffering, it recalls memories of your own suffering. You become very uncomfortable, through what I have called emotional resonance. To reduce your own discomfort, you act to help the other person. In some sense, it is a selfish motivation.

DALAI LAMA: Those human beings.

EKMAN: Yes.

DALAI LAMA: Not animals.

EKMAN: Darwin's basic position is that there is not much difference between humans and other animals in this regard; the only difference is of degree.

DALAI LAMA: That is right. I agree. I agree. I fully agree. A great example, now, in those animals, like turtles, no dealing with mother. I do not think they have the capacity to show affection.

EKMAN: What you are suggesting is that an animal where the infant is dependent on the mother—

DALAI LAMA: That is right!

EKMAN: For nurturance.

DALAI LAMA: Oh, that is right.

EKMAN: Then, you have the basis for affection.

DALAI LAMA: Yes, that is right.

EKMAN: And compassion.

DALAI LAMA: The affection brings them together. Without affection, there is no force to develop willpower to face difficulties or heavy tasks. The mother, you see, carries the baby. Of course, it is not easy. Twenty-four hours. Willing to sacrifice their own sleep. Like that. *I* do not know personally. (*Laughs.*)

(*Translated.*) Imagine someone who has been brought up in a very wealthy environment and has never experienced the pain of poverty or a lack in material resources. Compare that to someone who has been brought up in a family of limited resources or who has tasted the experience of poverty. In terms of their response to the suffering of the poverty of others, would not both be equally capable of empathizing? Or would they be different in the degree of compassion they experience?

EKMAN: We do not have scientific evidence to answer that very good question. I think it likely that if you have not felt it yourself, then the level or quality of your understanding may be different. But that may not be true. It may be that human beings do not need to experience suffering in order to completely understand and have emotional resonance with another person's suffering.

DALAI LAMA: (*Translated.*) I believe you do not need to experience it to be able to empathize. Sometimes you also see situations where people who are brought up under conditions of great hardship somehow become hardened, and then they are not able to empathize adequately with others' suffering. They should be able to empathize more strongly because they have experienced it themselves, as a personal, firsthand experience. But there seems to be another factor that is involved, because you do see situations in which people from underprivileged backgrounds do not empathize.

Darwin used the term "moral" rather than ethics. When he uses "moral," in the context here with animals, in what sense is he understanding the concept of morality?

EKMAN: I believe it was in terms of what you ought to do. He is trying to give an explanation.

DALAI LAMA: (*Translated.*) My own position would be to define ethics in terms of those underlying mental states and the actions that they motivate—which contribute toward the well-being of the individual. Or society. Or the community of that person.

EKMAN: That is a wonderful sentence that says so much so compactly. Can I ask you to expand on it? What are the underlying mental states? How does it contribute to well-being? Is it just an individual, or all individuals? I think you are going to say, if it contributes to all individuals, then it contributes to the individual.

DALAI LAMA: Usually, I describe, according to my limited vocabulary, the action or motivation, which ultimately bring happiness or comfort to one's self. Those are the ethics.*

EKMAN: Is ethics a motivation? Or is the ethics—

DALAI LAMA: Both motivation and action. Now, action here means physical action as well as verbal action. Ultimately bring positive happiness. Or, in a certain respect, I think happiness and comfort, that is considered ethics, because you want a happy life. So I think the ethics mean causes and conditions of comfort or happiness, long-run happiness and comfort. Sentient beings—we want that.

EKMAN: Yes?

DALAI LAMA: So, all the factors for that, of that, is ethics.

EKMAN: All the factors that contribute to it.

DALAI LAMA: Oh, yes. Ethics are something related with sentient beings. So, the action and motivation, which ultimately bring happiness or comfort. That is it.

EKMAN: To all people?

DALAI LAMA: *All people,* yes. Now, at the individual level, or family level, or community level, or national or international level, these are the ethics. I think it is true, also, all religious concepts or ethics are ultimately based on this. And for secular ethics. But some ethics, including religion, may be something, I think, based on their beliefs—that is something different.

EKMAN: Those are the religions, the branches, that say, "If you do not believe in *our* idea of a Creator, then your well-being is unimportant." There is that.

DALAI LAMA: Yes. That is right.

EKMAN: But in Islamic, Christian, and Jewish religions there are main branches that say that we are all the same people.

---

* Here the Dalai Lama is taking for granted the acceptance of interdependence, that one's own happiness cannot occur without others also being happy.

Dalai Lama: Mm-hmm.

Ekman: One more quote from Darwin:

> As man advances in civilization, and small tribes are united into larger communities, the simplest reason would tell each individual that he ought to extend his social instincts and sympathies to all the members of the same nation, though personally unknown to him. This point being, once reached, there is only an artificial barrier to prevent his sympathies extending to the men of all nations and races. If indeed such men are separated from him by great differences in appearance or habits, experience, unfortunately, shows us how long it is before we look at them as our fellow creatures. Sympathy beyond the confines of man, that is, humanity to lower animals, seems to be one of the latest moral acquisitions. This virtue, one of the noblest with which man is endowed, seems to arise incidentally from our sympathies becoming more tender and more widely diffused, until they are extended to all sentient beings.

Jinpa: He uses the term "sentient beings"?

Ekman: Yes, he does. (*Laughs delightedly.*) He is saying that it is the highest state of moral concern to extend one's sympathy to all sentient beings, not just to human beings.

Darwin was the hero of the animal rights movement in England. When I edited a new edition of one of his books, *The Expression of Emotion in Man and Animals*, people in England wrote and sent me copies of the books that animal rights' activists had published in the nineteenth century in honor of Darwin.[6] When I went through Darwin's files, I found letters from people who were concerned with the rights of animals from all over the world.

Darwin gave us a message that many people do not want to hear. The resistance to recognizing that animals have feelings resembles the wish not to know about how other humans in other parts of the world are suffering: You do not want to hear that "those people" in Darfur need help. Some people think *I need* help; I need a better school. Why should I be concerned with the people in Darfur? Let alone, why should I be concerned with the life of a chicken? We eat chicken. Who cares how much suffering they go through? To reach that state where your concern is for all sentient beings, Darwin said, is the highest level of moral development.

The other interesting thing, to me, is that in this quote he says we start with compassion for the family. We then extend it to the clan. We then extend it to the nation. But we must extend it to all human beings, and then to all sentient beings. I do not know whether Darwin was familiar with Buddhist philosophy; I doubt it.

DALAI LAMA: Wonderful.

EKMAN: Yes. What he is saying is that this is natural, that all human beings are endowed with this.

DALAI LAMA: Yes.

EKMAN: And that a full understanding, knowledge, will result in this. And yet, he is also saying that we know, unfortunately, such a concern for welfare does not extend to all sentient beings, even to all human beings, even though we are endowed with the capacity.

DALAI LAMA: Mm-hmm. Yes.

EKMAN: So the question is, how can we facilitate it? That is what we must talk about.

DALAI LAMA: Right. Okay.

EKMAN: It is the question, I think, of the twenty-first century, because we cannot afford to be selfish any longer.

DALAI LAMA: Once, some incidents, some pictures in books, they show two groups during the Spanish Civil War, or the First World War. You see, there were formally two groups fighting, killing each other. But in an individual case, the enemy soldier was dying, the soldier other side is taking care. So here, real human feeling is demonstrated. As far as their order is concerned, it is to kill the other. But as individual humans there—sympathy.

EKMAN: The last time research was done in combat, when people were shooting at them, only about half of American soldiers ever pulled the trigger. It is a very hard thing to do. The training is—

and you could see this in World War I, World War II, even now—
that the enemy is terribly evil. There is nothing good about them.

DALAI LAMA: Yes, yes.

EKMAN: It is to try to make it easier for you to kill them. If you
think of them as a human being, you cannot kill them. The problem today that makes it worse—

DALAI LAMA: Yes.

EKMAN: —is that technology allows us to kill at such a distance, we do not even see—

DALAI LAMA: That is right.

EKMAN: —the person we are killing.

DALAI LAMA: Mechanized warfare.

EKMAN: Seeing the suffering we inflict has restrained at least
some people from killing, but now we do not have to see the
harm. It makes it much more dangerous.

DALAI LAMA: True. Absolutely, absolutely.

ON ANIMAL MORALITY

by Frans B. M. de Waal

It is not hard to recognize the two pillars of human morality in the behavior of other animals. These pillars are ele-
gantly summed up in the golden rule—"Do unto others as
you would have them do to you"—which brings together
empathy (attention to another's feelings) and reciprocity (if
others follow the same rule, you too will be treated well).
Human morality as we know it is unthinkable without empathy and reciprocity—tendencies that are widespread in
other primates.

For example, it is not uncommon that, after one chimpanzee has attacked another, a bystander goes over to embrace the victim. We have documented hundreds of cases.
The usual effect of such consolation is that the screaming,
yelping, and other signs of distress stop. In fact, the tendency

to reassure others is so strong that Nadia Kohts, a Russian scientist who raised a juvenile chimp a century ago, said that if her charge escaped to the roof of her house, there was only one way to get him to come down. Holding out food would not do the trick: The only way would be for her to sit down and sob, as if she were in pain, and the young ape would rush down from the roof to put an arm around her, a worried expression on his face. This attests to the power of the empathic tendency in our close relatives: it beats the desire for a banana.

Reciprocity, on the other hand, can be seen in experiments on captive chimpanzees in which we give one individual food to divide with others. Before we do so, we measure spontaneous grooming in our colony: Who grooms whom for how long? Grooming is a pleasurable, relaxing activity, and being groomed is much appreciated. In our experiment, we found that if one chimpanzee had groomed another, this greatly improved his chances of getting a share from the other. In other words, chimpanzees remember who has groomed them, returning the favor later on. Like humans, they seem to keep track of incoming and outgoing services.

One of the momentous developments of our time is the effort to wrest morality away from Kantian philosophy and put it back in touch with evolution. This enterprise is not only supported by studies of animal cooperative behavior but also by modern neuroscience. Instead of attributing moral problem-solving to the latest additions to our brain, such as the prefrontal cortex, neuroimaging with human subjects has shown that moral dilemmas activate a wide variety of brain areas, some far older than our species. These areas are closely tied to the emotions. A recent report in *Science* only goes to show how far back some of these tendencies may go: mice show an intensified response to pain if they witnessed another mouse in pain.[7]

But continuity also exists with regard to rules of fairness. When Sarah Brosnan experimented with reactions to reward division, she found that one monkey will throw away a piece of cucumber—a low-quality food that she normally relishes—if a companion receives something much better, like a grape, for the same task. Apparently, we are not the only ones to judge certain social situations unacceptable.

Recently, I debated the animal origins of morality with philosophers in a book naturally entitled *Primates and Philosophers,* in which they insisted on the differences between humans and other animals.[8] I don't deny that differences exist, but philosophers have been emphasizing them for ages, and there is a great need to drop their usual celebration of the ratio. We need to first fully understand the vast similarity between human and animal psychology, including the emotional domain, before we are in a position to elaborate on the differences.

The author of numerous books, Frans de Waal is the founding director of the Living Links Center within the Yerkes National Primate Research Center at Emory University, in Atlanta, Georgia.

✦ ✦ ✦

ANIMAL INTELLIGENCE

EKMAN: The fact that you and Darwin are in agreement pleases me no end.

I want to come back to the examples that you raised. First, the easy one: the people who have never experienced poverty but are very philanthropic and devote their lives to helping people. If they have never felt poverty, why do they do it? I have an explanation, but I would like to hear yours.

DALAI LAMA: (*Translated.*) My understanding of this situation would be that although they have never themselves had firsthand experience of poverty, of what it feels like, they are as human beings fully aware of what suffering feels like. Everybody knows what suffering is. And so they have some understanding of the suffering of poverty.

In the case of animals, it may be harder to explain. Animals do not have the same kind of intelligence. Human intelligence plays a factor. Even among animals, the degree of intelligence probably makes a difference. For example, mosquitoes and butterflies: Their actions and states of mind are very much immediate—it is about survival. The degree of their intelligence compared to other mammals would be much lower. Their capacity for sympathy and compassion would also be lower. Maybe in order to feel sympathy or compassion, they need to also experience the pain themselves. But humans can use intelligence to understand.

EKMAN: You say in Buddhism the definition of living refers to sentient beings and that consciousness is the primary characteristic of life. This is in your—

DALAI LAMA: Life. This covers all living things. The sentient beings, not only with life, but also there is commitment or feeling. Feeling—pain and pleasure. (*Translated*.) Common sense leads us to believe that "life" encompasses not only the sentient beings, but also the animate things, like the plants, flowers, and these things. Because no one says, "But this blooming flower or this tree growing new branches is dead." In living things there is the faculty of discriminating among events. Life with feeling or—cognition. That we call "sentient being."

EKMAN: So, a sentient being must be aware of pleasure and pain.

DALAI LAMA: Yes.

EKMAN: Let's take a step further. Do you have to have memory for pleasure and pain?

DALAI LAMA: This same subject, we were just discussing, the mind or consciousness. We generally say, all living things, which have consciousness—that we call "sentient beings."

EKMAN: Yes, it is. Because if you take a fly—

DALAI LAMA: Yes—consciousness—yes.

EKMAN: A fly has a capacity for pain.

DALAI LAMA: Yes.

EKMAN: It avoids things it has learned will hurt it.

DALAI LAMA: Oh, yes.

EKMAN: And it knows what it likes.

DALAI LAMA: Yes.

EKMAN: But there is not much reason to think it is conscious.

DALAI LAMA: Maybe, yes. If the English word "consciousness" means a more sophisticated sort of thought, yes.

EKMAN: So when you say "conscious," do you only mean "experience?"

DALAI LAMA: Cognitive.

EKMAN: Just that they experience it or that they can think about it?

DALAI LAMA: (*Translated.*) From the Buddhist perspective, we say "the mind," which literally translated in Tibetan is *shepa*. It has the connotation of something that understands. Knowing. Something that knows.

EKMAN: Well, almost every organism, including amoebas, learn.

DALAI LAMA: Amoebas are sentient beings. The amoeba is very likely a sentient being.

EKMAN: A sentient being because it can learn.

DALAI LAMA: (*Translated.*) Yes. One time, debating in this room, we concluded that those things that can move from one place to another place, not by their mother but by their own initiative, are sentient beings. So at that time, we considered the amoeba the smallest sentient being, one of the smallest sentient beings. But then, you see, there are those germs. And, for example, sperm, bacteria. There is sort of movement—

EKMAN: Yes.

DALAI LAMA: —but that is mainly due to chemical threats. I don't know.

EKMAN: Let me tell you briefly about an experiment done with Macaque monkeys that raises a number of interesting points for us to consider that are relevant to the issues we have been discussing. The experiment is arranged so that a monkey has to pull a chain in order to get food. But every time it pulls a chain, it shocks another monkey, and the one that pulls the chain can see that the other monkey suffers. Monkeys literally starve themselves—one monkey for five days, and another for twelve days, would not pull the chain.[9]

That was if the monkey who would suffer was familiar. If it was a monkey it did not know, then it did not pull the chain for much shorter periods. Still a day or two, but not five to ten days. If it was not a Macaque, but a different kind of monkey, it postponed pulling the chain, but again not as much as if it was a familiar Macaque monkey who would suffer.

Monkeys act like many human beings. They are compassionate and self-sacrificing if it is a member of their own tribe, but not beyond that.

DALAI LAMA: (*Translated.*) But in the family, even in birds, you see some instances where mothers are willing to sacrifice themselves to save their offspring.

EKMAN: Sacrifice for offspring is really easy, it seems to me. Third cousins are harder, strangers are even harder.

DALAI LAMA: Yes.

EKMAN: The issue is, of course, where does intelligence come in? Is it solely an intellectual matter, in which I think, well, my welfare depends on everybody in the world. That is a thought. Or does it have an emotional basis? Is the cultivation of compassion simply an intellectual process? You teach people that your welfare depends on everybody else's welfare? You read a book, and then you become compassionate? Or does it have a different basis?

DALAI LAMA: (*Translated.*) It is a bit more complex. To a large extent, it is a matter of knowledge and the application of intelligence. I think according to wisdom.

Buddhists understand that there is a developmental process for cultivating compassion for others beyond one's immediate boundaries. It probably is not unique to Buddhists' understanding; in the Christians' understanding, it may be the same, that a process of development is required. First, you have to have some knowledge, whether on the basis of reading or hearing. In Buddhism, it is considering the interdependent nature of one's interest and others' interests, the shared humanity, the fundamental equality of desiring happiness and overcoming suffering.

So the first stage is the knowledge. You have to either hear it or read it, or someone has to tell you. Then, you need to constantly reflect and internalize this knowledge through reflection, constant reflection or meditation, to a point where it will become a *conviction*. It becomes integrated into your state of mind, and you are deeply convinced of it. Once you have that conviction, you cannot leave it at that: You need to constantly remind yourself and reflect upon it, familiarize yourself with it, cultivate the habit, make it part of your mental habit.

Then you will get to a point where it becomes spontaneous. The moment you think about others, compassion becomes effortless. At that point, emotion comes in, because it has now become an experiential part. There is intensity. It is no longer at the level of thought.

Similarly, in the case of a Christian practitioner, he or she has to either read it in the Bible, or hear it from somewhere, that all creatures are from the same Creator. There is a shared humanity, a shared creaturedness, or whatever you want to call it. On the basis of that, you then can learn how to empathize with others beyond your boundaries, internalize that knowledge, and get to a point where you feel deeply convinced. Then, when you have conviction, you will embrace that value and make it part of your life.

In a secular context, someone may read a passage like the one you read from Darwin that makes a case for the need for these high moral sentiments and the need for these to extend to all others. You can also complement that by reading modern medical science findings of how, in fact, compassion is deeply related to one's well-being, physical health, better health, a happier state of mind, and so on. Once you understand these benefits and constantly reflect upon them, you will get to a point where you will feel deeply convinced of its value. Then, on the basis of that conviction, there will be a genuine interest and willingness and enthusiasm to really make it part of your life. Again, that is when the emotion comes in. Compassion becomes infinite, unbiased only through training the mind.

UNBIASED COMPASSION

EKMAN: How does emotion come in?

DALAI LAMA: I believe emotion is a certain mental state, which you feel *very strongly*. So, there is the negative side also. You see, anger or attachment—very strong. Then your physical state also does some changing, and feel very strongly. So that same experience with compassion. But the difference is that the other emotion comes more or less spontaneously. Compassion, this infinite compassion, unbiased compassion, you see, only through training, through reasoning, through special effort. Once you experience, once you reach the high degree of that experience, then the same sort of effect on physical state or physiology changes.

EKMAN: I understand you to be saying that when you reach this stage of infinite, unlimited, or unbiased compassion, it becomes like an emotion in that it comes out without effort.

DALAI LAMA: Like emotion. Of course, our knowledge of emotion is very limited. You know better. I had an opportunity to visit some Muslim communities. One religious leader in that community welcomed me and he mentioned we should love not only human beings but also to extend to all creatures of God, or Allah, he mentioned. According to Muslim practitioners also, the emphasis: Our love or compassion should extend up to other creatures of Allah. I think that is nice.

EKMAN: What about an atheist? Would you extend it to an atheist?

DALAI LAMA: Atheists have true reasoning, true intelligence.

EKMAN: Do you have to believe in a Creator for Muslims to feel compassion for you?

DALAI LAMA: (*Laughs.*) So this is the "fundamentalist" thinking.

EKMAN: Yes.

DALAI LAMA: Christians, also. Is it not?

For a couple of years, I mentioned, you see . . . in early period, early stage of my sort of wish or my desire, having dallied with modern scientists, some of my friends or others, some Buddhists from America, they gave me some kind of warning: Science is a killer of religion, so be careful.

Then, I thought: Buddhism in general, particularly in the non-literal tradition [the tradition that does not solely rely upon the scriptures, but upon deep reasoning], places very much emphasis on investigation, rather than relying on literature or quotations. And Buddha himself gives us liberty to investigate his own word, and he clearly mentioned, "My devotees, my devotees should not accept my word out of faith, out of devotion, rather than investigation and experiment." That gives us liberty, you see, to investigate any object. Therefore, I thought a scientific approach and the Buddhist approach [not constrained by a literal reliance on the scriptures] is the same. Investigate. Experiment. So, then, I felt, you see, no problem.

So we are engaging in dialogue with modern science, or modern scientists or modern science, in this field—Buddhist science, which combines Buddhist philosophy and Buddhist practice. They are not discussing about, you see, whether there is salvation or not. We are not discussing about that.

EKMAN: Whether there is salvation, did you say?

DALAI LAMA: Yes, that is right.

EKMAN: See, I even had trouble hearing it.

DALAI LAMA: Oh. And, also, whether there is a next life or not, we are not discussing these things. Also, we are not discussing about karma.

EKMAN: Right.

DALAI LAMA: These are Buddhist sort of views, or Buddhist philosophy. The modern science is simply trying to know the reality. Buddhist science also similar. Now, within Buddhist science, there are two groups. The Buddhist science regarding the physical and another field, like mind, or time—these, not physical things.

We learn many valuable things from modern scientific findings, or scientific knowledge. As far as mind is concerned, or emotion is concerned, now Buddhist experience, Buddhist explanation also is making some contribution—to modern science.

EKMAN: Yes.

DALAI LAMA: In the field of Buddhist science now, there is real change in direction.

EKMAN: It is a partnership.

DALAI LAMA: Yes. Mutual benefit. Like that.

EKMAN: I was warned by scientists, "Do not talk to the Dalai Lama. He will ruin you as a scientist."

DALAI LAMA: Oh-h.

EKMAN: "You will become spiritual."

DALAI LAMA: Heh, that is right.

EKMAN: So, the same warning.

DALAI LAMA: Yes. Well, I think this, it reminds me, recalls to mind one occasion, in one city in California. One dialogue with scientists, on one occasion there. So, there one lady scientist. In our first meeting, that lady, you see, her attitude is that they are scientists and I am a Buddhist, religious person—"So, what do I have to discuss with you?"

Then, actual discussions were started. We are talking about a Creator—actually, we do not accept that—ha! Also, we do not accept "soul." Rather, there is compassion, or interdependency—or like that. So then, her attitude completely changed. Then she was showing eagerness to know about Buddhist explanations in certain fields.

EKMAN: There is one danger from the science point of view, and that is that almost all of the scientists who are currently studying meditators are either Buddhists or they are very closely aligned. That causes other scientists to say, "Well, you are biased." I have been trying to convince my fellow scientists that when you do a study of meditation, have one of the people on your research team be a skeptic, not a Buddhist, not a meditator. Let it be someone who says, "You have to prove it to me." Then, the results will stand more independently. But, of course, no one in science does research because it is something they think *does not* exist. So, every scientist, in a sense, is biased.

But typically in other fields of science, you publish your result and many other scientists try repeating and see if it really works. In the behavioral sciences and in psychology, that does not happen.

DALAI LAMA: Yes, that is right.

EKMAN: No one so far—I mean there are only about a dozen studies, serious studies, now on meditation that meet some scientific criteria.[10] But no one who is a skeptic would say, "Well, I will repeat it and see whether or not I could get it." And that is very important. That has got to happen at some point. It is just because that is how science works. You try to challenge it and confirm. And if you are already yourself totally convinced, then you may unwittingly not see errors you are making. I have tried to resist becoming a believer in the benefits of meditation, but it has become harder for me to do so, due to both personal experience and seeing the benefits that occurred in the "Cultivating Emotional Balance" research project that I initiated. But I did include a skeptic, my collaborator Robert Levenson, in the research we have done on Matthieu Ricard.[11]

DALAI LAMA: (*Translated.*) Even from a Buddhist perspective, there is a very explicit mention that in order for you to engage in the study of part of the text, you should become very skeptical, to make sure whether or not studying this topic has any benefits or has any long-term impact on you, or whether the content matter is something worthwhile to study, and similar things. Beforehand, you should be very skeptical in your approach. This is the basic criteria for someone to engage in the study of the texts. This very much corresponds to the scientific approach.

Also, the other thing that is mentioned in Buddhism, again from this tradition that is not constrained by a literal reading of scriptures, is that when you are trying to prove something, there should be two components: a person who is trying to prove and the subject to whom—I should say, "object"—the object to whom you would prove. So, there is an object and a subject involved.

In order for that reasoning to be successful, the opponent or the person who is going to listen to your reasoning, should be someone skeptical. One of the basic criteria for sound reasoning is that the person to whom this reasoning is put forth, that person should be skeptical.

(*Switching to English.*) Seriously engaging with scientists without losing the position of a Buddhist monk. (*Laughs.*) Last year I went to America. Some questioners rather religious-minded— believers. So, you see, asking some silly questions, something like, "miracle" or something, like healing power or some superstition. Then, I responded, "I am a scientist."

EKMAN: (*Laughs.*) You are welcome to join us. (*Dalai Lama laughs.*)

But, I want to take a further step. And encourage you, when you meet with the various scientists, which I know that you continually do.

DALAI LAMA: Yes.

EKMAN: Encourage them to always work with the skeptic, as well. It will be better science for us.

DALAI LAMA: Yes.

EKMAN: At this point, they are not listening to me. But, they will listen to you. If you say that, "As scientists I want you to be sure, when you do your science, that, just as in Buddhism, there is an opponent who is skeptical, you must in your science have someone who is skeptical. And it will make it better science." If *you* say that, they will do it. And if *you* say that, when I argue with them, "Why are all of the people on the research team meditators? Why don't you have someone who isn't?" I will be able to say, "And His Holiness says you should do that!"

CULTIVATING CONNECTEDNESS

EKMAN: Let's return to our discussion of compassion. Is loving-kindness meditation the key meditation practice for developing this mental state?

DALAI LAMA: (*Translated.*) Loving-kindness is used in the Buddhist literature in two different senses. There is one, which is, in a sense, the other side of the coin of compassion. Compassion is more focused on the suffering of the other, on the wish to see others free from suffering. Loving-kindness is focused on happiness, on the wish to have others happy. There is no sequence to them; in some sense, they arise together. When you wish others to be free from suffering, the wish for others to enjoy happiness comes side-by-side.

What is more crucial for the practice of compassion is the other type. It is translated as a sense of *connectedness*, a sense of endearment to others, where the idea is cultivating a state of mind that makes the sight of others' suffering unbearable to you. Cultivation of that is the crucial component of compassion. It is said that the stronger this sense of connectedness, the greater your feeling of unbearableness when you see others suffer.

EKMAN: It is unbearable to you?

JINPA: Unbearable to you, yes.

DALAI LAMA: (*Translated.*) When you reach that state of mind, then others are seen almost as an extension of yourself, as part of you.

EKMAN: So, their suffering is your suffering.

JINPA: Their suffering is your suffering.

EKMAN: The question is how to cultivate the feeling that *anyone's* suffering is unbearable for you, not just the suffering of your immediate family or friends.

DALAI LAMA: That is right. This is the reason why Buddhist teaching refers to all sentient beings as "mother's sentient beings." You deliberately try to develop attitude, "as dear as your own mother."

EKMAN: It raises an interesting side question for psychologists—which is, if you have a mother who is disturbed mentally, who abhors you, would that cripple your capacity for compassion? Or would you be able to overcome that? Perhaps just because your mother was so unkind you might develop a truly compassionate nature in your attempt to overcome her negative influence.

ON PARENTAL COMPASSION

by Paul Ekman

On further reflection, the Dalai Lama's reasoning suggests the possibility that giving birth to a child, or parenting a child even if he or she is not a biological offspring, might facilitate compassion. But in reaction to not being able to parent, or to not being parented, the opposite might also happen: People might compensate and be more likely to be more compassionate, too. Thus perhaps the better prediction would be that both extremes would be found. Still another possibility is that the capacity for compassion has evolved in mammalian species to the point where it does not require parenting experience, as either a giver or a recipient, for it to be expressed.

◆ ◆ ◆

DORJI: In the case of those not having a sound relationship with their mothers, they should not try to force it that way. One of the teachers of His Holiness quoted from Buddha: "To you, all beings are one's mother and one's father." So it is not really confined to the mother. For those having an unsound relationship with their mothers, they can think instead about whoever is really dear to them, whoever is kind to them, and then try to extend the same kind of sentiment toward all others.

EKMAN: The research on mother-infant relationships suggests that if the mother does not engage with the child, it has quite long-term consequences. The child grows up being a less engaging person.

DALAI LAMA: Yes, very harmful. (*Translated.*) The Macaque monkey you talked about—it is capable of being compassionate toward someone it knows within the same—

JINPA: Within the same kind. But it is not able to extend it beyond the species. For humans, that is what we need.

DALAI LAMA: (*Translated.*) We have to teach the monkey, first of all, to be able to extend this toward the members of the same species that are not directly related.

EKMAN: Right.

DALAI LAMA: (*Translated.*) Then the next step would be to teach it how to extend that to outside species. There, intelligence plays a role.

EKMAN: If I understand what you are saying, what I have termed "emotional resonance"—feeling the other person's suffering—is a key element.

DALAI LAMA: (*Translated.*) That is the key element, yes.

EKMAN: I thought that you said in our first meeting in Dharamsala in 2000 that when you hear about or read about some massacre of people, you feel the suffering, but it passes quickly. Now, the fact that it passes quickly—does that mean necessarily that you have to continue to feel the suffering in order to act to relieve the suffering?

DALAI LAMA: (*Translated.*) This is why, in the Buddhist literature, there is an emphasis on how compassion practice should be balanced with wisdom practice, because compassion needs to be accompanied by courage. If you focus simply on others' suffering, it can have a depressing effect.

There was a story of a great Tibetan meditator, the author of "Eight Verses on Mind Training," known as "Weeping" Langri. Apparently, compassion was his main practice, and the suffering of sentient beings was heavily bearing on his mind all the time. People said that when they would see him, he was always crying.[12] What is important from the Buddhist point of view is to complement that kind of practice with the element of wisdom. If you want to do something, with courage you will be able to do it. In the Buddhist path in life, the "Awakening Mind" is said to be brought forth by two desires. One is the desire to relieve others from suffering and lead them to Buddha-hood. The other desire is to seek that perfected state so that you will be able to bring this about. So there is both a courage element and the compassionate element, a desire to overcome suffering.*

EKMAN: For me, the new information here is the need to develop a conviction, after the first step of just knowing.

DALAI LAMA: That is right.

EKMAN: Then, you must continually reflect on it until you have changed your whole mental framework. Your mind is not the same. It has become deeply ingrained. You do not have to think about it.

DALAI LAMA: That is right.

EKMAN: It is part of you.

DALAI LAMA: That is right.

EKMAN: It is a whole restructuring of your cognitive framework, which comes from continual reflection on this knowledge. And that is the core, as I understand it, of meditative practice.

DALAI LAMA: That is right. I think on the negative side, also it is the same. That is why, you see—for indoctrination. Because the human mind, it can change through one-sided training.

CULTIVATING CONSCIOUSNESS

EKMAN: There is consciousness in humans, which we all have, with no need to cultivate. It is just part of us.

DALAI LAMA: Yes!

EKMAN: There is another kind of consciousness that, in both Western and Buddhist thinking, we believe you need to learn.

---

* The "Awakening Mind" refers the altruistic aspiration to achieve enlightenment for the sake of all sentient beings.

DALAI LAMA: Yes.

EKMAN: How do we characterize the second, cultivated consciousness? What should we call this?

DALAI LAMA: (*Translated.*) In Buddhist thought, when we speak about consciousness, we make a distinction between two things: The main nature of the mind, the clarity aspect, that is something innately existent. It is not something that can be acquired. What can be acquired is the capacity to understand objects. How much does the mind understand? What can be acquired? Through training, we can expand what the mind understands.

(*Switching to English.*) I think that the mere cognitive, that kind of consciousness is common in human beings and other animals or insects. But the second part—that, I think, due to different brains, due to different environments, different circumstances or different training, then you see change, or an increase of differences.

EKMAN: You said earlier that in the area of the mind and emotion, Buddhism has much to contribute to science.

DALAI LAMA: Yes.

EKMAN: I agree. When most people experience an emotion or act emotionally, they are not conscious of doing so. They could not tell you, because they do not know themselves, "What I am now doing is acting fearful," or, "acting angry." It is not that they are unconscious. But they are not observing themselves and realizing, Maybe that really is a coiled rope, not a snake, and I do not need to be so afraid. To be conscious of that, we would have to acquire this ability, which nature does not give us.

The walking meditation and breath meditation practices seem to help you become more "in the moment," to focus part of yourself on knowing and observing what you are doing.

DALAI LAMA: This is what can be technically described as an action done consciously.

From the Buddhist perspective, when somebody acts, even in the case of—a certain bad action, if your mind is normal calm, that means no *strong* emotion. But under the influence of negative stuff—emotion—then sometimes you consciously do certain things. Consciously.

EKMAN: But there is no part of yourself that is saying to yourself—

DALAI LAMA: (*Translated.*) In order to make clear these things you have to create more new English words. (*Ekman laughs.*) (*Switching to English.*) Then finalize or fix, and then we can discuss. Otherwise, it is no good to us!

EKMAN: Meta-attention is the word that is used for this. Meta-attention allows me to see the impulse to be angry arise. Do I want to engage, or let it simply pass? But I do not think nature gives that to us. We have to practice to get that ability. It's a skill.

Many Western Buddhist teachers emphasize meta-attention through breath work. My understanding is that you see that practice being used to bring or restore to calmness a mind that might not be calm, so that intelligence can operate.

DALAI LAMA: In the Burmese or Thai traditions, the special effort for training of mindfulness—walking, eating, every movement with awareness—that is highly necessary at the beginning, because our minds, even though they try to understand things using intelligence, but still our minds are scattered. Therefore, the realization or understanding or penetration into the reality is very limited, because our minds are scattered. Mindfulness brings mental energy to mobilize, to focus.

(*Translated.*) When you speak about whether or not this quality of the mind is naturally existent or acquired, it is this word "nature" that you're using: It is *Nature* as we explain it in the Buddhist context. For example, grasping at inherent existence is not the true *nature* of the mind; it is something temporary, and we can eliminate it. From that perspective, the cross mind is not naturally existent. But, in the Western meaning of nature, grasping at inherent existence is naturally existent.

ON THE NATURE OF MIND

by Paul Ekman

What emerged are two different views of what is fundamental to the nature of human minds, but our views do not differ in ways that have practical importance.

The Dalai Lama views the true nature of mind to be without afflictions, such as grasping or being susceptible to being seized by anger. I argue that it is in the inherent nature of our minds that we are not aware of what we are experiencing emotionally in those moments, so we are very susceptible to afflictions, that is, acting in ways we later regret. Regardless, we both agree that it is necessary to engage in practices to enable calmness of mind, to decrease susceptibility to actions that are destructive, and to cultivate compassion.

✦ ✦ ✦

EKMAN: But the individual can learn through practices not to be grasping.

DALAI LAMA: Yes, that is right.

EKMAN: Like an individual can learn to recognize impulses to become emotional, sparks before flames. That is the hardest thing of all—letting the spark go out without catching on fire. What I am suggesting, and trying to find out whether you agree, is that since we do not begin life with that ability, and that ability is not as easy to acquire as walking and talking, we have to engage in sustained practice to learn it.

DALAI LAMA: And experience.

EKMAN: What kind of experience?

JINPA: Your question is right. Is "meta-attention" something that naturally exists, a quality of mind, or should this necessarily be an acquired one?

EKMAN: I think it is a capacity of the mind. The mind is capable of it. But not without exercise.

JINPA: I see.

DALAI LAMA: The animals, obviously, they also have the capacity of being cautious.

EKMAN: Good point.

DALAI LAMA: So, you see, how to bring the cautious? This sense of caution is present even in the insects.

EKMAN: My understanding of many Buddhist meditative practices is that they are aimed at cultivating conscious awareness, so that there will be choice, so you are not simply the victim of your impulses, but you can choose what you do.

DALAI LAMA: (*Translated.*) Very likely this is true. In the practice of Buddhism, they basically train themselves to see the reality simply as it is and try to withdraw all elements of exaggeration.

(*Switching to English.*) I believe, as a Buddhist, training of mind is done to bring calmness of mind. Why? Not simply calmness of mind: but with the calmness of mind our intelligence can function more appropriately. The intelligence is the instrument to know what is good, what is bad, and what are the consequences— of the temporary and long-term. Basically, whether Buddhist or non-Buddhist, or human being or animal, everyone wants a happy life. No question.

EKMAN: Yes.

DALAI LAMA: So, at least for human beings, the many unwanted things due to our approach is unrealistic. As it is hurt, more trouble comes. So with unrealistic approach comes the wrong view; wrong view destroys. Wrong intelligence brings wrong views, an unrestful state of mind.

EKMAN: How does a wrong view come into existence?

DALAI LAMA: Wrong view, I think, generally speaking or basically, is ignorance.

EKMAN: Ignorance.

DALAI LAMA: Being uninformed is the opposite of intelligence, right? It is a kind of overtrusting or overconfidence that makes a person think there is no snake even though in reality there is one.

EKMAN: Human beings begin life without much knowledge.

JINPA: (*After a long discussion in Tibetan.*) His Holiness is wondering if in the human being, right from the beginning, from birth, if there is attached an incorrect view of the world.

EKMAN: Science suggests that young children have limits on their perception that lead to misunderstandings. The child believes it is the cause of everything.

For example, children often think their parents' divorce is their fault. That is an egocentric view, but it is part of being a child. So misunderstandings develop naturally, which is I believe what Buddhists term "ignorance," a distortion that has to be corrected through education.

DALAI LAMA: I think, that is what I think—"ignorance." Or, I think, "one-sided information."

EKMAN: How about, more gently, "with only limited information."

DALAI LAMA: That is very good. We have to act the diplomatic way.

EKMAN: We are being diplomats. (*Laughs.*)

DALAI LAMA: Now, scientists are supposed to be objective. Be objective.

EKMAN: Brutal. Brutal truth. (*Laughs.*) The term "ignorance," in English, is derogatory.

DALAI LAMA: I see, I see.

EKMAN: You could say "uninformed."

DALAI LAMA: Un-in-formed.

EKMAN: "Uneducated." But if I say you are ignorant, it is an insult.

DALAI LAMA: I see.

EKMAN: Does it have that meaning in Tibetan?

DALAI LAMA: I always use that word, "ignorance."

EKMAN: What I am asking is, Should I take out "ignorance" wherever you use it and put in "uninformed," to mean a lack of information, and "misinformed," to mean having wrong information or a distorted perception of reality? It is a question of whether you want to give the English reader the implication that not only do they not know but that there is something wrong with them; it is their fault. Do you agree with the derogatory implication if I call you ignorant?

DORJI: No.

EKMAN: There is an element of contempt in using the word "ignorant." I think it would be better not to have that, because I do not think that is what you intend to convey.

DALAI LAMA: That is right; that is okay.

EKMAN: The only virtue of the word "ignorance" is that it startles you, because it is not used very often.

DALAI LAMA: I see.

EKMAN: But it runs the risk of seeming arrogant. So, I think—

DALAI LAMA: Good.

EKMAN: I should take out "ignorance"?

DALAI LAMA: Very good, very good.

EKMAN: I have now eliminated ignorance in the world. (*Laughs.*) A great accomplishment in this meeting.*

DALAI LAMA: I think many concepts come through words. So, before speaking, I think at that time, the child's mind can think, but may often be uninformed and misinformed.

EKMAN: Earlier you said that strengthening positive emotions will weaken anger, hostility, and so forth. Are you referring here to developing calmness, or are you referring to something else?

DALAI LAMA: Calmness of mind. Then your intelligence can be used effectively. Intelligence basically has the capacity to know the reality. Most of the distracting emotions are very much connected with being uninformed or misinformed.

EKMAN: Yes.

DALAI LAMA: The counterforce of that is the awareness of the reality.

---

* Another substitute for the word "ignorance" that might better capture what the Buddhists are referring to is "incomprehension," what you understand about what you perceive.

EKMAN: And it is calmness that enables that awareness of reality?

DALAI LAMA: Yes, that is right. Generally speaking, for example, if someone, their state of mind is full of anger—or fear, or jealousy, or lust—during that period, their intelligence cannot function properly. During those periods, judgment often goes wrong.

EKMAN: Yes.

DALAI LAMA: Why? The lack of calmness of your mind. Your mental or natural capacity then no longer functions properly. Because of raw emotion, which is very much mixed with distorted reality and absence of knowledge.

THE BALANCE OF WISDOM AND COMPASSION

EKMAN: Let us consider an example that is relevant to the issues we have been discussing: a pediatric oncology nurse who works eight hours a day with young children who are dying of cancer and their grieving parents. Such nurses witness enormous suffering. Some children get helped, but many do not. It is said that if the nurse feels the suffering of all of the children and all the parents (what I term emotional resonance), that would produce burnout. The more general point is that you may not need to feel the suffering in order to be motivated to act compassionately to help try to relieve their suffering.

DALAI LAMA: (*Translated.*) This is what Buddhists refer to as the *discriminating* or *discerning awareness*. While you are capable of appreciating others' pain, it should be accompanied by discernment. You do your best to bring about the end of their suffering. If you are totally overwhelmed by others' pain, then you can be paralyzed by it; nothing happens.

There is a story told in the Buddhist meditation practice manual of a situation in which there was a famine in a region, and the whole family was starving. There was a real danger that everyone could die. But the family had a lump of meat. To be fair, this should have been divided among everyone, and everybody should have had their share. But the father, upon deep thinking, decided that he should have the whole thing. That way he was able to get some energy, and then he left to go a long distance in search of food. And he was able to bring back food and everyone survived. If the father had become paralyzed and everyone, thinking it is totally hopeless, had shared the meat, the family would not have survived.

EKMAN: I interpret the application of your idea to this nurse in that she may have a strong emotional resonance that motivated her to become a nurse, but that she must tone it down so that it does not interfere with helping her patients. Instead of sitting and crying with them, she does what she can do.

JINPA: Yes.

EKMAN: Her capacity for emotional resonance may play a large role earlier in the motivation, the choice to be a helper of people who are suffering, but it is not her daily experience.

DALAI LAMA: (*Translated.*) That is very true. The Buddhist understanding is that the role of discriminating awareness is to help provide a kind of resolution of conflicts among different mental states.

In the case of the nurse, there is emotional resonance, this unbearableness that makes her feel totally attached, and to identify with, her patients. But what is required is a degree of distance to be able to perform her role. You need to cultivate strong courage to work for the benefit of other sentient beings. These two states—humility and courage—may seem contradictory, but it is the application of wisdom that reconciles the two.

In the case of humility, the frame of reference is one's self: to remove the sense of ego, or self-importance. In relation to courage, the frame of reference is the desire to work for the benefit of others.

EKMAN: It is really a question of balance.

DALAI LAMA: (*Translated.*) If you look from the point of view of your own faults, then you tend to reduce arrogance and instill humility. Whereas the existence of the potential to achieve enlightenment can generate a deep sense of pride, a sense of confidence and courage, that "I can really get there." Here you must try to reduce your arrogance, so there is no conflict.

EKMAN: What I believe you have just been saying, and showing by holding up the last three fingers on your hand, is that different perspectives must and can be maintained on the very same object. If you go from the smallest finger to the largest one, you see increase in size; if you go from the largest to the smallest finger you perceive a decrease. Yet they are the same three fingers. The conclusion you draw depends on the angle, or perspective, from which you view it. You can—and must—view it both ways. So the very same object—the child dying of cancer—can be viewed with both humility and pride. It depends on your frame of reference.

DALAI LAMA: Perfect. (*Translated.*) It is about the need to consider, the frame, the difference. You can be very intelligent and unwise. Clearly. Clearly. Very intelligent.

DORJI: That is why His Holiness agrees with you so much.

DALAI LAMA: Very true. (*Laughs.*)

EKMAN: We are spending so much time together. We are agreeing maybe too much. (*Laughs.*)

DALAI LAMA: (*Translated.*) If the emotion of pride, or self-importance, is extreme, then you tend to view others as inferior to you. The old mode of thinking is: I am the best. When you slide into that kind of mental state, the tendency is to disparage others, so you slide into an extreme. If you cultivate humility by thinking, I am the inferior, I am the most inferior compared to all the others, if that goes to the extreme, then you feel totally demoralized. There is no sense of courage, no sense of energy and motivation. It is really a question of balance.

EKMAN: Yes. Balance seems to be a general principle.

DALAI LAMA: (*Translated.*) So the question is, What is it that brings about the balance?

EKMAN: Good question. What is the answer?

JINPA: Intelligence. That is it.

EKMAN: Intelligence?

JINPA: Yes, wisdom, the faculty of wisdom . . . (*Long pause.*)

DALAI LAMA: (*Laughs.*) Are you *thinking?*

EKMAN: I do not know whether to agree or disagree.

DALAI LAMA: Awareness.

JINPA: Probably "wisdom" is not the right word.

DALAI LAMA: Awareness.

JINPA: Again, it is a question of terms. His Holiness is asking, "What is the difference between, say, the faculty of intelligence and awareness?"

EKMAN: Oh, a huge difference. Awareness is simply to know what it is that is happening.

DALAI LAMA: Intelligence?

EKMAN: May I suggest that intelligence comprises both knowledge and skill, and wisdom is knowing how, where, and when to apply knowledge skillfully?

You can be very intelligent and unwise. You can be very smart, and have a lot of knowledge and skill, but when and how you apply them is bad.

DALAI LAMA: (*Translated.*) In that case, it is wisdom that brings about the balance.

EMPATHY, INTELLIGENCE, AND WISDOM

EKMAN: I want to see if we can reach agreement about the concepts of empathy, compassion, altruism, intelligence, and awareness. It is a big order. Let me begin by asking that we put aside the concept of empathy, and replace it with four more precise concepts, all of which are sometimes glossed by that term. Two of these terms I defined when discussing the nurse who works with children who have cancer.

DALAI LAMA: I see.

EKMAN: The first replacement term for empathy is what I have earlier termed *emotion recognition*—simply to know how another person is feeling.

DALAI LAMA: (*Translated.*) Why do you think of emotion recognition as empathy?

EKMAN: Because it is a necessary first step. You cannot have any concern or sacrifice for another person if you do not recognize when that person is suffering. Sometimes when people use the term "empathy," all they mean is knowing the other person's emotional state.

DALAI LAMA: (*Translated.*) In Tibetan, although it is quite a new word, new terminology, there is a word that says that there is a sharing with the feelings of the other.

EKMAN: You cannot share the other person's feelings unless you know what those feelings are. That is emotion recognition. When you actually feel—not just know the other person's emotion—I want to give it a separate name, because you do not always feel what the other person is feeling just because you know how they feel. I want to term that "emotional resonance." It cannot happen without emotion recognition, but emotion recognition does not necessarily generate emotional resonance.

"Compassion" is the third, separate concept. In compassion you want to relieve the suffering of the other person. You will not know they are suffering unless you have emotion recognition. It is arguable whether you must have emotional resonance to feel compassion. Compassion can follow emotion recognition without any emotional resonance, but often the emotional resonance is a motivator to act compassionately, and thereby reduce the suffering you feel when you witness another person's suffering. The fact that I recognize your suffering does not mean I will become compassionate. I may not care.

DALAI LAMA: (*Translated.*) In order to feel compassion, by your definition, the emotion recognition should precede.

EKMAN: Yes.

DALAI LAMA: (*Translated.*) While you are experiencing the emotion recognition, wouldn't you also have a kind of resonance of the emotion within you, and thus have compassion arise?

EKMAN: Probably that occurs often—at least initially—but it may not necessarily have to be there. A person may see another suffer and not feel that person's suffering. Maybe in the cultivation of compassion he or she did. But if compassion becomes an involuntary response, when it becomes totally ingrained, then it may occur without having any emotional resonance.

DALAI LAMA: (*Translated.*) For example, in the case of fear you can see the other person's fear—emotion recognition—without feeling the other person's fear. Then it is not necessary that you, as well, should experience emotional resonance, in order to feel compassionate.

EKMAN: That is what I am suggesting. When I taught medical students I would say, "A test of your humanity is to be able to be compassionate with a patient who is afraid of something that you know there is no reason to fear. Suppose a patient is afraid that a procedure is going to be very painful, and you know it will not hurt. You have to recognize the patient's fear and then act to reduce that fear. Do not brush it off as not worth your attention just because you know the fear is not based in reality. The patient is feeling fear; that is real. You do not feel the patient's fear, but you must act compassionately to reduce it."

DALAI LAMA: Yes. Now, four.

EKMAN: The fourth is altruism. All altruism is compassionate, but it goes a step further: It involves some risk to your own welfare when you relieve the suffering of the other person.

Let me give an example to show how I want to use these terms. I will use my wife, my favorite example, but this is not something that happened, it is something I made up. Let us say that my wife, in her role as dean of graduate students, had a meeting with the head of the university in which she asked him for more money for her students, and he was not sympathetic. She comes home and is still very angry at the chancellor. With obvious anger in her voice and face, she tells me what happened. Now, it would take very little skill on my part to recognize it is anger she feels. That is emotion recognition. It would take a bit more skill to be certain about whether she also had mixed in some feelings of disgust or contempt.

One kind of emotional resonance would be for me to get angry too. Not angry at her—*with* her. I could say, "That terrible chancellor! What a mindless person! How could he act in this way?! I am furious! I am going to write him a letter." That would be resonating with her anger.

Another kind of resonance would be to say, "My poor baby. How could he fail to see the merits of your argument?" I am being resonant, but I am not having her exact emotion. I am feeling an emotion in response to her emotion without *feeling* her emotion. People like to be the recipient of either kind of resonance.

A third response would be compassionate concern to relieve her suffering: "What can I do to help you think of other ways to deal with your problem with the chancellor? How can I help you? How can I help you with your anger, so it does not distract and distort you? Come over here and I will give you a massage." This is now compassionate.

I have not been able to think of an altruistic act I could do in this situation, that would help her but put my own welfare at risk.

DALAI LAMA: Yes. Good.

DORJI: His Holiness's tutor used to tell His Holiness, "So, whatever suggestion you might come up with, it is sure to be something correct and worthy." So, His Holiness says it seems that you are a great professor.

DALAI LAMA: An expert! In these fields.

EKMAN: You compliment me. I have been struggling for a long time to think this through.

DALAI LAMA: It looks, I think, very logical. And most of it is good.

EKMAN: Good. I would like to turn now to the concept of intelligence. The Buddhists use the term "intelligence" in a different way than it is used in Western psychology, where intelligence typically refers to a set of related intellectual capabilities, partly innate and partly learned. In contrast, you sometimes are referring to the capacity to learn, to remember, to make sound judgments about the nature of the world and human experience.

DALAI LAMA: (*Translated.*) I do not get the meaning of intelligence according to the Western perspective.

EKMAN: From the Western perspective, it is simply your mental capability. For example, one of the better tests of IQ is: "I am going to repeat the following numbers. You repeat them to me backward." So, I say, "7, 14, 6, 5, 3, 9," and you have to go, "9, 3, etc." Some people can do that much better than others, and everyone, unfortunately, as they get older, does not perform as well at it. Another test is to say, "Strike while the iron is hot—what does that mean?" That is a test of comprehension. Another is a test of vocabulary, where you require definitions of words that few people know. There is a general factor of mental acuity, the speed of thought. Having intelligence, in the Western sense, does not mean that you are wise. It means that your mind is very capable of making quick and difficult intellectual evaluations.

The Buddhist meaning of intelligence seems to have much more to do with wisdom: Intelligence is capacity. You can become very wise, but you do not have to be a genius to acquire wisdom.

DORJI: His Holiness is saying that perhaps it is the Buddha's intelligence that His Holiness has been referring to so often.

EKMAN: I think that he is always talking about what in the West we call wisdom: a basic understanding of the nature of life, of its impermanence and interdependence, an understanding on more than a superficial level, that becomes part of the furnishings of your mind. This has not to do with whether you are smart, average, or dumb; this has to do with whether you have *wise under-*

standing. And then, to take it a step further, whether you have developed this understanding to the point that it has become your outlook. Am I correctly describing your viewpoint on this?

DALAI LAMA: (*Translated.*) From a Buddhist perspective, there are four kinds of wisdom.

EKMAN: You never have a simple view! It is just wonderful that each of these concepts are so elaborated.

DALAI LAMA: (*Translated.*) The first one is the wisdom of the vastness. It is the capacity to tease apart, to understand things by one's own power, rather than learning through someone else. Paul, not relying on texts, memory, kept memory, like that. It is by one's own power, one's own wisdom.

The second is the wisdom of the clarity—the vivid wisdom. Not only are you able to understand things through one's own power, but you should be able to tease apart the subtle nuances.

EKMAN: Can you explain that a little more?

DALAI LAMA: (*Translated.*) Meaning that, whatever things you understand, you are so clear and so precise that you can tease apart and separate the subtle nuances.

EKMAN: How do you achieve that clarity?

DALAI LAMA: (*Translated.*) This has been stated as an innate quality of the wisdoms. Because people, compared to other species, have greater wisdom of this second kind.

EKMAN: More like the Western concept of intelligence.

DALAI LAMA: (*Translated.*) It can, as well, be cultivated, through true studying. Of course, learning, investigation, all this, increase these things.

The third is the wisdom of quickness, the understanding happens so quickly that you do not need to spend much time to gain it.

The final one is the wisdom of profundity. It is wisdom that understands, a wisdom so profound that you can infer things, very far.

ON THE FOUR WISDOMS

by John Dunne and Geshe Lobsang Tenzin Negi

The four forms of wisdom are: (1) *robust wisdom* that one uses to discern, through one's own intelligence, what needs to be done and what needs to be avoided in order to make spiritual progress; (2) *clear wisdom* that enables one to differentiate afflicted mental states from pure ones, even at the subtlest level; (3) *quick wisdom* that immediately eliminates misunderstanding, confusion, and doubt as soon as they arise; and (4) *profound wisdom* that reveals the deepest implications of the Buddha's teachings.

John Dunne is an associate professor of religion and the codirector of the Collaborative for Contemplative Studies at Emory University. Geshe Lobsang Tenzin Negi is a senior lecturer in Emory's department of religion and the chair of the Emory-Tibet Partnership.

✦ ✦ ✦

DALAI LAMA: (*Translated.*) All this is not found in the text. It is what is popularly being discussed [in the oral tradition of Buddhist scholarship]. Practitioners of Buddhist philosophy have, through their own experiences, identified three kinds of wisdom: one wisdom, which is good at memorizing things; another wisdom, which is good at debating and arguing; the third wisdom, which is good at comprehending things.

DORJI: His Holiness is sharing the story of a great scholar by the name of Tua Tashi. Of these three wisdoms, he lacked the first—very poor in memorizing. Because he was an abbot, he had to recite lots of texts. The students came to realize that what he was reciting did not correspond to what is found—

DALAI LAMA: In text!

DORJI: The actual wording was wrong. But in terms of the content—

DALAI LAMA: The meaning.

DORJI: It was so precise.

EKMAN: Am I right in thinking that these two different ways of looking at wisdom are really quite separate from knowledge? Knowledge has to do with things like the destructiveness of hatred, or the interconnectedness of all people.

DORJI: Yes. But from the Buddhist viewpoint, we have three kinds of knowledge: the knowledge derived through hearing; the knowledge derived through contemplation; and the knowledge derived through meditation. Here we have been speaking of the knowledge derived through studying, contemplation, *or* reflection.

EKMAN: It is a very interesting, complex account that has a lot of subtlety. So, I like it a lot—because the more distinctions you make, the happier I am. (*Dalai Lama laughs.*)

If I am not pushing my luck, one last point.

DALAI LAMA: Yes.

EKMAN: *Awareness.* That term, I am proposing, refers to that part of our experience which registers in consciousness. Alan Wallace's term "meta-awareness" refers to being able to observe one's conscious experience, as consciousness changes; being aware of those changes and thereby having the capability of being able to exercise choice. So awareness is simply the part of experience of which a person is conscious, but people are not conscious of a lot of their experience. Meta-awareness involves enlarging and observing awareness, monitoring awareness. Typically, I do not make the deliberate choice to focus on some aspect of experience and bring it into awareness. I do not even know what part or process of my mind selects what rises to my awareness.

Let me give an example. Until I tried to think of an example, I was not aware of the pressure of the bottom of my foot against the floor. But I can bring that into my awareness, and I can be totally aware of the sensations in my shoe. Before, what was happening in my shoe never entered my awareness.

There was an American Buddhist practitioner [whose name unfortunately I cannot remember] who used the phrase, "the watcher." He was referring to a part of your awareness that watches what is in your awareness. It is an interesting idea; I am watching my awareness to see that I still feel my foot. (*Dalai Lama chuckles.*) But who cares about what is going on in my shoe? So the watcher is saying it is irrelevant; it is not part of the discussion.

DALAI LAMA: Oh-ho-ho-ho-ho.

6

GLOBAL COMPASSION

It has always been a Buddhist tenet that compassion should be cultivated so that it extends to all living beings, not just the members of your family, tribe, or nation; indeed, it should extend to all sentient beings, not just to people. For many people this seemed to be an appealing but impractical ideal.

But matters have changed. Television now brings the suffering of other people, including those in far distant places, into our living rooms every night. Not only do we hear the facts of their stories, we see them express their suffering on their faces and in their voices. It has become less plausible to argue that starvation or devastation in another part of the world is the rightful concern only of those who are suffering. On the other side, our actions, and those of others, have an increasingly large impact. Environmental insults—such as the burning of large sections of forest land or oil spills—are not local events. The source of the energy people consume, and in what amounts, affects how other people live around the world. Although some still argue about how serious the environmental problems are, few argue that starvation or devastation in another part of the world is only the rightful concern of those who are suffering. Our fates are linked together.

Our discussion focuses on new possibilities for combining exercises arising from Buddhist practices and Western techniques for cultivating emotional balance and compassion.

EXTENDING THE LIMITS OF COMPASSION

EKMAN: The problem of our time, of our century, is to achieve a global compassion; otherwise we run the risk that we will destroy ourselves. We are talking about influencing all the people in the world, who are, to a large extent, brought up in exactly the opposite way, with a national, or even worse, a tribal concern, and nothing beyond that. We are not starting on neutral territory; we start with a need to counter tribal-bound compassion. How do we do this? What are the first steps?

DALAI LAMA: (*Translated.*) It would be very helpful if we could have research undertaken on how best to promote compassion and intensive workshops dedicated to this.

EKMAN: To planning the steps?

JINPA: Yes.

EKMAN: Do you think that the first step is to achieve some personal emotional balance?

DALAI LAMA: (*Translated.*) The first step is to be able to educate people to see the downside of a completely individualistic rather than a global concern, to recognize the pros and cons, the benefits and the disadvantages, of compassion for all living beings. (*Switching to English.*) Here, the narrow-mindedness to think of one's own nation, one's own country, one's own tract. Or only the West—America and Europe—not thinking about Africa, Latin America, Middle East, or Asia. And the Asians say, "Oh, we're Asia"; there is a sense of rivalry with the West. So, what is the benefit of that? For us to think globally is a positive benefit:

the economy, the environment, and also the political system. I think with politics, there is, how do you say?

JINPA: Rivalry.

DALAI LAMA: Rivalry, based on the national feeling, policy commitments, and concern about power. (*Translated.*) The first step is to appreciate really and deeply the pros and cons, the benefits and the disadvantages of narrow-mindedness, nationalism, tribalism, provincialism, whatever it is, as opposed to a global consciousness, a unity of humanity. How do we do this on a global scale? Here it becomes very important to reflect deeply upon the interconnected nature of the modern economy, and how environmentally our fates are all intertwined. And a need for responsible consumption of natural resources. And an appreciation of the dangers of nationalist-based international politics.

(*Switching to English.*) I think many problems that we are facing today are due to the one-sidedness. "We" and "them," and they do not consider themselves as a part of *we*. As a result, the unnecessary problems now happen. In the United States and many other countries, up until recently, they do not think globally. American resources, everything, they go sometimes: "Mine!"

JINPA: In the case of the United States, if there was a greater global awareness, then there would be a greater willingness to share the material resources the United States has with the poorer parts of the world.

EKMAN: We can attack the United States in our discussions, because many Americans like being attacked and criticized, and we need it, but I should note that we may have to be more careful about criticizing other countries.*

DALAI LAMA: Recently, I think in Denver, some Nobel laureates—total around ten—found fault: They criticized America, and particularly Bush. I defend it. (*Ekman laughs.*)

It is a certain policy, you see, that is wrong. I also feel like that. But America as a whole: I love America. I defend it. President

---

* Some criticisms of other countries were excised for diplomatic reasons.

Bush as a human being, very nice person. I like him. I become the defender of America. But here [not sharing natural resources, and using so much of the world's resources] is some criticism.

EKMAN: What you have just said about America and George Bush will startle some people. One of the worst problems in America—not just in America, everywhere—is *demonizing*. If you disagree with a person, then you think they are a demon. Yet, though you did not say anything favorable about Bush's policies, you said you like him "as a person."

To me, this is very Buddhist. You are recognizing the good in the person. That is different from whether you would agree or disagree with what his actions are. I don't think people realize the cost of hatred, how it not only corrodes the person feeling it but makes the possibility of persuasive conversation with the hated person impossible. Hatred has only one object: hurting the target. (*Dalai Lama chuckles softly.*) In my view, we can oppose Bush's policies on Iraq, but not hate him.

When I teach, I use an exercise in which I ask people to form into pairs. Where I live, nearly everyone is opposed to Bush, so I instruct the pairs, "One of you is going to be President Bush. The other person must tell Bush what is wrong with his policies. But if the critic says anything that is personally insulting, the person playing Bush must stop the critic and ask the critic to start again." It is enormously hard for people, because there is so much anger and venom. Afterward, people tell me that learning how to express disagreement with respect is very useful.

I think it is very important to disagree without venomous hatred, without insult. No one changes their views, or even considers a differing view if it is presented as a personal attack.

DALAI LAMA: That is right.

EKMAN: You might as well forget it. Why talk to them?

DALAI LAMA: I met one American, a cop, he told me before he heard my talk at Buffalo, at the university or something like that there, he had hate toward George Bush and Dick Cheney, because of his disagreement with their policy.

After he had listened to my talk, he changed his attitude. He still disagreed with their policy, but he no longer held any anger toward these two persons. He told me that.

EKMAN: Many people think we should not have gone to war in Iraq; others thought it was right, at least at that time. In a sense it does not matter now. The issue now is: How can we stop the killing? If we spend all of our time looking at the past, if you focus on who to blame, I do not know that this helps you with the immediate problem.

DALAI LAMA: That is right.

EKMAN: The other side of it is we have to learn from mistakes. So, that is the job for the historian—to go back over and teach us what mistakes were made so that the next leaders do not make exactly the same mistakes.

DALAI LAMA: That is right. Mm-hmm.

EKMAN: One of the things that makes it so difficult to reach agreement in the Middle East generally is that there is so much hatred from the past.

DALAI LAMA: True, true.

EKMAN: To stop the bloodshed going forward, we need to recognize that there have been terrible injustices, but that it cannot start with hatred. Only war comes with hatred.

DALAI LAMA: True.

In the Arab world, if they were thinking globally, then many of the problems—social, political, and so on—that they are facing now could be avoided. And in Africa as well. This is my view.

This reality, I think, is totally different than the reality of the nineteenth century, eighteenth century, seventeenth century. At that time, the Western nations had more advanced technology than other people, and so they exploited some other countries. The reality was "we" and "them"—this was the basis.

Today, the reality is much different. Everything is heavily interdependent.

EKMAN: So it would appear that the world has been changing in the last century to better fit a Buddhist view. In the sixteenth century, the Buddhists had the same view as they do today, but the world did not fit it. You could live your life without much regard for how other people on the planet were living their lives. Now it is a fact of life that what one person does has effects on others; we are all interdependent.

JINPA: (*After a long discussion in Tibetan.*) His Holiness feels that there ought to be detailed research done on understanding how many of the problems that we experience internationally are really, in one way or another, related to narrow-mindedness.

DALAI LAMA: If all the scientists, the medical scientists, in America would collaborate with scientists in Europe or Japan, or the like, there would be a distinct advantage—

EKMAN: Yes, right.

DALAI LAMA:—if all the scientists had a sense of internationalism.

JINPA: And collaboration.

DALAI LAMA: Is it not?

EKMAN: Scientists compete with each other; it is not nation against nation, but against whomever the scientist believes will make a discovery before him- or herself. It does not matter if they are Japanese or German. It is all individual. It is not tribal or national. There are a few exceptions, but it is not like the Olympic games, where the tallying of gold medals is by nation, with less focus on individual accomplishment.

DALAI LAMA: They have, in some sense, transcended the national.

EKMAN: Yes, transnational.

DALAI LAMA: I think in competition, there is positive competition and negative competition. There are two kinds of competition.

I think with a lot of businessmen—within China, within India, within America, within Africa—it does not matter. Or take environmentalists—for them, there are no differences between Europe, America, or Asia.

So, we need a new reality.

JINPA: If we look at the business world, the multinationals are, in some sense, moving toward the new reality. The same happens among environmental activists and the environmental movement. And among scientists—

DALAI LAMA: A new reality. (*Translated.*) But the problem is that the politicians are not able to follow that trend. No.

EKMAN: I see what you are pointing to. There are two destructive forces to contend with. One of them is historically grounded resentment. In areas like the Balkans, the hatred goes back for centuries; it is living your life now in terms of what happened to your father or your uncle. But facing realities today is not so easy to achieve. Much is based on equalizing the score for past resentments. Resentment—a long-term, harbored sense of injustice and unfairness—is a real obstacle.

Another obstacle is a concern with the short term rather than the long term. Politicians generally are only concerned with what happens in the short term, because that is what is going to affect them.

DALAI LAMA: Yes.

EKMAN: What is going to affect the next person down the line? Bush is going to try to leave it to the next president to have to deal with getting out of Iraq, and to the next president to deal with global warming.

If you are thinking short term, then you are not thinking global. We may get to a point where things get so bad that the short term is global. But by then some things may be irreversible.

DALAI LAMA: (*Translated.*) But, in another sense, many of the problems that we are facing right now, even in the short term, are results of not being able to appreciate the global dimension.

EKMAN: Absolutely.

DALAI LAMA: For example, the Chinese Communists. They are not thinking about the global. Same thing with the United States and the Arab world as well. So, "we" and "they" very strong. As a result, the short term is the thought.

(*Translated.*) On a global level, we need to have a deeper

appreciation of how many of the conflicts and problems that we face today are really the consequence of an inadequate appreciation of the global dimension, and that this is the result of narrow-mindedness, of one form or another.

More than a century ago, Darwin had already pointed out the need for this kind of global sentiment. Even on the individual level, it may be helpful to bring to people's attention the health dimensions of the more positive emotions, like compassion. How thinking more globally, thinking about others, provides an outlook within which the individual may no longer get caught up in the petty issues and problems that often become stumbling blocks.

To give an analogy, there is an admonition in the Buddhist texts to appreciate that basic existence itself is subject to personal dissatisfaction. This natural "unsatisfactoriness" is a fundamental condition of existence. This is like global awareness. When you have a better appreciation of global awareness, then, with relation to specific instances of pain (whether it is physical pain or emotional pain), you have a greater ability to deal with it. Whereas if your understanding of suffering is confined to a specific instance of the pain in the present, if you keep thinking about it and thinking about it, it could actually make you feel hopeless and helpless.

EKMAN: Yes. There is always some dissatisfaction with the nature of life. It is fundamental to life. It is not all honey and sweetness; there is difficulty.

RELEASING RESENTMENTS

DALAI LAMA: (*Translated.*) Perhaps it is more clear to give this anecdote. In the eleventh or twelfth century, a great Tibetan master by the name of Geshe Potowa said, "Even if there is the suffering of sickness, aging, and death, I do not care. Because this very body is under the control of sickness, decaying, and death. What is there to be so surprised about?"

EKMAN: A slightly more positive Western version of this saying is, the sun does not shine every day. We do not just have health; we have sickness. We do not just have fortune; we have misfortune. We have life; we have death. It is the nature of our existence that there will be difficulties we will encounter. There is only a problem if you have an unrealistic expectation.

DALAI LAMA: This is good. It is known by common sense. That is, I think, useful.

EKMAN: It turns our focus back to one of the fundamental truths, it seems to me. It is amazing that I, as a scientist, am using a phrase like "fundamental truth," but it is a fundamental truth that you need to have a realistic view of the world.

DALAI LAMA: The First Noble Truth.*

EKMAN: If you do not have a realistic view of the world, life is nothing but trouble. Today, a major form of psychological treatment in the United States is cognitive behavior therapy. The goal of this treatment is to help you see that it is your view that is making you miserable. It is just a *view*—and you can *change* that view. I am oversimplifying it a bit, but I know Aaron T. Beck, one of the founders of this form of treatment, will be very enthusiastic about this meshing. One of the more recent developments is to combine cognitive behavior therapy with meditation: It is called mindfulness-based cognitive behavior therapy, and has been especially effective in the treatment of depression.[1]

DALAI LAMA: Good. (*Translated.*) Similarly, there is an emphasis in the Buddhist texts on thinking about others more than one's self alone. For example, if your mode of thinking is confined to self-centeredness, then anything and everything that happens to you seems to have significance beyond reality. Even a tiny problem may seem unbearable. Whereas if you are able to think about

---

* The Four Noble Truths—the nature of suffering (*dukkha*), the origin of suffering (*samudaya*), the cessation of suffering (*nirodha*), and the path to ceasing suffering (*magga*)—are one of the core Buddhist teachings. Later, as the discussion of cultivating global compassion unfolded, the Dalai Lama expanded on their role.

others as well, then you have a global consciousness. Like Darwin, if you are able to think about the welfare of all sentient beings, then you have a better ability to deal with it if you situate your own problem within that framework. You have a global perspective on your own situation.

To apply this in the secular context, people can appreciate that if you have a global perspective on things, then you will have a better position to appreciate the specific problems of one's self, within the wider context and in the right proportion. Then you will be aware of past history. Sometimes our memories are very useful. Sometimes our memory is harmful. In India on one occasion, I was on a television program. The interviewer wanted to ask me about the conflict between the Muslims and the Hindus in India in the past—

JINPA: Many centuries ago.

DALAI LAMA: (*Translated.*) He wanted to say something about this past. I told him, "It is no use. Now we are facing today's reality, where referring to past experience, past history, is of no use to solving present-day problems."

The other day, talking with Muslims, I told them frankly that in some periods in the past the people in India suffered a lot due to sectarian conflicts—Hindus and Buddhists suffered at the hands of Muslims, but that is in the past! Today it is a new reality. Now, we have to accept this new reality and, according to this new reality, handle these problems. The past—forget it! (*Claps his hands together.*)

JINPA: That is how His Holiness deals with issues. Because you might be aware that, historically, the Islamic invasion of India was detrimental to Buddhism. Many of the temples and monasteries were totally destroyed by the invading Islamic hordes.

DALAI LAMA: (*Translated.*) Referring to the past and holding on to resentment is done not just by emotion alone. It is a memory and intelligence that is—

EKMAN: Yes! I think it is taught. Some schools in Muslim countries, especially in Saudi Arabia, teach the past history of terrible treatment to motivate the students to want revenge, cultivating their resentment.

DALAI LAMA: (*Translated.*) If you dwell on the past and respond to events today on that basis, then you are responding primarily from an emotional stance, to a felt sense of injustice or resentment. On the other hand, if you recognize the past and choose not to respond on the basis of that past, then you are using your human intelligence to make a choice to respond in a different way—with wisdom. (*Laughs warmly.*)

The Chinese have an expression, although they do not put it into practice themselves: "There are no judgments about what has been done in the past."

EKMAN: Three issues are raised by what you have said. One is to develop ways of diminishing resentment, instead of encouraging it. At this time, in different parts of the world, resentment is explicitly encouraged. Children are taught resentment for the sins of the past. It is not going to be an easy matter to encourage people to drop their resentments of past cruelties or injustices. It will probably be just as hard as changing what triggers an emotion. Once a resentment is well established, it is not easy to change, and we don't have much research to draw upon about how to do it.

DALAI LAMA: Right. (*Translated.*) It is not a question of forgetting the past; the question is not holding on to that resentment.

EKMAN: There may be some lessons, but they may not be the right lessons. They may be the wrong lessons from the past, because the world is different, as you were saying.

The second issue is that most of the time that human beings existed on this planet, they lived in small groups, like the village in which I lived in Papua New Guinea in 1967 while I was doing fieldwork. There were one hundred or two hundred people in the village. If you saw someone suffer, you could immediately console them.

DALAI LAMA: Yes, yes.

EKMAN: Now we live in huge cities. On television, we see suffering all over the world. Some people—political commentators—have suggested that this makes you feel helpless. But if you look at the response on an individual level to the South Asia tsunami or to Hurricane Katrina, many people, without being asked, voluntarily wanted to comfort and console very distant suffering. You can see a positive side to this, a cause for hope. These acts of compassion were often outside a person's own clan, or even the person's own nation.

We have to find a way to foster that reaction.

LEARNING ALTRUISM

EKMAN: The third issue is to focus on what we can do to work out both a research and training program on compassion. Because it is so vital. It is probably the most vital thing. With what practices do you cultivate compassion?

DALAI LAMA: One of our methods is to see those beings, those sentient beings who are suffering. There are some helpless, poor people; spontaneously a strong feeling of compassion will come.

Now people see on television Iraq's violence. Day by day, some people then maybe feel it become something normal, but often, usually when these things are often seen, you get the feeling, Oh how bad, violence—bombings, how bad. Also through books you may learn violence is bad. But if you just saw people suffer as a result of violence, you really feel sorry, and share in their suffering.

EKMAN: Just seeing the suffering of others will increase your compassion?

DALAI LAMA: That is right. (*Translated.*) It is the same as the recognition that just as you desire to have happiness, others desire happiness. And seeing suffering in others—though you do not experience suffering yourself—creates the feeling of personal unbearability. We are one family of human beings, so a person must take concern about the well-being of everyone in society.

There are different ways to increase your compassion. Usually television avoids showing actual killing. But in the human mind, seeing someone bleeding and dying makes you uncomfortable. That is the seed of compassion, of the development of its central concern.

EKMAN: Typically television does not show the suffering that results from violence or revenge; you do not witness the misery caused by violence. If television was to show that it might make people more compassionate, but if you show violence with no consequences it could encourage aggression.

DALAI LAMA: If someone is dying or suffering, even if enemies, still, on a human level, you see: taking care. If you see millions of people suffer, remember that you cannot be happy. Is it not? You have the moral responsibility to help as much as you can, in order to find one's own happiness.

EKMAN: Do you think that you need to have cultivated compassion in order to have that response or do you think that there is a natural human response that most everyone will have?

DALAI LAMA: This quality is within us. We need a sense of care for others.

EKMAN: Would seeing films about many people suffering help in developing compassion?

DALAI LAMA: I think that what is important is when we saw a lot of suffering, there are two possibilities. As you are seeing these horrible things, you are discouraged and have the feeling of helplessness. (*Translated.*) In some cases, when the enormous amount of suffering has been shown to someone, instead of feeling compassionate, he or she feels discouraged and despondent. In order to make sure that you do not feel discouraged, people can be shown or learn the direction by which you have the capacity to overcome the suffering. Instead of feeling discouraged, the person gains a sense of confidence and courage.

EKMAN: *Yes.* It was a natural experiment, not planned by scientists, but the tsunami is the best example we have, because for the most part it happened to people far, far away.

And for the majority of Americans, to people not of our religion and not of our race. But when people saw the level of suffering, they responded to the information at the bottom of the TV screen that provided something they could do: You can give clothes. You can give money.

DALAI LAMA: The response was immediate.

EKMAN: Hopelessness is encouraged if suffering is presented without anything that can be done in response. If suffering is presented so that the person can take an action that will be of help to others, then the suffering builds compassion.*

DALAI LAMA: Then the knowledge of the suffering turns into enthusiasm, to an extent. Research on compassion needs to look at the destructive side of the emotions that prevent it.

EKMAN: I believe that we should do this research, but we should also start trying out interventions. We should not sit back and wait for research results.

Let me tell you about the research of a political scientist, Professor Kristin Monroe. In her book *The Heart of Altruism,*[2] Monroe proposed a six-part definition of altruism:

1. You cannot just think about what you should do to help someone; you must act.
2. Your action may be taken without thought or consideration, almost reflexively, or by deliberate choice.
3. Your goal is to further the welfare of another person.
4. Your action has consequences for that person (it might not succeed, but it is intended to have consequences).
5. There is a possibility that your actions may diminish your welfare; there is some personal risk.
6. You act without anticipation of reward or recognition of your actions.

---

* The initial actions to relieve suffering are easier to achieve than the sustained commitment that is often required, for such sustained commitment may require sacrifice.

Monroe studied two groups of altruists. The first group she called heroes, who acted without consideration to help someone in danger, for example, a person who may not be a very good swimmer and therefore risks drowning to save a child who is about to drown in a lake. The second group she called rescuers, and their acts were not impulsive but carefully planned, and their risk was more than to themselves, but might jeopardize their family or entire village; she looked at people who hid Jews in Europe during World War II.

She compared these two groups of altruists with more usual philanthropists and entrepreneurs. She found no significant differences in education, religion, or occupation across the groups. The only difference she found through her interviews was in what she called their worldview. Here are quotes from some of the interviews with the altruists: "You help people [be]cause you are human and you see a need." "There are things in this life you have to do, and you do it." "We all belong to one human family." It sounds as if they were studying Buddhism. But they had not.

Two characteristics stood out in her interviews. First, there was this perception of shared humanity. "There is no concept of an in-group or an out-group. We are all one group." "All people have value. There is no one who doesn't have value. No group of people is better than any other group." The second characteristic was a belief that they had no choice, they had to act altruistically. "You ask, 'Well, what made you choose to do it?' I didn't choose. They needed help! I did it. I had to do it." We need research now to compare such people with people who grew up in similar circumstances but did not act altruistically to discover what might account for the differences.

Earlier you raised the example of the wealthy person who responds in a compassionate way to the person in poverty who is suffering, and yet that wealthy person may never have personally experienced the suffering of poverty. My explanation of why that could happen is that when you see someone suffer, you see what is on his or her face, you hear what is in his or her voice, it immediately connects to a compassionate motive to help. We may not know what elicited the suffering, but if we see and hear the signals of suffering, we begin to feel it within us, and that makes us want to console the person who is suffering. (This, of course, was what Darwin pointed out in the quote I read earlier.) The emotions are key to eliciting compassion, so it seems to me this is natural to humans.

DALAI LAMA: You are right.

EKMAN: Here is something that I do not understand at all; maybe you will help me understand it. Thirty years ago I had surgery on my back. For a variety of reasons, they could not give me any pain medication and for about eight or nine days, for twenty-four hours a day, I had terrible pain, and no relief.

If I could have taken my life, I would have done it immediately; I could not stand the pain. But there was no escape. The unanticipated consequence was that afterward, if I read in the newspaper about an unhappy event, I would begin to cry. Having suffered seemed to have totally and permanently intensified my emotional resonance to the suffering of others. I do not know why that occurred, and clearly that is not the kind of intervention we would want to put people through.

How does that work? Why should such intense suffering so open my heart to the suffering of others?

DALAI LAMA: (*Translated.*) Generally, we do see that people's lives are changed as a result of some experience. Even their personalities can change. There are instances where individuals, who previously were very haughty, self-righteous, and arrogant, who tended to be oblivious to others' suffering, completely changed as a result of some great tragedy in their lives. Certain experiences tend to open up the individual to others. Maybe you had a similar kind of phenomenon. Whatever it may be, in your case it was a wonderful thing. (*Everyone laughs.*)

EKMAN: I do not think I would choose it, but it had a benefit. Totally unexpected.

ACHIEVING EMOTIONAL BALANCE

EKMAN: What I have been able to distill from our discussion is that there are three different things that we need to achieve to make for a better emotional balance, and there are three different possible benefits to be achieved by them.

The hardest one is increasing the gap between the impulse and the action or increasing your awareness that an impulse has arisen and you are about to become emotional. Matthieu Ricard told me that sometimes when an emotion arises, he recognizes it simply as a cloud that passes by and does not engage it. I use a visual image. When I see anger arise—sometimes, though not always, unfortunately—I envision it as a rolling ball of cactus. I simply step to the side and let it go past me so it does not seize me. With such awareness, you have a choice to be emotional or not emotional, to say, "I am not going to respond." Or when you are aware of the impulse arising, you can choose to be emotional but guide *how* you are going to be emotional.

There are two different approaches to achieving that awareness of an emotional impulse arising. One approach is to develop an awareness of your experience *at that moment* through meditation exercises, such as focusing on the breath. Another, very different approach is to develop acute knowledge of the triggers that lead you to become emotional, that lead you to superimpose a script from your past life that does not apply and instead distorts reality. This second approach is, in my opinion, more knowledge-based than skill-based, but the two can work together. Another variation on this recognition of the triggers that lead to regrettable emotional episodes is to try to avoid such situations when possible.

In a more knowledge-based approach, I encourage people to keep a diary of regrettable emotional episodes. Keep the diary for a month or two months, and then look at the common themes that underlie it. With that knowledge and with the greater awareness of this automatic process, you will be able to have choice. By this means, you aim to bring into your awareness choices that you have, so that you can select the one that is most beneficial to you and others.

Separate from the need to be aware of the impulse to become emotional—which is very hard to achieve—is what to do when you begin to act emotionally. As we have emphasized several times in our discussions, then the goal is to become aware that you are behaving emotionally and to shorten the *refractory period*, that period when you cannot get new information from outside events or from your own memories and knowledge or from seeing an alternative explanation of what is occurring. When this refractory period is over, and hopefully it will only be a second or two, you can reevaluate what triggered the emotion. You can see that it is not a snake, it is a rope; you can see that it was not meant as an insult, it was meant to be helpful.

There are three techniques for trying to achieve that. The first is heightening your awareness of the other person's emotional reaction. You can learn that you are becoming emotional if you are sensitive to how someone else is reacting to you. Without saying anything, the other person becomes a source for awakening your awareness of how you are behaving. We have a very good way, an efficient way, of teaching people how to become more aware of signs of emotion in another person.[3]

The second technique is a little harder. It comprises exercises that teach you to be more aware of the sensations in your body that happen when an emotion occurs. As you become more familiar with these sensations, the goal is to become more aware of the fact that you are acting emotionally and then to consider whether you want to do so and whether you want to act in the way you are acting. These two different approaches to shortening the refractory period are described in detail in my last book, *Emotions Revealed*.

In terms of Buddhist practices, I do not know of anything to help this other than meditation that focuses on the breath. Is there another practice that we could employ that would help people become aware that they are acting emotionally?

DALAI LAMA: (*Translated.*) In the Buddhist psychology, there is an understanding that each emotional episode will have a preparatory stage—we call it "preliminary"—and then the actual event and its consequence or outcome—or "concluding event," as it is sometimes called. Some of the techniques that you mentioned earlier seem to be dealing with the preliminary stage.

For the techniques dealing with the actual events themselves, one practice that is recommended in the Buddhist texts is awareness of the rising of emotions. The problem is that when an emotion arises in you, at that instant, your entire being becomes that emotion. You are completely overtaken by that emotion. There is no separation between you and the emotion. The goal of this kind of awareness practice is trying to recognize that the emotion is arising in you, and to immediately bring the separation—

EKMAN: I completely agree with your characterization, and especially find useful the distinction about the two parts of an emotional episode. Can you explain the practice to bring about this separation?

DALAI LAMA: (*Translated.*) Some of the practices that you are describing seem to be doing this, having the effect of being able to become aware: Now, I am emotional.

It is really a matter of habit. Because the more habituated you are to this awareness of the rising of emotion, the awareness in itself creates a separation between you and the emotion, and that reduces the emotion immediately. One of the key factors for this is thought to be the basic attitude of the person. In relation to a specific emotion like anger or hatred, if you have a basic attitude that the emotion is undesirable, that it is bad and destructive, then the chances are that you are in a better position to recognize and be aware of it when it arises.

EKMAN: In my terms, you are talking about using knowledge.

JINPA: Knowledge, yes.

EKMAN: Do you think that focusing on the breath exercises will help the second process?

DALAI LAMA: (*Translated.*) In the second context, when you adopt mindfulness practice, focusing on the breath, it is more a kind of a diversion.

EKMAN: Oh no, I am not saying that you should focus—I do not think in the midst of an emotional episode you can start focusing on the breath—but will engaging in that meditative practice make it more likely that you will be aware of when you are being emotional?

DALAI LAMA: (*Translated.*) That is true, that is true, because you are cultivating the skill of mindfulness in general.

EKMAN: So it will transfer.

JINPA: Yes.

DALAI LAMA: (*Translated.*) In dealing with what Buddhists call "afflictions," it is very important to recognize the destructiveness of these emotional afflictions and their potential for harmful consequences but also to complement that with an understanding, or an awareness, that you *can* overcome them. You should see the benefits of the opposite side. Otherwise, it becomes morbid.

Take the example of Buddha's teaching of the Four Noble Truths. If the emphasis on the contemplation on the nature of suffering is not accompanied by an awareness that there can be freedom from suffering, then that contemplation would only lead to a greater sense of discouragement and helplessness. In the example of the nurse that you gave earlier, her empathy with others' pain should be complemented with an awareness that she can do something to help them. Even in the extreme case where she may not be able to help the patient to fully recover, she can understand that she can help and that if she doesn't help, the child may suffer more.

Reflection on suffering needs to be tempered with an appreciation of its opposite: what it must feel like not to have it, or freedom from suffering. What is important is to have a basic attitude based on a recognition of the destructive consequences of certain emotions and also some understanding that there are ways in which you can actually help yourself to avoid these situations.

ON THE FOUR NOBLE TRUTHS

by Geshe Dorji Damdul

The Four Noble Truths form the foundation of all the Buddha's teachings. They are based on the idea that all beings have the innate wish to be happy and not suffer; furthermore, that we have the *right* to achieve happiness and avert suffering.

How can we go about fulfilling this aspiration? This leads us to the teachings on the Four Noble Truths—the truth of suffering, the truth of the cause of suffering, the truth of the cessation of suffering and its causes, and the truth of the path leading to the cessation of suffering. The first two truths are about the cause and effect of suffering; the third and fourth about the cause and effect of happiness. The teachings also describe two states of being: *samsara*—the painful state—and *nirvana*—the state of ultimate peace. Beings under the power of undisciplined, disturbing mental states are entangled in the state of samsara, whereas beings who are purified of their disturbing emotions are in the state of nirvana. There are three kinds of suffering (or states of unsatisfactoriness): evident suffering; suffering of change, referring to all worldly pleasures which are prone to end in pains; and conditioned suffering, referring to our state of being under the control of disturbing emotions and their respective actions.

What is the significance of the sequence of these four truths? Unless you know that you are suffering, your desire to be free of suffering will not arise at the outset. Thus the first thing to do as a practitioner is to know the state we are in, full of unsatisfactoriness and frustration. The deeper our understanding of our suffering nature, the stronger is our sense of the wish to be freed of it.

After having identified suffering, the wise thing to do, the Buddha says, is to identify and eliminate the root cause of suffering. The Buddha points to our fundamental ignorance as the trigger of all problems: It blinds us to a clear vision of reality; all our actions that are motivated by ignorance turn out to be unrealistic, and acting based on this unrealistic view is the immediate cause of suffering. All disturbing emotions—such as afflictive attachment and hostility—come through ignorance, which in turn motivates our respective actions. So this fundamental ignorance, along with afflictive emotions and their corresponding actions, constitute the second truth.

What is this fundamental ignorance? It is the misconception of the reality of yourself and all other things. It is through exterminating fundamental ignorance that we can be freed of all forms of suffering, the third truth. This state of freedom from the fundamental ignorance is nirvana, the ultimate peace. Is there really such a state as nirvana? If yes, is it achievable?

This leads us to explore the fourth truth: the path leading to nirvana. Just as darkness can be eliminated fully by introducing the contrary force, which is light, in the world of mind, introducing a mental state that is contrary to the undesired mental state—ignorance in our case—allows us the chance to eliminate it fully. Unlike physical things, two minds are said to oppose each other if they have contrary objects of apprehension in relation to a single object, say white or non-white. In the case of ignorance, viewing things to exist independently as opposed to the reality, it would be another mind, which sees the emptiness of independent nature. This mind that understands reality is known as the wisdom that realizes the ultimate truth—the emptiness of independent existence, the fundamental nature of interdependence.

The wisdom realizing the ultimate truth in the most re-
fined way—technically known as direct non-dualistic experience of ultimate reality—is the actual remedy to
ignorance, which leads us to nirvana. The wisdom which is
developed to that extent forms the fourth truth.

◆ ◆ ◆

DALAI LAMA: As for the actual method in the Buddhist tradition, the first stage is to somehow avoid the circumstances that
would normally trigger these afflictive emotions. The Buddhist
language used is "guarding the gateway of the senses."

EKMAN: That is a nice phrase.

DALAI LAMA: (*Translated.*) This is more of an avoidance, making sure that you do not put yourself in a situation where you
confront the triggers that will lead to the emotions.

The second stage in the Buddhist texts is described as not responding, even when the signals are there in the environment.
You are not avoiding the triggers—you are confronting the situation, but you do not respond in an emotional way, even though
you recognize these triggers, which are often harmful emotions
being expressed by the other person. In the Buddhist language,
the term used is "not willingly inviting" the afflictions, somehow
not giving credence to them. Also, you need to avoid bringing up
the memory of past emotional experiences. Here, with mindfulness meditation, the breathing may be helpful, an awareness of
the arising of the emotion that we spoke about. These things can
be helpful in the second state, but the first stage is this avoidance
of the trigger.

EKMAN: When you say that breathing may be helpful, do you
mean it may be helpful in having prepared you beforehand, helpful right at the moment you are experiencing an emotion, or helpful before that, when you sense the emotion is arising?

DALAI LAMA: Right at the moment, in order to avoid, the consciousness is just on the breathing. When the emotions have

already arisen, the best method is to try to cultivate the opposing mental state in yourself, to overcome the emotion. But the initial stage, of course, is difficult. Also, it depends on the force of the afflictive emotions. In the practitioner's initial stage, the afflictive emotions are strong. Then, an immediate switch to positive emotions—it is difficult. (*Laughs.*) (*Translated.*) A complete change, a hundred-percent change, it is very difficult. Therefore, in order to reduce the strength of forces of the negative emotions for the time being, you forget and just think about the breathing, and then the mind grows a little calm, and then the switch to the positive mind.

EKMAN: If someone does something rude or insulting and you feel anger, would you focus on your breathing for a moment, to calm yourself, before saying something?

DALAI LAMA: That is right.

EKMAN: As I listen to this, I think that what you are saying applies to affliction. Some feeling of the suffering of another person is not an affliction, unless one is overwhelmed by it and does not maintain any feeling of hope. There are many emotions, some that are not pleasant to experience but yet are non-afflictive.

JINPA: Yes.

EKMAN: I am also reminded of the nurse example because I have had six operations over the last five years and the nurses were just wonderful. They made such a difference. I never saw them in any way burdened by my suffering, but they knew of it. They understood it. I do not think, in their dealings with me, they had any emotional resonance, and I did not miss it. I wanted help, not a sharing of my agony.

Passivity itself creates problems when you experience certain emotions. Nurses report that if they simply watch, rather than help, during surgery, it is much harder for them. That fits with a memory I have of a severe fear experience. In 1967, in the last part of my first journey to New Guinea, I chartered a single-engine plane to reach my meeting place with my host Daniel Carleton

Gajdusek.* At that time, I was very afraid of flying and I was in a single-engine plane for the first time in my life, with an eighteen-year-old pilot. Soon after take-off, the airport radioed to inform him that the wheels had dropped off the plane. We had to come back to land at the strip, where they would have a fire truck waiting for us. The pilot told me that I should practice opening and closing the door on my side—while we were in the air—so that as we scraped into the ground, I would be able to quickly get the door open; otherwise I might not be able to escape if the plane caught on fire. Hearing this in the abstract, you would think I would be terrified. But I had no fear at all, because I had something to do. Once we landed, *then* I was afraid. (*Dalai Lama laughs.*) I was terrified about getting into another plane, but I did it despite my fear.

When a person is able to engage in action, it changes the nature of the experience. Psychologists talk about this as "coping," but it is more than coping: It is an engagement with the emotion in a constructive fashion, and is a factor in not becoming overwhelmed by it.

DALAI LAMA: (*Translated.*) When you are *doing* something, the mind is not focused solely on the pain.

EKMAN: Particularly with fear, in which we often feel helpless. We are most afraid of a danger when we are helpless and unable to protect ourselves. But if there is something to do, we do not feel afraid. Instead, we engage with the source of the fear.

To contradict myself, I now find the most relaxing time is when I am on an airplane because then my fate is not in my hands. I enjoy the fact that, for this flight, I have no responsibilities at all. That is totally different from actively coping, but that is how I now deal with it.

---

* Gajdusek was studying the means by which a central nervous system disease, Kuru, was transmitted. To do this work he had set up a base camp and other facilities, which he invited me to use for my work. He later received the Nobel Prize for his discovery that Kuru was caused by eating the brain tissue of someone who had died of the disease.

ON EMOTION AND MEMORY

by Paul Ekman

It may be intrinsic to the nature of emotional experience that our immediate memory of what transpired is distorted in a way that justifies the emotion we just experienced. To the extent that occurs, we would be less likely to learn from reflecting upon the emotional episode, unless we were to discuss it with someone else who was involved in the experience.

Research by my former student Erika Rosenberg and me found another problem in memory for emotional experiences: Most emotional episodes arouse a sequence of emotions, not just one emotion; yet memory tends to focus on the last emotion that was felt, or only the most intense of the emotions that was experienced.[4]

◆ ◆ ◆

EKMAN: The last emotion felt is, of course, the easiest to recall, but not necessarily what you will understand easily. For instance, if you can only remember the last thing that happened when you talked to someone, but not all the things that led up to what was said, it is going to be more difficult for you to learn from the emotional experience. The less self-centered you are, the more likely I think it would be that your memory would be fuller, and less self-justified.

Many people, when they remember an action that they regret, do not seem to learn from their memory of what went wrong. There are many reasons why this occurs, but one of them might be that they did not remember fully. It can be very helpful if you have a partner with whom you can, without rancor, discuss and fill in the holes in your memory.

Earlier, we talked about what you could do to increase your awareness as the impulse arises. Then, what you could do once you become emotional to bring that awareness to bear on the situation, so that you can choose whether to continue to be emotional and how to express the emotion in the most constructive fashion. And last, after the emotion, what you could do to bring skilled knowledge to the analysis of what occurred.

It still amazes me how little understanding people have about their emotions, since emotions are such a central part of life. But learning from a regrettable emotional episode after the episode is easier to achieve than becoming aware of being emotional as an episode unfolds, which is easier than becoming aware of the impulse to become emotional before the emotion has begun.

DALAI LAMA: (*Translated.*) This is partly a result of a culture in which people experience various mental states but do not give much thought to the experiences themselves. People like you are helping by drawing others' attention to the need to be more aware and to pay attention to emotion.

EKMAN: We need a book for parents on how to raise an emotionally skilled child, because that is when most of what we learn about emotion occurs, and most of what we learn badly occurs in the home. The first chapter would insist that you have to become emotionally skilled yourself if you are going to raise a child who might have a balanced emotional life.

I hope that those who are conducting research on the impact of meditation will examine not just the meditator, but if that meditator is a parent, whether it has beneficial consequences for the children, who presumably would be dealing with a less impatient, more understanding parent.

GRATITUDE AND REJOICING

EKMAN: I would like to mention two other emotions that I think are relevant to the development of compassion.

Often, though not always, when someone is thanked profusely, especially if it is done while others are present, the person being thanked can become overwhelmed and speechless, and tears may flow. The person who is expressing thanks feels "gratitude," but should we use the same word for the person being thanked? Certainly that person is grateful for being thanked, for being acknowledged.

My wife recently retired from a senior administrative post at the university, to return to being just a professor. At a public ceremony in her honor, many of the people thanked her; some of them broke down into tears, and so did my wife. I have never seen her cry so much. She was exhausted at the end. But they were tears of overwhelming joy.

DALAI LAMA: (*Translated.*) If I am quite thankful to you, and I say, "I am so thankful. You have been so kind to me," and these things, the gratitude is within me. Then you, the person being thanked, in turn might respond with a sense of joy, feeling grateful for being thanked. It is a kind of exchange.

Two things are happening. From one side, a feeling of gratefulness or gratitude, and from the other side, a sense of responding to and recognizing the gratefulness that is felt. In these two cases, the object is different.

EKMAN: It is much more common for the person who is thanked to become overwhelmed and unable to speak than for the person who is doing the thanking. If the thanking occurs in front of an audience, then it is even more likely that the person being thanked will be overwhelmed.

When I retired, many of my students made speeches. I remember one of them said, "I have Paul Ekman in my head. And whenever I have to make a decision, I have a conversation with him about what he would say about this decision." It was nice just hearing that—see, it is starting to happen again (*Becomes tearful.*)— I could have had such a positive influence on someone else, that it produces tears. What are those? We still do not understand. Is it just that you are overwhelmed?

DALAI LAMA: Again, again—

EKMAN: With joy?

DALAI LAMA: Many other factors involved. There is also the indication that you are basically a very good person. I think in the case of Mao Zedong or Stalin, I do not think they have that kind of response. (*Ekman laughs heartily.*)

The person's basic way of thinking makes a big difference.

EKMAN: There is something related to embarrassment in this, particularly when it occurs in public.

DALAI LAMA: (*Translated.*) Embarrassment, and social habits. This embarrassment comes from social conditions.

EKMAN: Darwin stated that embarrassment occurs most commonly when you praise a person, especially if you praise his or her appearance, and particularly his or her face. If you say, "Oh, what a handsome face you have—it just emanates wisdom, kindness, and judgment . . ." (*Dalai Lama chuckles.*)

You are not taking me seriously. But Darwin would say that at those times when you get embarrassed, you should begin to blush. I will blush for you. (*Ekman laughs.*)

DALAI LAMA: That, also, I think, applies in the person who is not arrogant. (*Translated.*) An arrogant person would say, "Of course!"

EKMAN: "Of course! Why didn't you say that earlier?!" (*Both laugh.*) "More!" or "Without a doubt."

Let me suggest that the exchange of gratitude may help to move people toward becoming more compassionate. Helping is a compassionate act, and being thanked and feeling appreciated should strengthen the inclination to respond in that fashion.

In addition to gratitude, there is another emotion that seems related to cultivating compassion. The anthropologist John Haidt has written about what he calls "elevation," the feeling you have when you see someone else engaged in a compassionate act. It makes you feel good. It is different from other feelings of goodness. Do you have a name for this?

JINPA: We call it "rejoicing."

EKMAN: In another person's compassion or exemplary act . . .

JINPA: In someone else's good act.

EKMAN: That is nice. It is a better term than "elevation." The word "rejoice" has "joy" within it, and the prefix of "re" refers to something else. So it is a better word than "elevation," which is going up to the ceiling, unlike your joy. (*Laughs.*)

DALAI LAMA: (*Translated.*) When I watch nature television or see a mother express affectionate dedication to her offspring, I feel a sense of rejoicing, because they are confirmations of the value of compassion.

EKMAN: When my wife and I attended Dick Grace's Heroes of Compassion ceremonies, and we heard Dick read what each "hero" had done, tears came into our eyes, for each person, again and again.* As you know, thirty or forty people are honored in the ceremony, yet with each one, perhaps because each person had done something different, it was very moving. We were not suffering, yet we had tears. It feels good to know that there are such compassionate people in this world: We were rejoicing.

DALAI LAMA: And you are seeing! (*Translated.*) If you look at a weeping face, it begets tears; a laughing face begets laughter. If you see someone yawn, you start yawning too.

EKMAN: Very much for yawning.

DORJI: When His Holiness works on the discourses that he is giving to the public, he often yawns.

EKMAN: Yes?

DORJI: The people at the front are also yawning. (*Burst of laughter from everyone.*)

EKMAN: They yawn back! (*Exuberant laughter.*) My wife considers me the Olympic athlete of yawning. Very big yawns. You have not seen me do that. (*Dalai Lama laughs warmly.*)

At the Dick Grace ceremony, when these people come onto

---

* Dick Grace is a philanthropist whose contributions include organizing an annual ceremony to honor people from around the world who he feels have engaged in a compassionate life. They are brought to San Francisco to be recognized in public and congratulated by the Dalai Lama.

the stage and Dick reads what he or she has done, they are not crying—but everyone in the audience is crying at the inspiration of human beings acting lives of great compassion. The heroes are ordinary people. They are not exceptionally educated, or different from anyone else in some remarkable way, except that their lives are dedicated to compassion.

The thing about attending this event is that afterward, for hours, you feel much more hopeful about the world. That is why I suggest incorporating such events in a program to cultivate compassion.

DALAI LAMA: (*Translated.*) So, what is the essence here?

EKMAN: The essence is that we rejoice and are inspired by the compassionate actions of others.

DALAI LAMA: Oh, yes, clearly.

(*Translated.*) When you have a very strong and intense good feeling, it can immediately bring about a physiological change, which can bring about tears. But there can be a diversity of underlying causes for tears: There could be army generals who would cry because of having failed to kill an enemy.

Instead, what we are discussing are the tears and physiological changes that happen because of virtuous or positive emotions. But even within that domain, there can be two kinds of people. One type is prone to shedding tears, even for small reasons. There is a very popular expression—it says that someone who is so prone to tears is like a baby with the spit coming out. The other type is, a solemn person, deep in thinking and intent in feeling, who is not really prone to shedding tears. But if at some time the person sheds tears, it really means something.

EKMAN: You are always bringing to our attention how individuals differ, and how difficult it may be to know from an external manifestation what is happening inside. And you are always thinking of ways to draw further distinctions in what at first may seem unitary. I like that. I used to think that I had an excessive need to make more and more distinctions. But, yours are beyond me, and always useful. (*Dalai Lama laughs.*)

You further unpack each point into another set of classifications. I think we need to do that in order to understand the world. There is an opposite emphasis in science—to arrive at the simplest explanation—but in my judgment that is often at the cost of missing important individual variations.

DORJI: Should your gratitude make His Holiness cry now? (*A lot of laughter.*) His Holiness says that he never cries.

DALAI LAMA: That is, if it involves altruism or certain things. Almost always after practicing major teaching, I always cry. I am actually moved, and I cry, cry.

EKMAN: You cry about what *someone else* has done. When people thank you for what you have done, you do not cry. But one of the reasons *you* may not cry when people express all their gratitude is that it happens so often. (*Dalai Lama laughs delightedly.*)

It may be that whenever emotion is aroused to a very high level of intensity, tears are produced—whether it is anguish or rejoicing. There are also tears of anger. I have seen them in women and children much more often than in adult men; the reasons for why this is the case are complicated, and I will resist the temptation to speculate about that.

MENTAL TRAINING GYMNASIUMS

DALAI LAMA: (*Translated.*) If you look at the idea behind modern educational systems, there is a certain universal recognition that being uninformed is bad for you, that it will lead to suffering later in life, and that knowledge is a good thing: Knowledge will give you the tools to lead a happier and successful life. Human civilization probably can be said to be based on this recognition that knowledge is good for you and leads to happiness, that ignorance leads to suffering and impoverishment. On that basis, educational systems are developed and children are taught.

In the basic Buddhist teachings, there is also the idea that being misinformed or uninformed is the source of suffering; such a condition is painful. Recently, in my meeting with the group of Muslim scholars, one of the scholars said that Islam holds the same view, and it became very clear in our discussion that many of the emotions are grounded in a distortion of reality, perhaps arising from a lack of understanding of the situation.

It is this dimension of not having accurate or sufficient information, of lacking an understanding of reality that leads to many of our excesses; our emotions give rise to the pain of suffering. In contrast, the mental states that are grounded upon some form of understanding, knowledge, and wisdom tend to promote happiness, success, and well-being. If we can convey this idea to people and develop it into training for children to receive, that education would be helpful.

EKMAN: I believe we cannot get rid of emotions; they are built into us. But we can be more intelligent in our understanding of our emotions—that is the knowledge we need. We can develop skills so that our emotions are not enacted destructively. That is a first step, a fundamental step.

I think we now are close to having evidence that people can make changes in how they experience each of their emotions. This is harder for people with emotional profiles in which there are very short fuses and very strong reactions, but they still can acquire knowledge about what is needed and learn skills for managing emotions. They need both.

I like to use the example of wanting to learn to play tennis. You have to read the rule book, but doing that is not going to get your ball over the net: you only have knowledge about how to play the game. To get your ball over the net, you need to practice and develop your skills. And you need a coach; you need someone who will help teach you.

Emotional skills are similar. In my view, the key opportunity to introduce mind training is in adolescence, because adolescents are often unhappy—all the changes they are going through make this time a wonderful entry point for developing emotional skills. Adolescents are wondering what life is about and how they are to live their life, questions not often considered again until the signs of aging appear in late middle age.

Many areas need to be developed. One aspect is knowledge of the global nature of our existence; another is the dismissal from the mind of the resentments held from past experiences. And if you are being seized by emotions without realizing it, you are not going to be able to use any of that knowledge.

DALAI LAMA: (*Translated.*) It really comes down to wisdom, and the prudent use of it. For example, sometimes reflecting or dwelling upon the past can have a beneficial effect, in teaching us a lesson, and then we *do* need to dwell on the past and understand it. But if turning back to the past is going to lead to destructive consequences, we need to let go of it.

Whatever the pursuit, if it goes to an extreme, it always leads to problems. Also, the judgment of what constitutes an excess, an extreme, is a function of a person's wisdom and discernment.

EKMAN: Should the effort to generate global compassion be focused on an antidote to narrow-mindedness or on an intervention to bring about more compassion? To get one, you do have to get rid of the other.

DALAI LAMA: (*Translated.*) My approach is to bring light, powerfully, onto the downside of narrow-mindedness, which then provides a powerful rationale for having a more broad-minded, global perspective and concern for others. So they are related, a kind of a premise. (*Claps hands together.*)

In Buddhist meditation practice something analogous, where in order to practice compassion, first you reflect deeply upon the downside of narrow-minded self-centeredness. Then you reflect upon the positive consequences and the potential of more other-centered perspectives. On the basis of these reflections, you cultivate compassion.

Otherwise, if you simply admonish others to cultivate compassion, and if you do not give them the resources—particularly the rationale for its need—it is just wishful thinking. Whereas, if you explain from the point of view of self-interest—it is for your own interest and well-being; it is essential—it makes a difference.

There are two kinds of self-interest. (*Switching to English.*) Without self-interest, generally speaking, there is no basis for development of determination. But extreme self-centeredness, is foolish, selfish interest.

EKMAN: If we put two advertisements in the newspaper, one stating that we are holding a weekend workshop, free of charge, to develop compassion and the other that we are going to have a weekend workshop, free of charge, to reduce your narrow-mindedness, I think the compassion advertisement would draw more people than the narrow-mindedness ad. Coming to a "narrow-mindedness workshop" requires you to acknowledge that you are narrow-minded, which most people would be reluctant to do.

DALAI LAMA: (*Translated.*) Compassion is what we are aspiring for. The whole notion of narrow-mindedness, the downside of being narrow-minded, is part of the argument for the need for compassion.

When you advertise if you talk about "dealing with narrow-mindedness," people might think, What is it for? Whereas, if you say, "cultivation of compassion," people can relate to it. But the problem is that, though most people may share the idea that it is a very valuable thing, a precious thing, sometimes people have a rather naive understanding of what compassion is. But people might also feel that it is a noble idea and it is a noble value. We need to give people a deeper understanding of compassion, grounded in a real appreciation of its need and value.

EKMAN: I totally agree. I would prefer to say, "removing the obstacles to compassion" because if you have to think of yourself as narrow-minded, it might be insulting.

JINPA: Yes.

EKMAN: But removing the obstacles, recognizing what they are, might be more acceptable.

DORJI: Paul, perhaps in the case of the second advertisement, instead of saying, "We are going to remove your narrow-mindedness," you could say, "We are going to *increase* your sense of *openness?*"

EKMAN: Yes. That would be excellent.

DALAI LAMA: In order to feel happy. Then maybe, more attention. The same meaning, but the different way of presentation.

EKMAN: A positive presentation.

DALAI LAMA: One way of cheating.

EKMAN: There used to be a song, "Accentuate the Positive." What was the second line of that song? "De-emphasize the Negative."

But there is the serious challenge of scale: How do we do this on a global level? For instance, we have to address the disproportionate use of the world's resources. Americans are not the majority of the world's population, but in terms of the world's oil consumption, they consume a disproportionate amount.

DALAI LAMA: (*Translated.*) It is partly because America has quite a large land mass, so you have to drive long distances. (*Ekman laughs.*) If it were a smaller country, there would be less scope for consumption.

EKMAN: We eat a lot of beef, which requires an enormous amount of energy to produce compared to diets that are more common in other parts of the world. If we were to make things more equitable worldwide, in order for the poorest to not be so poor, the richest might not be able to live so luxuriously as they now live. Some economists argue that is not true. But some argue that it is very true, that people do not want to give up either their individualist aspirations, or the fact that they can drive huge cars, go wherever they want, and eat steaks every night. "And you are telling me I have to maybe only have steak once a week? Or I have to drive a smaller car? Is that what compassion requires?"

I say this with a bit of a smile, but I think it is a serious problem to confront, how we share the world's resources equitably when we have an inequitable situation to begin with, and a very powerful nation that is benefiting from the inequity—this may be a very large obstacle to achieving global compassion.

DALAI LAMA: (*Translated.*) One of the things that people can consider or have brought to their attention is the question of the sustainability of their current lifestyle. If we were to continue on this path of consumption, at this current level, how long could this last?

EKMAN: Some might think, As long as it lasts for me and my children, why should I be concerned? That is the problem, as I see it.

DALAI LAMA: Oh.

EKMAN: Matters are getting to the point where people are beginning to worry: "Maybe my children will have a burden if we do not change things now." For example, America is mortgaging itself with a deficit that may be a burden to our children. I believe that we should recognize this as bad selfishness.

DALAI LAMA: Mm-hmm.

EKMAN: It is a perversion of the individualistic culture: "It is me that matters, not everyone else. Not even everyone else in my own country. Why should I care about the homeless? If they wanted a home, they'd get one!" That is the attitude that has to be overcome.

As a parent with children, I realize that if I give up a little bit of my standard of living, it will be better for my children and grandchildren. It will not benefit me, but if I make some reductions, it will benefit them. From a Buddhist view, giving up attachment—to material comfort or lifestyle or whatever—is accomplished freely, not begrudgingly, there will be psychological benefits in the state of the person's mind as a consequence of this compassionate act.

DALAI LAMA: Yes.

EKMAN: So, it is the built-in compassion we have for our offspring that may help to save the world. It may be difficult to care about the children in Darfur, but worrying about my own children and grandchildren is easy. I better start reducing the inequity, for my own children's sake. So, it is building on what is already there.

DALAI LAMA: Yes. That is how we start: family level. (*Translated.*) Part of the tension here may be arising from a fairly standard Western attitude for dealing with problems that you want to solve.

The world has many problems, and the idea that all the problems can be solved is probably not very realistic. There were great teachers in the past, across many cultures, who have taught certain ways of being, but if you look carefully, it seems that none of these teachers premised their teaching on the assumption that everyone is going to listen or going to change themselves and follow them.

Similarly, Darwin expressed very powerful sentiments [about the need for the welfare of all sentient beings]. He probably did not expect that they would be achieved. (*Ekman laughs.*) He probably did not write them on the assumption that everybody was going to listen to him.

The same applies to us. Our responsibility is to try our best and do what we can. Then that will be a part of things that we may achieve. Ten people follow a practice—good. One hundred—better. A thousand—still better. Not all six billion.

EKMAN: Maybe over time.

DALAI LAMA: Modern education.

JINPA: We are not dealing with matters of religion here, nor are we propagating religion; we are basically dealing with problems in a secular context. We have a basis for hope.

One of the ways in which His Holiness was saying he would like to see this done is to really make these kinds of things an integral part of education. For example, consciousness of hygiene is now universal. Everyone recognizes its value, the need to do it. Hygiene deals with physical health. And this is like mental and emotional hygiene. So he would like to see training on compassion integrated into the educational system.

EKMAN: Public schools are not easily changed, but it can happen from within. The teachers we provided with practice on meditation and emotional skills are all now dedicated to continuing it and to having their children benefit from the practice. But I totally agree with you that the long range has to involve reaching people earlier in life, in more formative periods of life, before they get on the wrong track. It is also important, if it is to be accepted within public schools, that religious terms are not used. Which is why I talk about mental exercises, not mindfulness.

DALAI LAMA: (*Translated.*) What we need are pilots like yourself, who will do a project, an experiment, and demonstrate the efficacy and feasibility of these trainings so that they can be gradually incorporated into the curriculum.

EKMAN: Six years ago you said exactly the same thing: We should work with children. And I said, "But what about us, who are already adults? We are the ones who are making the decisions that are endangering the children." Alan Wallace responded, "Well, we can get spiritual gymnasiums." Alan noted that we accept the idea that we go to gyms to develop our muscles and get in good physical shape. Why couldn't we do this to develop emotional balance?

When you go into a physical exercise gym, you often get on a scale to weigh yourself. For the mental training gymnasium,* we need to find a way for you to measure your levels of compassion and emotional balance, to see how much progress you have made since your previous visit. Scientists like to measure things.

ON COMPASSION TRAINING

by Charles Raison

Beginning in 2006, my colleagues and I have studied sixty-one healthy college freshmen who were randomized to either six weeks of training in a compassion meditation protocol, designed by Geshe Lobsang Tenzin Negi, PhD, or to a health education discussion group control condition. Following these interventions, the students participated in

---

* At first I described this as a *compassion* gymnasium, but the training necessary to achieve compassion involves other mental processes.

a laboratory test designed to mimic many of the features of stress that are especially problematic in our daily lives. Students who spent the most time in the compassion meditation had reduced autonomic nervous system responses to the stress test, as measured by heart rate during the stressor. There was also a strong correlation between practice time and reduced inflammatory responses to the stressor in the meditation group, and those who practiced the most had lower inflammatory responses to the stressor than did either the control group or those who spent less time meditating.

Although in need of replication, these results suggest that young adults who practiced compassion meditation for six weeks had a change in how they perceived and responded physically to stress, such that they felt less threatened and distressed, and because of this they responded to the test with less stress system activity and less activation of the body's inflammatory system. Because chronic activation of these systems has been associated with the development of a number of diseases, the results suggest that the practice of compassion meditation might, over time, provide protection against a number of physical illnesses.

Charles Raison is an assistant professor in the Mind-Body Program, Department of Psychiatry and Behavioral Sciences, at Emory University School of Medicine.

◆ ◆ ◆

DALAI LAMA: Yes, that is right.

EKMAN: There are many scientists now working on how to measure compassion. We also need what I call, for the moment, a *stressometer,* a device that can quickly assess your level of physiological arousal when you first enter the gym. I have just received a pledge of financial support to bring together a small group of scientists to plan how to construct and evaluate such a device. We are also considering the feasibility of a stress decompression chamber that could, perhaps through biofeedback, help you return to a calmer state, guiding you by a visual or audible display, to focus on what to do to lower your physiological arousal level. The development of either the stressometer or the decompression chamber will require a research program involving a number of years of work, but I believe the benefits it would have make it worth pursuing.

We need inspiration rooms, in which you can see films of people who have acted heroically. It makes you feel good to witness such actions, and the rejoicing should motivate participants to become more compassionate.

We need meta-attention rooms, perhaps with biofeedback, to help you learn how to become more aware of your emotional experiences on a moment-by-moment basis. When your mind is distracted and scattered, this type of information can restore your focus and equilibrium.

We need a loving-kindness exercise room. We should have video games in which you face conflicts and learn how to resolve them respectfully. Other games could offer the opportunity to make compassionate acts; still others would reward collaborative engagements rather than competitive ones. For example, there is an Israeli game that I first saw played on a beach in Tel Aviv in which you hit the ball back and forth between the two players as long as you can, rather than hitting the ball in such a way that it cannot be returned. It is a cooperation game. There might also be group exercises that you do with other people. In these groups you would receive encouragement and support to engage in a more compassionate life.

I have just presented an outline, but I think this is something that could be done and should be tried—with children as well as adults. Efforts are now being made.[5]

DALAI LAMA: If the work is something that is worthwhile, then, regardless whether we can achieve it or not, make attempt. That is, I think, important. Courageous.

[For a further discussion on whether global compassion can be learned, visit www.emotionalawareness.net.]

7

PERSONAL TRANSFORMATION

Sometimes, for seemingly inexplicable reasons, and without seeking or expecting it, a major change occurs in how one experiences life. For me, when such a change occurred around the turn of the millennium, its impact was startling and perplexing because none of the tools I had spent a lifetime perfecting as a research psychologist equipped me to make sense of what had happened. Given the mysterious nature of my change, I would have dismissed it except that the benefits were quite great, not just to me but to those who dealt with me on a daily basis.

The change in my life was a dramatic shift in how I experienced emotion—my very own professional bailiwick. It occurred during my first meeting with the Dalai Lama in Dharamsala, India, in 2000. It was a riddle. As a scientist, I was used to seeking explanations but also comfortable when some things could not yet be explained, which was one of the reasons I had never been drawn to any religion, let alone Buddhism.

I had to find out if the Dalai Lama could explain what had occurred.

CHANGING THE
EXPERIENCE OF EMOTION

EKMAN: I would like to discuss something that is very personal and difficult to understand from a Western viewpoint. Yet if you and I can begin to comprehend it, others might be able to obtain similar benefits. What I am going to talk about opens the possibility of misunderstanding, so I will try to be careful in what I say.

It again goes back to our first meeting in Dharamsala, in 2000, which was an experience that changed my life course in very unexpected ways. It changed me from being a pessimist to being an optimist. Some months after the meeting was over I examined the videotapes of the fourth day of the meeting, I heard myself say, spontaneously, "Well, I am not feeling my usual pessimism. I think we can do something." That was a different me speaking.

I remembered that on the fifth day, I had noticed that for the previous two days I had not experienced any feelings of frustration. That day, Francisco Varela spoke at length on matters that I could not understand; I just could not follow him. Usually I would get impatient in such a circumstance, but I had no impatience. I did not wish to be impatient, but it was very noticeable that impatience was gone, frustration was gone.

The most dramatic change in my emotional life was that over the next seven months, I never had an angry impulse—not one. So, when and how did this begin? What produced this change in me?

Overly intense anger had been a plague in my life until then: It began shortly after the last time my father hit me, when I was eighteen. I warned him that if he hit me again, I would hit him back. He regarded this as a threat and called the police to arrest me for threatening his life. I had to flee my home forever. Since then, very few days would go by without my having an angry impulse on which I would act in a way that I regretted afterward. I was constantly on guard, trying not to yield to such impulses and often failing. I do not think a week of my life went by, from the time I was eighteen until the time I was sixty-six [in 2000] that I did not have a couple of regrettable episodes of anger. Not a wonderful way to lead your life.

Then, for seven months, not one angry impulse. Not one. I was freed; it was a wonderful relief. I asked Alan Wallace, "What's happening?" and he said that this was "not at all unusual—but expect it to fade over time."

He was right. It did fade over time, but never back to where it had been. I do have angry impulses, and I do sometimes act on them, but not all the time. Sometimes I recognize the impulse and just let it pass by me, even when provoked. I am not able to do this all the time, but my experience of anger is very different than before. The chief exceptions are when I am very tired, having not had enough sleep, or when I am experiencing physical pain due to some medical problem. Even then, my anger is not as severe as it typically was before my visit to Dharamsala.

In an attempt to understand how this came about, I interviewed other people who have had similar experiences, and there are some commonalities. But let me first describe my own experience, and how this change may have come about.

During that meeting in Dharamsala, you did not get up during the breaks. Everyone else got up, stretched, and drank some tea. You remained seated so that the observers could come up and talk to you for a few minutes. My daughter, Eve, wanted to ask you a question. And if you knew her well, you would know that she is a fairly rambunctious—

DALAI LAMA: What is that?

EKMAN: A not-shy, spirited person. Yet she felt very reluctant to approach you. I dragged her up and I introduced Eve as my spiritual leader, telling you that it was because of her that I had come to Dharamsala. When I made the decision to seek an invitation to the meeting on destructive emotions, I had no interest in Buddhism and virtually no knowledge; I knew Eve did. She had lived in a Tibetan refugee camp in Nepal with a Tibetan family for two weeks, during the summer when she was fifteen. She became very concerned about the plight of the Tibetan people. When she returned from Nepal, Eve organized a Free Tibet club in her high school, as well as boycotts and other political activities. When I learned that if a scientist was invited to meet with you, he or she was allowed to bring someone as an observer, I volunteered so that I could provide such an experience for my daughter.

During one break, Eve and I sat down on either side of you, and I told you in just a few words (not as much as I said now) about her. She asked and you answered her question: "Why do we get the angriest at those we are in love with?" Your reply suggested it was because they fail to meet our unrealistic, idealized expectations of them; focus on and accept their flaws and you will not be disappointed, and that source of anger will fade. You and she talked for about eight minutes.

During this whole time, you held my hand in one of your hands. I never said another word after introducing Eve, but I had two unusual experiences. One was that I had a very strong physical sensation for which I do not have an English word—it comes closest to "warmth," but there was no heat. It certainly felt very good, and like nothing I have felt before or after. The other experience was that looking out into the large room was like looking at the world through the wrong side of the binoculars. Although people were quite close, maybe four feet away, so they could watch what was happening, it appeared to me as if they were hundreds of feet away.

DALAI LAMA: Sometimes you actually experience that kind of vision—distant vision.

EKMAN: It was as if the three of us were encapsulated, tightly bound, and everyone else was off in the distance.

I told a number of people about this experience and asked them if they knew of anyone else who shared it. I asked Jinpa, and I asked Alan Wallace, and I asked Matthieu Ricard. They were all familiar with what I described, each of them saying they had witnessed it many times. They gave me the names of other people they had observed having the same experience.

I interviewed eight of these people. None of the other eight had their child with them, so that cannot be necessary to it. They all described a transformation of their lives, a change in the direction of their lives, and a change in their emotional lives; that was common. They were also all at a transition point in their lives. One or two had just recovered from a life-threatening illness; another had just had a divorce; another was just about to change jobs. It was a transition point for me also: I had made the decision to retire from the university, which I subsequently postponed for four years so that I could organize research that you asked be initiated at the meeting.

I think many Americans lead their lives in such a way that they cannot see anything on either side of them. It is as if they are in the Olympic event called the luge, in which there are high walls on either side. You are moving very fast; if you look to the left or the right, you might crash. You just speed ahead as fast as you can. That is how I was leading my life, how most scientists I know lead their lives. They never see alternative paths in life once they start on the race to discover. But each of these eight people were at a transition point, able to look to the left and to the right, seeing alternative paths in life.

And one more characteristic—they each had a severe emotional wound in their lives that had never healed. They reported that after their meeting with you, the wound did not disappear, but was enormously improved.

I remain a skeptic about how to explain what happened, but I am convinced a major reorganization in my emotional life occurred. I am a little worried that many Western scientists might think I have gone nuts, especially when they read what I am now going to tell you about what it felt like. (*Dalai Lama and Jinpa laugh.*)

What I was experiencing was an intense, very unusual feeling, which felt very good; it felt as if it was radiating. The other eight people I interviewed also used the term "radiate" when describing their experiences.

I have given you my first-person, phenomenological description. As a scientist, I do not know how to explain it, but that does not mean it is not susceptible to scientific explanation; I just do not know where to start, and I suspect we do not yet have the proper tools to examine this phenomenon objectively.

The change that occurred in me was very dramatic. When I left Dharamsala, I met my wife in New Delhi so that we could spend two weeks traveling in India. My wife said, "You are not the man I married."

DALAI LAMA: Really?

EKMAN: She said, "I had not asked for a change." Then, the next day, she said, "Oh, I am so glad. You are so much easier to be with," and she still says this. In fact, I talked to her last night, and she again said, "Be sure to thank His Holiness, because the last seven years have been our happiest."

I now believe that this experience was involved in the end of my hatred; the platform for my too-ready anger was no longer in place, and so the anger itself receded. In the last seven years there have been maybe two incidents where I would say I could have handled anger better. Now most of the time, when my wife gets angry at me, I do not get angry. Most of the time—this is the funny part—I avoid it. I say, "I can see you are angry. Let us talk about it when you are not angry. I do not want to talk now because your anger might get me angry. I do not want to get angry." (*Dalai Lama chuckles.*)

I used to think, I am being a coward. Now I am going to say to her, "I am being a Buddhist. I am going to avoid dealing with your anger now. We will talk about it when you are over the anger." Angry people do not like that. They want to fight.

DALAI LAMA: Yes. That is right.

EKMAN: Why did these changes occur in my life? Why did they happen to the other people I interviewed? Some people who have heard my account have said, "Oh, it is because you look up to the Dalai Lama so much." It is not true. I had zero knowledge of Buddhism. I thought you were, from what I read, an advocate of nonviolence, like Gandhi, and I respected that, but I had little sympathy with Buddhism. But before coming to Dharamsala, there was a meeting of the participants, in which I met Alan Wallace. Alan later told me he was convinced they had made a terrible mistake in inviting me to Dharamsala because I was so close-minded about Buddhism. So it cannot be that I was in a receptive mind intellectually. It was not because I was expecting a miracle. I do not believe miracles occur; that is religious, and I am not religious.

How do you explain it?

DALAI LAMA: Of course, from the Buddhist viewpoint, I do not know. From common sense . . . I do not know. I think your base nature is a pleasant nature, I think, more honest, and a person who recognizes what is positive—I think that is the main factor. The very nature of our discussions also; they are dealing with emotions, and these things, and automatically focus on the value of compassion and the recognition of the destructiveness of anger or hatred. So that also is one factor. Then, by my side, of course, it is not only me; I think the whole atmosphere also makes the difference; and all the other persons generally make for a more calm mind. Anyway, I think the secular—regarding simpler principles—most of our talk has been more spiritual-minded.

Not necessarily *religious* faith, but awareness about the values. From Buddhist viewpoint, of course, the karmic factor is also there. Whether you are from a Buddhist viewpoint, or whether you accept or not, or whether you know or not that there is limitless life, there is some acquaintance; that is also there. I do not know. So, now what is important is finding satisfaction.

Some benefit there, some positive things there: that is enough. (*Laughs.*) I am not to say, to find the answer of how it happened, why it happened, or how it happened, in this case.

THE MYSTERY OF GOODNESS

EKMAN: As a scientist, I cannot ignore what I experienced. It is not that I had not earlier tried other approaches to ameliorate my problems with anger. Three times in my life I was a patient in psychoanalysis, in part to try to deal with this terrible problem of anger. Yet, no change.

DALAI LAMA: Hmm.

EKMAN: I think the change that occurred within me started with that physical sensation, whatever it was. I think that what I experienced was—a nonscientific term—"goodness." Every one of the other eight people I interviewed said they felt goodness; they felt it radiating and felt the same kind of warmth that I did. I have no idea what it is or how it happens, but it is not in my imagination. Though we do not have the tools to understand it, that does not mean it does not exist.

I have to mention another thing, which is that during our first meeting in Dharamsala, I had this feeling—in the West, we call it déjà vu—as if I had known you all my life.

DALAI LAMA: That is right, that is right.

EKMAN: The only people who can explain this that I know of are Buddhists: that I would have known you in some previous life. That is not part of my belief, yet I do feel as if I have known you all of my life!

DALAI LAMA: That is, I think, a very clear sign, some kind of imprint, I think, from the past. So that means within this lifetime, you see, no, it did not happen. So, that means some previous life.

EKMAN: The experience is closest to how I feel toward my sister and my aunt. I have known them since I was born. I have not known you since I was born, but it is as if—

DALAI LAMA: And also the attitude, I think, of being a scientist, thinking more widely, more open. That also makes a difference.

DORJI: (*After a discussion in Tibetan.*) His Holiness is saying that when he is giving a public talk or public discourse, His Holiness often has that kind of instinctual feeling, that he is seeing someone whom he knows so well.

DALAI LAMA: That is right. Like a close sort of friend. Like that.

DORJI: It does not mean, or guarantee, that His Holiness met all these people in his past lives.

DALAI LAMA: I think that is my own attitude. I am thinking, These people, who are just like me, just like myself, not like the differences. I always look from the angle of *sameness* rather than *differences*. That also makes a difference.

EKMAN: Alan told me that he has witnessed that sometimes when people have a meeting with you, just the opposite occurs. They fall totally apart, into anxiety attacks or despair. I think that some people come to see you and expect a miracle; it is their last hope.

DALAI LAMA: That is right.

EKMAN: And no miracle . . .

DALAI LAMA: Ah, too much expectation.

EKMAN: There is a second explanation, and that is some people have spent their lifetime hiding their own inner life from themselves. It is too unbearable.

DALAI LAMA: Yes.

EKMAN: When they encounter you, that curtain falls down, and they are overwhelmed with the demons in their head that they have been avoiding.

It is a paradox, but very typical of Western thinking, that I can explain the unfortunate but I cannot explain the fortunate: It remains a mystery.

ON "GOODNESS"

By Paul Ekman

Discussing this question with my closest friend, Paul Kaufman, who has known me for more than thirty years and, not by coincidence, is a long-time meditation practitioner as well as an atheist, I suddenly thought of a second explanation, though it does not rule out the explanation I provided to the Dalai Lama during our conversation.

I had experienced a very unfortunate relationship with

my father. His favorite curse was, "I only hope that your children will bring you as much misery as you have brought me." As a result, I both wanted to have children (to show that I would not be victim of his curse) and feared having children (because I might become as bad a father as he was, and his curse would come true). When I became a parent, these hopes and fears weighed on me.

Initially I did experience some problems with Tom, my stepson, but with time I was able to overcome them. My relationship with my daughter is the easiest relationship of my life. I have been able to be the parent I never had. And there I was in Dharamsala, sitting with her, having introduced her to the Dalai Lama, a person I knew she greatly admired. This for any loving father would be a priceless moment; for me, it was the final freedom from my father's curse. That freedom released me also from the platform of hatred that I had developed in order to not allow him to hit me anymore and to fight back more generally, against him and other obstacles in pursuit of my goals.

This explanation of my emotional transformation comes from a much more Western and psychological perspective. I suspect it holds true, but that the experience of goodness may also have been crucial. So this shift remains, at least in part, a mystery.

◆ ◆ ◆

EKMAN: When I asked Jinpa, Alan Wallace, and Matthieu Ricard, they all said, "His Holiness knows about the changes some people experience in his presence. He may not want to talk to you about it, but it is not going to be foreign to him that some people experience important changes in their lives—sometimes positive, sometimes negative—after an encounter with him."

DALAI LAMA: (*Translated.*) It is a kind of mystery, actually. One of the characteristics of mysteries, of anything that is a mystery, is that it is not untrue—it is a fact.

Yet its underlying conditions and explanations are opaque and hidden to us. Maybe scientists would not have much to say about this phenomenon; it is not connected to science; it is not your business. (*Several people laugh, including the Dalai Lama.*) Something happened—okay. It is positive; it is good.

JINPA: His Holiness was saying that in his own case, of course, he experiences deep moments of being inspired and being moved when he reflects upon the past teachers, like Buddha or Nagarjuna, and their compassionate actions and teachings. He sometimes feels moved to tears and is deeply inspired. In relation to actual human beings, he does not seem to have that kind of life-changing experience, but he has been informed by numerous other people that they have had experiences of this kind in their interactions with him.

DALAI LAMA: So from the Buddhist viewpoint, the karmic link, not only in this life but also in previous times or in past lives, that is also a factor.

One of the key inspirational prayers that Buddhists make on a daily basis is: "May anyone who comes into contact with me, whether they hear about me or they see me or they think about me, experience a benefit and happiness." That is an important part of the daily prayer. Maybe there is some effect of this kind of prayer on people who do it continually, on a daily basis. But then, of course, among the Tibetans there are hundreds and thousands who do these kinds of prayers on a daily basis!

EKMAN: I agree with you that if it is a mystery that does not mean it is not a fact. And I agree with you that just because science at this time cannot explain something does not mean that we should not try to do so. I suspect that there is something about contemplative practice that generates, in some people, a small number of people, a *goodness*—I cannot think of another word, though this is not a twenty-first-century word—but a kind of goodness that is of benefit to others. Historically, there have been accounts of such experiences.

There are many mysteries still. Some people think that if it is a mystery, it cannot be, but that is not my view. It is a mystery, but I do not know whether it will always be a mystery or whether some day we will be able to understand it. It would be nice to better understand this experience, which had such benefit, so that we could provide a similar benefit to other people.

DALAI LAMA: (*Translated.*) This is not exactly at the level of mystery that we were talking about, but it is kind of . . . semimystery. (*Laughs.*)

EKMAN: I have been asking you many questions. Do you have questions you want to ask me?

DALAI LAMA: (*Translated.*) Emotion is part of the mental experience. We have thoughts and other mental states, as well. The question is, With all this entire spectrum of human experience, of different mental states, can they be explained on the basis of the brain?

EKMAN: Ah-ha! I have read your last book, *The Universe in a Single Atom,* carefully, so I know that you think the mind is not explainable totally by the brain, either what we know now or will ever know.

We have seen it in our lifetimes again and again, that when we do not have the tools or methods to scientifically study something, we ignore it—or even worse, claim it does not exist. I was originally trained by a protégé of the very influential psychologist B. F. Skinner, who spent most of his career at Harvard. In Skinner's time, there were no methods to examine thinking, and so Skinner ignored thoughts; they did not exist for him because they could not, at that time, be studied scientifically. I believed that for a while—(*Laughs.*)—I had the thought that thoughts did not exist. I soon came to realize how silly and foolish that was.

I think that a lot of the brain research that is now in fashion has not taught us as much as is sometimes claimed. That is not because understanding the brain is unimportant. I think everything we do and think is, as best I can understand, directed by our brains. To know what lights up in the brain from an fMRI scan tells us something, but not a great deal. The crucial questions about how the brain is operating, what processes are occurring, are still opaque to present methods. Maybe in the lifetime of our children we will begin to be able to examine mental processes scientifically through some new measurement devices—discovering not just where they are occurring, but how they work, what they are doing, and how they are doing what they do, and even the content of the thought processes.

JINPA: His Holiness is referring to a discussion that took place at Stanford in 2005.[1]

One thing that came up was that at the level of brain expression, no differentiation was found in the brain measurements between a person feeling unbearable about his or her own pain and a person feeling unbearable in response to another's pain, through compassion. In terms of the content and the experience, there is a huge difference. But in terms of the brain level of expression, there does not seem to be much difference.*

EKMAN: I think you have to be more careful to say "in terms of what they were looking at in the brain." When we develop ways of looking more fully at brain activity, we might see a difference.

We need to avoid an antagonism between what we can examine scientifically and what we have reason to believe happens that we cannot examine at this point. These need to continually interact with each other. That is why I think His Holiness's engagement with science has been very good for science. I hope it has been as good for him.

---

* I neglected to mention my theory that emotions once triggered do not reflect differences in how they were triggered; for example, the facial expression triggered by reading about an outrage versus the expression triggered by hearing someone say something outrageous. From that vantage point, it would not be surprising that the brain activity would be the same, regardless of how it was triggered.

DALAI LAMA: (*Translated.*) As a person I benefit, but also the Tibetan Buddhist tradition benefits enormously. As a result of my dialogues with scientists, I am questioning many of the descriptions and assumptions of Buddhist cosmology. Some could say I have become a heretic!

On a serious note, what becomes evident is that, through dialogue with scientists, Buddhists can learn a lot in terms of refining their worldview in areas where science has empirical evidence to demonstrate—to refine, to expand, to update. This is a process that Buddhists need to go through. In fact, partly as a result of my series of meetings with scientists, we now have an ongoing systematic scientific education program in the monasteries.

EKMAN: I have heard of that.

JINPA: In South India, His Holiness recently gave a massive teaching, at which there was a large number of student monks from all the different monastic universities, colleges, and monasteries.

DALAI LAMA: Over ten thousand monks.

JINPA: There were three days of preliminary teachings on basic Buddhist thought and philosophy and practice. His Holiness expressed much skepticism about the various elements of the traditional Buddhist cosmology in the classical texts and argued the case for accepting modern cosmology and taking the evidence of science seriously. He was in the science camp, not in the Buddhist camp. (*Laughs.*)

He asked, "Listening to my lecture today, do you now consider me a heretic?"

EKMAN: What did they say?

DALAI LAMA: No response. It was a big gathering.

JINPA: On the second and the third days, he was talking about compassion.

DALAI LAMA: Interdependent theory.

JINPA: Then, of course, he was very squarely in the Buddhist camp. (*Dalai Lama laughs heartily.*)

THE PATH OF REASON

EKMAN: Scientists benefit enormously from your questions. Sometimes you ask us questions about our own work that we have not thought of and that do not seem to particularly come from a Buddhist perspective. They come just from a very sharp, attentive mind, listening to something for the first time, accepting nothing without testing it for alternative explanations or exceptions.

I also believe that from a Buddhist perspective, you raise questions that we need to think about in science. The dialogue has just been wonderful.

DALAI LAMA: (*Translated.*) One of the things that has become quite clear, as a result of these discussions, is that in the Buddhist texts there is a lot of attention paid to the specific afflictions, their causal mechanisms, and the antidotes that need to be cultivated to respond to them. Yet there does not seem to be enough attention paid to the developmental process. At what stage, and what kind of specific antidote should be applied? When is this appropriate? That kind of developmental process does not seem to be identified in the texts.

Buddhists probably need to think through carefully, reflect, and then see these developmental stages. Of course, there are numerous meditators who engage in these practices, who benefit from them, who have transformational experiences but do not seem to have articulated the actual step-by-step sequence in which their transformations take place. If I look at my own process of transformation, what seems to be evident is that I continue my meditation on emptiness, on the interdependent nature of everything, and on infinite altruism. These together seem to provide a big framework within which a cumulative, transformational effect takes place. But as to exactly at what stage, what transformation is occurring, I am not able to say. Maybe the Buddhists need to sit down, like the scientists, and be a bit more specific.

EKMAN: It is such a difficult thing to do—to examine, over

time, the sequence of what occurs. Yet, it seems to me that people such as you and Matthieu Ricard are uniquely able to do this. We can learn from that because you are what Varela talked about: highly skilled observers of your own mental processes.

Most of us are not such highly skilled observers of our inner thoughts and feelings. The issue, of course, is for us to learn some of those skills from those who are highly skilled, to be able to learn how to develop the skills, and become more observant of the sequence of our subjective experiences.

DALAI LAMA: *(Translated.)* Part of the monastic educational training is debate-oriented, always looking for inconsistencies and posing critical questions. Thus some of the Western teachers who have taught science in the monasteries have said they enjoyed teaching the monks very much because they are always asking critical questions, challenging and stimulating one another. Maybe it is that monastic debate background that makes a difference.

Tibetans have inherited an intellectual culture from the great Indian masters of Nalanda University, who have provided us with avenues of critical reasoning and methods of analysis. But we should not confine the scope of our analysis simply to the fields that we have been familiar with for thousands of years. We now need to somehow expand this scope, and continue to use the same analysis in other areas.

JINPA: And in the monastic debate culture, often one of the—

DALAI LAMA: Drawbacks.

JINPA:—is that it tends to rely heavily on citations from authoritative texts. His Holiness has expressed the hope that one day, a new—

DALAI LAMA: Now!

JINPA: From now on, we should modify the system, so that we do not rely on any statements from the authoritative texts but rather more on the reasoning, the path of reasoning.

EKMAN: In 1949, at the age of fifteen, I went to the college of the University of Chicago, which then would admit students after two years of high school. Their goal was to teach you to think critically, to accept nothing on authority: Question and find your way to the truth. There were no lectures—discussion only—and no textbooks; you read the primary sources themselves, but not what somebody in a textbook thought about it. We sometimes carried this to excess. We could believe in nothing and criticize everything. The idea was that to live in a democracy, we had to critically evaluate alternatives. I think that is very much what you are talking about.

When I worked with students, they had to learn that I liked to change my mind. Today, I would argue this point of view, and tomorrow I would argue just the opposite. I was not attached to any of the viewpoints; I wanted to try each one on and see how it worked.

Each time I think about something, I am starting from a different place, having thought about other matters in the interval. I try to make use of that to regard things anew, rather than trying to resurrect what I had previously thought. I am keenly aware that as I enter the last phase of my life, there is a temptation to rigidify my thinking, to begin to cling—if I may use that Buddhist term—to my own views of the world rather than to continually question them. I deliberately work to resist that temptation.

DALAI LAMA: (*Translated.*) There was an eighteenth-century Tibetan master who wrote beautiful advice, in verse, to his students. One of the statements he makes is, "Make sure that you have a position of your own." On the part of the teacher, it is very skillful, to point out different perspectives.

EKMAN: I do believe that theories are more useful if you do not become committed to them. All too often, I see in science, particularly in psychology, that people think of a theory that to begin with is a very interesting way of explaining a set of facts. They become committed to their theory; they do not want to know any facts that do not fit it. Then their theory, instead of opening new questions, closes their vision. That is terrible; it is what we have to guard against. One wonderful value of contact with Buddhist thinking is that it is a framework, a set of very developed ideas that comes from a different direction, one that I did not anticipate.

DALAI LAMA: (*Translated.*) I found a statement made by one of Francisco Varela's teachers very helpful. The teacher said that as scientists we should not become attached to our research. I often tell my fellow Buddhist colleagues that as Buddhists we should ensure that we do not become attached to Buddhism. (*Breaks into laughter.*)

EKMAN: Not so easy.

DALAI LAMA: (*Translated.*) There are historical examples in the Buddhist world, for them: Critical questioning and analysis were crucial, not an attachment to a particular creed. That opens the way to questioning the literal truth of statements attributed to the Buddha. It is considered an affliction to have a clinging attachment to one's views or standpoint; it is actually listed as an affliction, and this is referred to as the superiority of one's views.

EKMAN: I want to thank you for spending all of this time. Over the three meetings in which we have pursued these discussions, we have spent thirty-nine hours. I have never spent so much time with anyone discussing a topic of mutual interest.

This has been a remarkable gift to spend so much time exploring with you the ideas that have occupied me in my life. I have found your interest and enthusiasm more than I can express in words—I am very, very grateful.

I think it was Jinpa and Alan Wallace, in particular the two of them, who, when I first raised the question, "He is such a busy man, with so many important demands made on his time, am I being presumptuous, to ask for so much of His Holiness's time?" said, "No, what you are thinking about could really be useful to many people." Now, having spent this time over the last sixteen months, I am very convinced that they were right that our conversation will help open people's minds to a better understanding of their emotions and capacity for compassion.

I thank my family for sitting through the first three days of our initial meetings. It made such a difference for me. (*Tears flow down Ekman's cheeks.*) I am glad they could be here.

DALAI LAMA: Your family members. (*Shifting his gaze toward them, smiling, he nods.*)

JINPA: It seems, Paul, you have the credit of bringing up nice children. (*After an exchange in Tibetan.*) Sorry, sorry. I got it wrong. The fact that you are wonderful now is probably the result of the children.

EKMAN: Yes! Of course! Oh, yes!

DALAI LAMA: Children are life! (*Arises.*) Thank you.

At the conclusion of the last conversation, the Dalai Lama asked for a thangka to be brought into the room. It was unfolded, to reveal a beautiful hand-painted image of Tara, a female Bodhisattva regarded as "the mother of liberation," who represents the virtues of success in work and achievements. The Dalai Lama then wrote an inscription on the thangka in Tibetan, which was afterward translated by Dorji: "To my dear friend and scholar Paul Ekman. After many years of acquaintance we have developed a very close and genuine friendship with which I am so delighted. I pray for your long life and that your activities proliferate."

Notes

INTRODUCTION

1. Daniel Goleman, *Destructive Emotions* (New York: Bantam Books, 2003).

2. His works include *The Monk and the Philosopher: A Father and Son Discuss the Meaning of Life* (New York: Schocken Books, 1999), by Ricard's father, Jean-François Revel, and Ricard; *Happiness: A Guide to Developing Life's Most Important Skill* (New York: Little, Brown, 2006), by Ricard; and Ricard's books of photography.

3. Paul Ekman, Wallace V. Friesen, and Ronald C. Simons, "Is the Startle Reaction an Emotion?" *Journal of Personality and Social Psychology,* vol. 4995 (1985): 1416–26.

4. I thank Erika Rosenberg, Cliff Saron, Margaret Cullen, Margaret Kemeny, Sharon Medrick, and the psychiatrist from Marin, who were the most regular attendees at the yearlong sessions.

5. Scholars who wish to hear the entire thirty-nine hours of our discussions, including all of what was said in Tibetan but not translated, can obtain a copy from paulekman.com.

1. EAST AND WEST

1. Paul Ekman, *Emotions Revealed: Recognizing Faces and Feelings to Improve Communication and Emotional Life* (New York: Owl Books, 2007).

2. Ibid., pp. 39–40.

3. See E. Diener, "Subjective Well-Being: The Science of Happiness and a Proposal for a National Index," *American Psychologist*, 55 (2000): 34–43; D. G. Myer, "The Funds, Friends, and Faith of Happy People," *American Psychologist*, 55 (2000): 56–67.

4. Dalai Lama, *The Universe in a Single Atom* (New York: Broadway Books, 2005).

5. Helena Cronin, *The Ant and the Peacock: Altruism and Sex Selection from Darwin to Today* (London: Cambridge University Press, 1991).

6. Oliver Curry, "Morality as Natural History: An Adaptionist Account of Ethics," unpublished dissertation, London School of Economics, 2005.

7. B. Alan Wallace, *Contemplative Science: Where Buddhism and Neuroscience Converge* (New York: Columbia University Press, 2007).

8. Paul Ekman, Richard J. Davidson, Matthieu Ricard, and B. Alan Wallace, "Buddhist and Psychological Perspectives on Emotions and Well-Being," *Current Directions in Psychological Science*, 14, no. 2 (2005): 59–63.

9. In late 2007, plans were under way for a conference of Tibetan and English language scholars, who will discuss the terminology of mental experience and elaborate a better common vocabulary, thus one hopes, decreasing misunderstandings that result from what the Dalai Lama calls Buddhalogical English.

2. EXPERIENCING EMOTION

1. Paul Ekman, "All Emotions Are Basic," in Paul Ekman and Richard J. Davidson, eds., *The Nature of Emotion* (New York: Oxford University Press, 1994).

2. See chapter 4 in *Emotions Revealed* for a fuller discussion of this matter. Paul Ekman, *Emotions Revealed*, rev. ed. (New York: Owl Books, 2007).

3. I am grateful to Jonathan Schooler for this example.

4. Personal communication from Steven Souci, National Institute of Mental Health, 1980.

5. First reported in Paul Ekman, Robert W. Levenson, and Wallace V. Friesen, "Autonomic Nervous System Activity Distinguishes Between Emotions," *Science*, 221 (1983): 1208–10.

6. Described in Daniel G. Freedman, *Human Sociobiology: A Holistic Approach* (New York: Free Press, 1979), and Daniel G. Freedman, *Human Infancy: An Evolutionary Perspective* (New York: John Wiley & Sons, 1975).

7. "Emotional Profiles," http://www.paulekman.com.

8. Dalai Lama, *The Universe in a Single Atom: The Convergence of Science and Spirituality* (New York: Broadway Books, 2005), p. 178.

9. For more information on these practices, see Sharon Salzberg and Joseph Goldstein, *Insight Meditation: A Step-By-Step Course on How to Meditate*, audio program (Louisville, Colo.: Sounds True Publishers, 2002).

10. James Carmody and Ruth A. Baer, "Relationships Between Mindfulness Practice and Levels of Mindfulness, Medical and Psychological Symptoms, and Well-Being in a Mindfulness-Based Stress Reduction," *Journal of Behavorial Medicine*, published online September 25, 2007, http://www.springerlink.com/content/n26838t52m727u13/.

11. Thich Nhat Hanh, *The Miracle of Mindfulness* (Boston: Beacon Press, 1975), p. 14.

12. Jon Kabat-Zinn, *Coming to Our Senses: Healing Ourselves and the World Through Mindfulness* (London: Piatkus Books, 2005), p. 108.

13. Jack Kornfield, "Finding My Religion," *San Francisco Chronicle*, November 28, 2005.

14. Nyanaponika Thera, *The Heart of Buddhist Meditation* (York Beach, Me.: Samuel Weiser, 1988). Originally published 1956.

15. "Mindfulness: The Heart of Buddhist Meditation? A Conversation with Jan Chozen Bays, Joseph Goldstein, Jon Kabat-Zinn, and Alan Wallace," *Inquiring Mind: A Semiannual Journal of the Vipassana Community*, 22, no. 2 (Spring 2006): 5.

16. Bhikkhu Bodhi, ed., *A Comprehensive Manual of Abhidhamma: The Abidhammattha Sangaha* (Kandy, Sri Lanka: Buddhist Publication Society, 1993), p. 86.

17. Thera, *Heart of Buddhist Meditation*, p. 9.

18. Ibid.

19. Ibid., p. 6.

20. Paul Ekman, *Telling Lies*, rev. ed. (New York: W. W. Norton, 2002).

21. Paul Ekman, Robert W. Levenson, and Wallace Friesen, "Autonomic Nervous System Activity Distinguishes Between Emotions," *Science*, 221 (1983): 1208–10; Robert W. Levenson, Paul Ekman, and Wallace Friesen, "Voluntary Facial Action Generates Emotion-specific Autonomic Nervous System Activity," *Psychophysiology*, 27 (1990): 363–84; Paul Ekman and Richard J. Davidson, "Voluntary Smiling Changes Regional Brain Activity," *Psychological Science*, 4 (1993): 342–45.

22. Paul Ekman, *Emotions Revealed*, rev. ed. (New York: Owl Books, 2007), p. 39.

23. Harry Stack Sullivan, *Interpersonal Psychiatry* (New York: W. W. Norton, 1953).

24. Kunzang Pelden, *The Nectar of Manjushri's Speech: A Detailed Commentary on Shantideva's Way of the Bodhisattva*, translated by Padmakara Translation Group (Boston: Shambhala Publications, 2007), chapter 4.

25. Silvan S. Tomkins, *Affect, Imagery, Consciousness* (New York: Springer, 1962–1963).

3. EMOTIONAL BALANCE

1. M. E. Kemeny, C. Foltz, P. Ekman, and P. Jennings, "Contemplative/Emotion Training Improves Emotional Life" (in press).

2. The psychologist John Gottman discovered this. See L. L. Carstensen, J. M. Gottman, and R. W. Levenson, "Emotional Behavior in Long-Term Marriage," *Psychology and Aging*, 10, no. 1 (1995): 140–49.

3. Shanti Deva, *A Guide to the Boddhisattva Way of Life*, translated by Vesna A. Wallace and B. Alan Wallace (Ithaca, N.Y.: Snow Lion Publications, 1997).

4. An example of this can be seen in Heleen A. Slagter, Antoine Lutz, Lawrence L. Greischar, et al., "Mental Training Affects Distribution of Limited Brain Resources," *PLoS Biology*, 5, no. 6 (2007): e138, doi:10.1371/journal.pbio .0050138.

5. The Dalai Lama and Victor Chan, *The Wisdom of Forgiveness: Intimate Journeys and Conversations* (New York: Riverhead Books, 2004), p. 110.

4. ANGER, RESENTMENT, AND HATRED

1. Stone Mountain Zendo, http://www.stonemountainzendo.org/textsbodhisattva.html.

2. Geshe Sonam Rinchen, *The Bodhisattva Vow*, translated and edited by Ruth Sonam (Ithaca, N.Y.: Snow Lion Publications, 2000).

3. I am grateful to Clifford Saron for this suggestion.

4. Emotion researchers do not completely agree about the definition of anger. I have theorized that anger is triggered by a perceived block to a desired goal that may or may not involve a wish to harm the person responsible for the obstacle.

5. Arne Ohman, "Fear and Anxiety as Emotional Phenomena: Clinical Phenomenology, Evolutionary Perspectives, and Information Processing," in M. Lewis and J. Haviland, eds., *The Handbook of Emotions* (New York: Guilford Press, 1993), pp. 511–36.

6. This change in view occurred between March and June 2007.

7. Paul Ekman, *Emotions Revealed* (New York: Owl Books, 2007), p. 119.

5. THE NATURE OF COMPASSION

1. This is an extension of work reported in an article by Tania Singer, Ben Seymour, John O'Dogherty, et al., "Empathic Neural Responses Are Modulated by the Perceived Fairness of Others," *Nature*, 4396 (January 26, 2006): 466–69.

2. Charles Darwin, *The Descent of Man* (New York: D. Appleton and Company, 1871), p. 77.

3. Frans B. M. de Waal, "On the Possibility of Animal Empathy. Feelings and Emotions: The Amsterdam Symposium," *Studies in Emotion and Social Interaction* (2004): 381–401.

4. The legitimate concern to not interpret animals as if they were humans led to an extreme of denying that animals could have emotions.

5. Darwin, *Descent of Man*, p. 492.

6. Charles Darwin, *The Expression of Emotion in Man and Animals*, 3rd ed., Paul Ekman, ed. (New York: Oxford University Press, 1998). Originally published 1872.

7. De Waal is referring to Dale J. Langford, Sara E. Crager, et al., "Social Modulation of Pain as Evidence for Empathy in Mice," *Science*, 312, no. 5782 (June 30, 2006): 1967. For an overview, see McGill University, "New Pain

Research Shows Mice Capable of Empathy," *ScienceDaily*, June 30, 2006, http://www.sciencedaily.com/releases/2006/06/060630100140.htm.

8. Frans B. M. de Waal, *Primates and Philosophers: How Morality Evolved* (Princeton, N. J.: Princeton University Press, 2006).

9. Ibid.

10. For recent reviews see Shauna Shapiro and W. Alan Wallace, "Mental Balance Well-Being: Building Bridges Between Buddhism and Western Psychology," *American Psychologist*, 61, no. 7 (October 2006): 690–701; and Roger Walsh and Shauna Shapiro, "The Meeting of Meditative Disciplines and Western Psychology: A Mutually Enriching Dialogue," *American Psychologist*, 61, no. 3 (April 2006): 227–39.

11. Unpublished study.

12. The Kadamapa Buddhist master Langri Thangpa lived from 1054 until 1153. His "Eight Verses on Mind Training" read:

> *Determined to accomplish/The highest welfare of all sentient beings/Who are more precious than wish-fulfilling jewels,/I will practice holding them supremely dear.*
>
> *Whomever I accompany,/I will practice seeing myself as the lowest amongst them,/And sincerely cherish others supreme.*
>
> *In all my actions, I shall examine my mind,/And the moment a wild thought arises,/endangering myself and others,/I shall face it and prevail.*
>
> *When I encounter those overwhelmed/By strong misdeeds and sufferings,/I shall hold them near as if I had discovered/A precious treasure difficult to find.*
>
> *When, out of jealousy, others treat me badly/With abuse, slander and the like, I will practice taking all loss/And offer the victory to them.*
>
> *When someone I had benefited in great hope/Unreasonably hurts me badly,/I will practice regarding that person/As my most excellent and holy guru.*
>
> *In short, I will learn to offer help and happiness/Directly and indirectly to all my mothers,/And secretly take upon myself,/All their harmful actions and suffering.*
>
> *I will keep all these practices/Undefiled by the superstitions of the eight worldly concerns,/And by understanding all the dharmas as like illusions,/I will practice, without grasping./To release all sentient beings from bondage.*

6. GLOBAL COMPASSION

1. D. A. Clark and A. T. Beck, *Scientific Foundation of Cognitive Theory and Theory of Depression* (New York: John Wiley and Sons, 1999).

2. Kristen Renwick Monroe, *The Heart of Altruism: Perceptions of a Common Humanity* (Princeton, N. J.: Princeton University Press, 1996).

3. The MicroExpression Training Tool and the Subtle Expression Training Tool quickly teach people to be more aware of how another person is feeling.

For individuals interested in training in this technique, online interactive training is available at www.paulekman.com.

4. Erika L. Rosenberg and Paul Ekman, "Coherence Between Expressive and Experiential Systems in Emotion," in Paul Ekman and Erika L. Rosenberg, eds., *What the Face Reveals: Basic and Applied Studies of Spontaneous Expression Using the Facial Action Coding Systems (FACS)* (New York: Oxford University Press, 2005), pp. 63–88.

5. Victor Chan and others are attempting to develop mind-training gyms.

7. PERSONAL TRANSFORMATION

1. From the conference, "Growing, Suffering and Choice: Spiritual and Scientific Exploration of Human Experience," held November 5, 2005, at the Stanford School of Medicine, presenting His Holiness the 14th Dalai Lama, and moderated by Dr. William Mobley. See also Mark Williams, Zindel Segal, and Jon Kabat-Zinn, *The Mindful Way Through Depression: Freeing Yourself from Chronic Unhappiness* (New York: Guilford Press, 2007).

Acknowledgments

·❊·

In chapter 7, I thanked all the people responsible for these conversations: the Dalai Lama himself, Dorji Damdul, Richie Davidson, Dan Goleman, Thupten Jinpa, Matthieu Ricard, B. Alan Wallace, and the Mind and Life Institute. Here I would like to thank Adam Engle in particular, as I would not have met the Dalai Lama without the help of his organization, the Mind and Life Institute. I also want to express my appreciation for those who helped me turn those nearly forty hours of conversation into a book.

Sally Frye was dedicated in her transfer of the audio materials into an initial manuscript. Paul Kaufman and Cliff Saron read an early version and provided invaluable suggestions. I thank the small group of colleagues and friends who listened to the audio recordings of our first meeting and raised many of the questions that I pursued in subsequent meetings: Margaret Cullen, Patricia Jennings, Margaret Kemeny, Erica Rosenberg, Cliff Saron, and Marc Schwartz. I am grateful to all those who wrote commentaries that have been added to the text. Each of them did so cheerfully and promptly: Margaret Cullen, Dorji Damdul, Richie Davidson, John Dunne, Bob Levenson, Lobsang Tenzin Negi,

Charles Raison, Matthieu Ricard, Cliff Saron, Marc Schwartz, Alan Wallace, and Frans de Waal. My literary agent, Robert Lescher, provided what I now know to be his standard, very high level of encouragement, as well as his skill in negotiating the difficult contractual issues in a coauthored book.

Robin Dennis at Times Books/Henry Holt edited my previous book, *Emotions Revealed*. On this current book she accomplished the impossible, providing even more diligent, insightful, constructive help and examining each word, not just every sentence. It would have been a different, less incisive book without her dedication and commitment.

—Paul Ekman

Index

About the Authors

✴

Tenzin Gyatso, His Holiness the 14th Dalai Lama, is the recipient of the Nobel Peace Prize and is the temporal and spiritual leader of the Tibetan people. The author of *The Art of Happiness,* among many other books, he is the head of the Tibetan government-in-exile and resides in Dharamsala, India.

Paul Ekman is the world's foremost expert on facial expressions and is a professor emeritus of psychology at the University of California-San Francisco School of Medicine. The author of fourteen books, including *Emotions Revealed,* he lives in northern California.